John Bascom

Philosophy of english Literature

A Course of Lectures delivered in the Lowell Institute

John Bascom

Philosophy of english Literature
A Course of Lectures delivered in the Lowell Institute

ISBN/EAN: 9783337081348

Printed in Europe, USA, Canada, Australia, Japan

Cover: Foto ©ninafisch / pixelio.de

More available books at **www.hansebooks.com**

PHILOSOPHY

OF

ENGLISH LITERATURE

A COURSE OF LECTURES DELIVERED IN
THE LOWELL INSTITUTE

BY

JOHN BASCOM

AUTHOR OF "PRINCIPLES OF PSYCHOLOGY," "SCIENCE, PHILOSOPHY AND
RELIGION," "ÆSTHETICS"

———

G. P. PUTNAM'S SONS

NEW YORK   LONDON
27 WEST TWENTY-THIRD STREET   24 BEDFORD STREET, STRAND

The Knickerbocker Press

1893

Press of
G. P. Putnam's Sons
New York

PREFACE.

THERE are, in each department of knowledge, central facts and germinant principles. If we reach these early and well, the labors of acquisition are greatly lightened. They serve to explain to the mind, and to hold for the memory, those multitudinous minor facts which otherwise confuse the one and burden the other. It is a secret of wise acquisition, to learn the most in learning the least, and we do this by directing attention at once to leading, fruitful facts. The ground is thus outlined; we know where to look for particulars; and these, as they come to us by direct search, or as incidents of growing information, fall at once into their place, strengthen our general hold of truth, and are themselves securely rolled in and bound up in the compact bundle of knowledge.

The object of the lectures herewith published is to put the general reader and the student of English Literature into early possession of the leading influences operative in it, and thus to enable them to peruse and to study its numerous productions with more insight, more pleasure, a better mastery of relations, and a more ready retention of facts. A net-work of forces is here given, which, covering the entire field, may enable them easily to in-

close and attach the ideas each day furnished in
this range of knowledge. We have termed our
work a Philosophy of English Literature, as indicating a discussion of causes, of controlling tendencies, and leading minds, rather than a presentation
of details, a reproduction of facts in their chronological connections.

A class pursuing English literature by the aid
of text-books like Craik's, Shaw's, Spalding's,
Angus', Gilman's, might, we believe, carry on a
review to advantage in connection with these lectures. The last impression would thus be one
more organic and living than that ordinarily
reached.

It is not necessary to suppose what is said in
these lectures is wholly proportionate, or entirely
sufficient, in order that the student may, by means
of it, reach the end here proposed. It will be
enough if the lines of thought struck out, and the
considerations brought forward, are those which in-
terlace and occupy the field. Each reader will then
easily make such additions and modifications as his
own mind suggests, and the facts before him seem
to require. We have followed freely the bent of
our own thoughts, and our conclusions therefore
will not be found exactly parallel with those which
others are reaching. If they provoke question,
they may not for that reason be less valuable, provided the discussion leads to a better insight into
principles.

CONTENTS.

———◆———

INITIATIVE PERIOD.

LAST HALF OF THE FOURTEENTH CENTURY.

(v)

LECTURE III.

RETROGRESSIVE PERIOD.

THE FIFTEENTH, AND FIRST HALF OF THE SIXTEENTH, CENTURY.

Due to

LECTURE IX.

SECOND TRANSITION PERIOD.

LAST PORTION OF THE EIGHTEENTH CENTURY.

LECTURE XII.

ENGLISH PHILOSOPHY.

THE PHILOSOPHY

OF

ENGLISH LITERATURE.

LECTURE I.

Literature.—Its Essential Characteristics.—Variable Use of the
Word.—The Initiative Period in English Literature.—Last half
of Fourteenth Century the Date of the English Nation, Language and Literature.—Anglo-Saxon Element.—Norman Element.—Norman Superiority.—Early Relation of the Two.—
Causes which United Them.—English Character.—Foreign Influences: First, Classical; Second, Italian; Third, Norman.

THE literature of a nation is the embodiment of
that which is most artistic and complete in its intellectual, literary life. There are many practical
products of composition, records, chronicles, works
of instruction, of science, and of reference, which
contain the material of knowledge, the raw staple
of art, but are not literature. These change with
succeeding years, and reappear in altered and enlarged forms, as the progress of events and investigation determine. Many books, in each generation,
are the seed which is returned to the soil as the
condition of farther increase. No work is a part of
national literature, in its more specific sense, till it
is possessed of such merit of execution, aside from

mere matter, or it were better to say in conjunction
with matter, as to give it permanent value. Thought
alone, the substance of wisdom merely, cannot
save a work to literature. It may be rather the occasion of its speedy disappearance. More skilful
laborers will swarm around the sweet morsel, let
fall as it were in the highway of thought, and each
bear off a portion of the unidentified product. It is
some completeness, symmetry, excellence of form
that gives identity, ownership to a product; and a
permanent interest in its careful, exact preservation.

There are in literature three forms of value, an
intellectual, an emotional and an expressional one.
The thought-value is the most stable, residuary element; the emotional and expressional values are
the constituents most changeable and volatile.
These two are thoroughly interdependent, and according as merit passes to this end of the scale, is
the literary excellence of a work declared.

Thought as thought is saved, no matter how often
it is altered in expression, and reappears in new relations. Form alone, in subtile fellowship with
emotional power, necessitates careful transmission.
Gold as bullion waits momentarily on the arts for
working up; stamped as coin, or wrought as orna-
ment, it has a new character, an enhanced value,
that everywhere attend upon it, and guard it.

In proportion as the excellence of the form
transcends the value of the matter, does the literary
work gain perpetuity. The poems of Shakespeare
and Milton hold their present position, not from any
new truths they announce, not from facts of history

or of science they contain, but through the superior, inimitable workmanship which belongs to them. Material, for the most part fanciful, thus acquires an interest, and receives an estimate, that fall to no records of history, no facts of science, however valuable these may be. Indeed, in proportion as th very substance of a literary work, the thought it contains, becomes important, is it difficult for it to claim and hold a place in literature. The material of history in so large a measure confers upon it its value, that each succeeding work, the product of more investigation, tends to displace preceding ones; and only rare excellencies of style can keep the early historian in possession of the national mind. The very interest of the facts stated stimulates farther inquiry, and this pushes into the background those who first contributed to it. The hard workers, the investigators and compilers, in the fields of knowledge, descend by genesis only to those who come after them; their discoveries, their theories, like wind-sown flowers, enrich many who are ignorant of their origin.

Literature, then, is essentially of an artistic character; poetry is its chief product; and all its creations hold their ground by completeness and beauty of form. The material is as often imaginative as historical, and must, even in the essay, get its peculiar character and coloring from the mind of the writer. There must be in the literary work, as in the crystal, something which cannot be broken in on without loss, something in itself specific and final. It is, in fact, the individual mind which the nation treasures up in literature; and he who has only common truths, that which is or may be the spoil of all, to bring, can find no entrance to this gallery of art. His contributions are valuable, but they have other and coarser storehouses than those in which beauty garners her own. He must bear his useful things to the markets in which like products are bought and sold.

There seems, at first, something a little unequal and harsh in this, that the patient laborer is so easily thrust back by the artist, he who gives bread by him who gives visions; yet we are willing to accept it as one more proof that spiritualities, inspirations, creative touches, though they be mere traces of light, are more to man than the solid, coarse-grained comforts of being. Those who bring us these fare as servants, and those who fling carelessly to us those rarer gifts are sought after, and entertained as angels; yet at times a little too much on the light food of posthumous praise.

The word *literature* is determined in its breadth by its connections. When we speak of the literature of one department of knowledge, as chemistry, the artistic quality is comparatively overlooked, and all works of merit that have been written on the subject are included. If we refer to the literature of a particular century, as of the sixteenth century in England, we then gather up in the word more carefully all the literary products of that period, though some of them may since have sunk out of sight. In the words, *English literature*, we should comprise only those works whose artistic merit has put them in permanent possession of the mind of the nation; which hold on their way, not through years, but through centuries. Yet few even of these would reappear in the world's literature, as working for themselves an abiding-place in the educated thought of different nations. While the word, therefore, is always inclining towards merit of form, and the more with each extension of it, the theme, the time and the territory in which the literary success has been achieved are indicated by the qualifying adjective, and our definition becomes a conjoint one. English literature is made up of those English writings which have gained a permanent place in the regard of the English people. This position has been won by artistic excellence, and hence our literature is, in letters, our national art-gallery. The broader the field which the collection covers, the more select are its constituents; while restriction in time or place makes lighter the conditions of admission.

We have pushed this point clearly out, that the pleasures of literature are essentially æsthetic, because it will aid us in a just estimate of the merits of English literature, and of the forces which have affected it. We hold it to be a general truth, that moral influences, the ethical tone of sentiment, the spiritually perceptive powers are pre-eminently united to works of literary art. This seems to follow from the fact, that nothing mounts into the region of art without undergoing some transformation, receiving buoyancy and color from the mind that wings it for flight. Art is not literal, is not commonplace, mere copy; but owes much to selection, arrangement, infused character and infused life. Now this infusion which goes mantling through the new, the beautiful product is the intellectual, spiritual life and movement of the artist; and as the artist himself is known in his temper and moods by their relation to the supreme element of his nature, to the ethical temperature of his own soul, so are his works. What the light is to the landscape, grading it in its every degree of emotion, lifting it up to the key-note of highest joy and exultation; or depressing it to the deepest sadness and unmingled fear; or leaving it in the midway region of commonplace comforts; that is the moral revelation to the literary work, revealing men, revealing things and thoughts even, under a sportive and jocular, a serene and reflective, or a stern and portentous aspect, according to the soul that is in it. We are not to be understood, of course, as restricting the word ethical to precepts of conduct, more or less numerous, but rather as referring by it to that tacit declaration which every man makes of the nature of life, its delights, its insights, its achievements; and of the ministrations of God, society and nature to it. The soul of man is centred in his moral constitution; that is in his perceptions of the objects and forms, and hence of the beauties, of rational action. He can gain no orbit of thought; he can reach not even the conventional excellencies of character, the courage of manhood, the gentleness of womanhood; he can give no interpretation to the voices of nature, save as he does it by one or more of those

ethical sentiments that spring from the depths of
his being, that belong to him as man, under larger
joys, and severer sufferings, and sterner laws and
more enduring hopes than those which fall to the
animals about him. As man sinks in action, in
emotion, in intuition, he loses high art; as he as-
cends he regains it, effecting a new entrance into
that which is peculiar to himself, to a moral being
with springs and laws of life hidden in its superiorly
perceptive constitution. Even comedy cannot
thrive on mere trifles. Unless its laugh has elation,
election, taste, sense and sensibility in it, it sinks
to low burlesque, in which the animal appetites so
predominate, that we find ourselves in action and
impulse facing downward toward the brute. The
poet Schiller seems to have been possessed of this
principle in a more tense form than we have ventured on. "There was in him," says his biographer, "a singular ardor for truth, a solemn conviction
of the duties of a poet, a deep-rooted idea on which
we have been more than once called to insist, that
the minstrel should be a preacher. That song
is the sister of religion in its largest sense ; that
the stage is the pulpit to all sects, all nations, all
time." * The difference between men is great; it
lies here. To one nothing is religious which is not
coldly, formally preceptive ; to another nothing fails
of religion, which at all reaches the heart. It is,
then, of English literature in its associated artistic
and ethical forces, of necessity gathering strength
and beauty from that which is in man most beauti-

* "Bibliotheca Sacra," Oct. No., 1871, p. 716.

ful and strong, that we are to speak. If it has been at times like a tropical forest, infested by a rank undergrowth of briars, we may be sure it was because the hot and reeking atmosphere engendered them, entering in to obstruct and hide the majestic life above them.

It is not our purpose to give the facts of English literature, we shall assume a general knowledge of them, and strive to trace their dependence. We shall start with the earliest works of pronounced merit in our literary history, and shall speak of authors only as their productions are themselves a distinct force, giving character to the periods under discussion.

The initiative period in English letters covers the last half of the fourteenth century. Literary periods have no definite bounds. As the slopes of mountains may gently rise and gently descend again to the plains beyond, leaving their midway line and general trend to be determined by isolated peaks and bold ridges; so periods in literature are defined, not by definite dates, but by persons scattered through them, characteristic tendencies that stretch across them.

The initiative period was one of vigorous poetic life, whose chief representative was Chaucer. In an effort to understand this introductory era, we shall need to inquire into the national character, into the foreign and domestic influences prevalent, and into the traits of individuals whose productions constitute its chief intellectual strength. The national and the individual elements can never be separated in literature, nor do they maintain any uniform ratio to each other. In writers of ordinary power, the conditions under which they compose their works exert a controlling influence; in writers of genius, this influence, though still felt, is over-shadowed by personal qualities. The direction and general character of their labor may be settled by external inducements, but its method of accomplishment is to be referred to their own powers. Our first inquiry is into national character. It is through those general conditions which surround and envelop the individual, and whose force he cannot but feel, either in assent or dissent, that we at length approach the seat of art in the soul of the artist.

An English nationality, like an English language and an English literature, was beginning to appear in the last half of the fourteenth century. The three sprang up together; they had one birth, nationality, language and literature; and held in union the same elements. The root of our language is Saxon. It has furnished, though in connection with revolutionary changes, the grammatical frame-work of our speech. The foreign tongue, which for a time overlay and at length largely melted into our language, saturating it with its vocabulary so far as one language can be saturated by another, was Norman French.

So too the nation, in bulk and staple Anglo-Saxon, was permeated, put in active ferment everywhere with Normans, first as rulers, afterward as leaders and fellow-subjects. The popular literature, hitherto chiefly Norman, began, as the

1*

fourteenth century drew to an end, to be English in form and theme.

The two elements, then, in English nationality, of very unequal prevalence and unlike characteristics, were the Saxon and the Norman. The first remained throughout, the substance into which the second, as a color or quality, was received; constituted the material shaped by the latter into new forms, and enlarged into new offices. The Saxon character, though less brilliant and dominant than the Norman, was superior to it in patient strength. The Anglo-Saxon, of Low-German origin, seems to have possessed the qualities which belong to his kinsmen of the continent. Known abroad as Saxons, early spoken of by themselves as Angles or English, they have, in the more careful historic use of the present, been designated as Anglo-Saxons. For six hundred years they had held by extirpation and expulsion, rather than by conquest, of its inhabitants, the larger share of Britain, leaving to the Celts the mountains of the west and north. At the time of the Norman conquest, they were possessed of less enterprise and less cultivation than their invaders; but more equality, greater liberty, and the hardihood of stubborn strength: Their rights were ill-defined, as those of a rude, independent people are wont to be; but centuries were required after the conquest to win again for the general voice of the nation the influence that fell to it under the Saxon constitution. The sturdy array of foot-soldiers and the heavy battle-axes with which they met the horsemen and bowmen of tne

Normans presented in a visible form their tough, unyielding temper.

The Normans were in many respects the reverse of the Saxons. These had occupied England for six centuries by displacement, with comparatively slight alterations of character and language. The Normans, in less than a third of that time, gained in the north of France, a new speech, and gave rise to a new national development. They did not, as the Saxons, expel and exclude those whom they invaded, but included them in a fresh life. Not only did they become a leading element in the formation of the French monarchy and people; that portion of them which was transferred to England, in a period but little longer, accepted new conditions, again changed their language, and once more gathered, with vigorous, organizing force, a new, diverse and independent nation.

"Above all men," says one, "the Norman was an imitator, and therefore an improver; and it was precisely because he was the least rigid, most supple, plastic and accommodating of mortals, that he became the civilizer and ruler wherever he was thrown. In France he became French; in England, English; in Italy, Italian; in Novgorod, Russian. ❀ ❀ ❀ Wherever his neighbors invented or possessed anything worthy of admiration, the sharp, inquisitive Norman poked his aquiline nose. Wherever what we now call the march of intellect advanced, there was the sharp, eager face of the Norman in the van. He always intermarried with the people among whom he settled, borrowed its language, adopted its customs, reconciled himself to its laws, and confirmed the aristocracy of conquest, by representing, while elevating, the character of the people with whom he closely identified himself." *

We give, as another illustration of the flexibility of Norman character, the control soon gained over the Irish by those to whom lands were apportioned on the first invasion by Henry II. This Norman nobility became rapidly Irish in character, outstripping native chiefs in indigenous traits, won an easy and complete ascendancy over the primitive population, and were cordially sustained by them in later rebellions against English rule. "Some most powerful families rooted themselves in the soil, and never forsook it; the Geraldines, of Munster and Kildare; the Butlers, of Kilkenny; the De Burghs, the Birminghams, the De Courcies. This complete absorption of the Norman into the character, customs, feuds, revolts of the Irish was expressed in the phrase 'Ipsis Hibernis Hiberniores.'"† It was this subtile, diffusive, adaptable, and spirited element that was infused by the conquest into the sluggish, phlegmatic Saxon society; and became the nervous system in the body politic, with wide awake senses and a rapid interchange of influences calling to instant service and active subjection the solid bone and brawny muscle which composed the staple of English strength.

* *The Examiner*, for 1848, as given in Stephen's "Literature of the Kymry," p. 429.

† Froude's "History of England," vol. ii. p. 238.

The points at which the Normans surpassed the Saxons, and were thus prepared to contribute new impulses to the national character, were three. The first of these was in weapons and warlike enterprise. They used the bow, and fought on horseback, and were thus ready for more aggressive and nimble movement, for skirmish as well as encounter. The were also of so martial a turn as to give promise of the ultimate unity and sure defense of Britain. No portion of Europe, and not even the new world, were withheld from the wild adventure of this race. Cape Cod is set down as the western limit of their explorations as early as the commencement of the eleventh century.

A second superiority was found in culture, more particularly in poetry and architecture. They had shown gains in both of these directions, and were to become, in Gothic architecture, the most skilful builders in Europe. England and Normandy possess many of their magnificent structures. In poetry also they were relatively cultivated, their minstrels dividing with those of southern France the honors of the national Romance literature.

Their third point of excellence, worth more perhaps than either of the other two, was the piety and intelligence of their clergy. Such men as Anselm and Lanfranc, transferred from the celebrated abbeys at Bec and Caen, were more superior to the native Saxon clergy in the grounds of just influence than were the Norman lords to the Saxon thanes. The conquest was thus attended with a new religious rule, and took possession of authority in both of its great branches. The leading ecclesiastics, of whichever portion of the nation, became identified with the Normans. We find among them, at that time and later, men of great ability, such as Thomas à Becket and William Wykeham. Though there was occasionally a bitter struggle against ecclesiastical influence in secular affairs, the superior clergy, directly and indirectly, exercised a strong civil authority, and were parties to the power of the state.

For the first two hundred and fifty years succeeding the conquest, the pride and arrogance of the Normans, sustained by these points of superiority, kept them aloof from the Saxons. The oppression also which these suffered from their rulers embittered the division, and made the inferior party, as is wont to be the case, even more hostile than the superior one. French was the language of the court and of polite intercourse, and Saxon speech became a badge of inferiority and dependence. Cultivation and rank shrank away from it, and though it remained unshaken as the popular tongue, it soon began to undergo those changes, incident to grammatical decay, by which it passed into English. Resting for support upon the ignorant, and, from a literary point of view, the indifferent and the careless; living on the lips of the people, Saxon speech suffered a rapid loss of inflections and construction. These, dropping off by misuse and disuse, left the English the most bald, but one of the most simple and serviceable of languages.

The hostility of the Saxon subjects to their rulers was maintained, in the earlier reigns, by the

connection of the English throne with ducal authority in Normandy, making the fortunes of the former
dependent on the latter; and by the severe rule of
the Normans, especially in the extension of forests,
and preservation of game.   Little was done to consolidate the nation till after the loss of Normandy
under king John, and the final identification of th
conquerors with England as the exclusive seat of
authority, and centre of all possessions.

There were indeed influences which began at
once to abate the hostility of the Saxons and Normans, and prepare the way for their later union in
one nation.   The clergy, never altogether partisan
in its character, constantly became less so.   The
Englishman, Saxon or Norman in descent, found an
open path to preferment in the church; and thus
the Norman features of authority rapidly softened
in that most influential body, the clergy.   Thus
both Becket and Wykeham came up from the people, and won by talent the prominent positions they
held.

The wars also of the Normans in Wales, in Ireland and on the continent, made them more dependent on the Saxons, and their common victories
served to unite the two races.   Add to these causes
the softening influences of time, and of intercourse
between parties of very unequal opportunities and
rank, indeed, but characterized alike by solid endowments, and we are prepared for that ultimate
subsidence of the flexible Normans into the mass
of the community, by which the nation became one
again in its dissolved and evenly diffused elements.

The Norman provinces being lost—a fresh indebtedness of the nation, like that for the first charter of its liberties, to the tyranny and weakness of John—the two divisions of the English people, enclosed in one kingdom, and one island, and one set of interests; too closely interlocked to render separation either desirable or possible, were, in the reign of Edward III., firmly compacted and welded together by their common national victories on the continent; and by the commencement of that bitter warfare with France which evoked a rivalry and hostility of the two nations, from that time onward shaping the history of both of them. Already, then, in the fourteenth century, had there begun to be a movement toward liberty at home, interesting Norman lord and Saxon thane alike, while that century beheld the two, side by side, as Englishmen, gaining great victories on French battle-fields, and consolidating their national unity by a prolonged conflict with those who had been to the Norman kinsmen and fellow-subjects. In the battle of Cressy, the English yeomen, a Saxon branch of the service, became a recognized national feature and national power by the stubbornness with which they held the field. This sense of superior unity, this growth of English influence are evinced by that national jealousy which compelled Edward, on opening the conflict, to declare, "We will and grant and stablish that our said realm of England, nor the people of the same, of what estate or condition they be, shall not, in any time to come, be put in subjection nor in obeisance of us, nor of our heirs and successors, as kings of France." We find also a similar concession to national feeling in the law that all pleas "shall be pleaded, shewed, defended, answered, debated and judged in the English tongue." This was not only a step toward nationality, it was equally one toward justice and liberty, by bringing the action of the courts more immediately under the knowledge and criticism of the people. We know indeed that all legal and legislative proceedings were not at once thereon transferred into English, but for a time bore a mixed character. So decisive a movement could not complete itself instantly. In France, it was two centuries and one-half later, when a kindred transfer into the vernacular was effected.

What, then, are the features of English character, appearing in this new nation, whose political, social and literary elements were, in the fourteenth century, passing into permanent union? The English are a reflective people, as opposed to an impulsive, passionate one. Herein they are the reverse of the Irish, and unlike the sprightly, intuitive French. They have not the enthusiasm for a sentiment which stirs the French to such extreme and contradictory action; but they have a dogged policy, a predisposition settled in interest and conviction, which render them the most calculable and patient, and ultimately the most irresistible, force in European politics. It is inspiration to an army of France, that forty centuries look down on it from the pyramids; it nerves an English fleet to be told, in severe phrase, that England expects every man to do his duty. What the sentiments are to one nation, the interests of life are to the other; and if there is here some want of brilliancy, there is none of substantial good. If there is less to nourish taste, there is more to feed affection; if the fire does not flame in every wind, it is well raked in, and keeps warm the national hearth from century to century.

The cast of English character is also of an external, objective type, rather than of an internal, subjective one. In this they are opposed to the Germans. English thought issues in a physical good, a social gain, a practical view, with one foot upon the land and one upon the sea; German thought issues in a theory, a speculation, a criticism, whose locality and bearings are scarcely asked for; which traverses the air, or, touching the earth, does it at times with a cloven foot. The fruits of the German mind are subtile spirits, that spring out of great heat of thought, bent, in wayward fashion, on any or no mission; the fruits of the English mind are spirits of a cold, tame, and serviceable cast, that, at the worst, can, like Caliban, be pinched and whipped into hard work. Thus idealism has found few disciples in England, and the entire drift of her philosophy has been materialistic. For the most part she has grounded morals in utility, and thus made her theory the reflection of her practice. Amid all her plodding, patient virtues, she has rarely had a bold, brilliant ideal, plucking at the heart, and lifting society into revolution. This reflective, external cast of English character has colored her literature and history, and, united with her insular, protected position, has given rise to a social and civil growth, slow, safe and continuous; a growth that renders her institutions the most instructive and interesting in the record of modern nations.

Having defined the national character, everywhere effective in English literature, we shall consider the foreign influences at work in its initiative period, the last half of the fourteenth century. Indirectly, modern Europe is deeply indebted to the literature and cultivation of Greece and Rome. These were the seeds left in the soil; and when the first savage, rugged growth of barbarism was cleared away, it was these that occupied the field, and slowly beautified it. The Latin influence was wrought into Latin Christianity, and spread, therefore, with the evangelization of the Gothic races. Moreover these races came in their conquests everywhere in contact with the laws and civilization of Rome, laws which slowly resumed sway in those provinces in which they had become indigenous. Latin was the only universal language of western Europe in the Middle Ages; contained the works of religion, science, philosophy, the products of the times; and transmitted also the classical works of earlier Rome.

Grecian philosophy and poetry were more remote and indirect in their influence. The logic of Aristotle gave shape to the scholastic philosophy, but in a secondary form as it had found transmission through Arabic, Jewish, Latin mediums. The direct influence of classical authors on English literature in the fourteenth century would seem to

have been slight. It was most immediately indebted to the Latin for those stories of earlier times,
which reappear so often in the works of Chaucer
and of later poets. These tales, increased by those
of Oriental origin, and by others, native to the west
of Europe, furnished a stock in trade to all the
poets. They were transmitted in Latin collections,
and also transferred to the vernacular tongues of
the West. It was the hold they had secured on the
popular mind by constant repetition, and the semi-
historical character they bore in that credulous age,
that fitted them to the purposes of the mediæval
minstrelsy, and gave them, by steady accretion, that
flexible form and controlling influence which ren
dered them, even to such men as Chaucer and
Shakespeare, a constant source of material. These
themes were already in possession of a popular interest denied to a purely literary creation; and the
subjects of literature had thus a conventional existence and force to which all readily yielded. The
growth of history and invention has slowly pushed
aside these stories, that thus presented new versions
with every transfer, though even in our day we occasionally return to them with fresh zest.

The second foreign force, which was especially
operative in English literature, was Italian influence.
As was to be expected, Italy was the first division
of Europe, after the barbaric overflow, to regain
the arts of civilization. In commerce, in freedom,
in the industrial and fine arts, in literature, and,
later, in science, she took the lead, a position she
has failed to maintain, chiefly through political di-

visions and ecclesiastical tyranny. No real liberty of thought, or settled polity, has found foothold on her soil. The three great poets of the fourteenth century were Dante, Petrarch, and Chaucer, two Italian and one English. The first of these in time was Dante. He was much less influenced than the other two in the form of his poetry by his own period. There was more moral elevation in his theme, there were more ethical force and sentiment in his execution, and he aspired, under the guidance of Virgil, to the breadth and dignity of a great poet. Next came Petrarch, with whom Chaucer may have met. His poetry was of that lyrical cast which chiefly affected English literature later than the time of Chaucer. Chaucer, the last of the three, stands in more immediate sympathy with Boccaccio, whose rehearsal in the Decameron of mediæval tales has won for him his chief reputation. Some of these Chaucer has borrowed, or both have taken them from common sources. We may well believe that Chaucer was quickened by his Italian contemporaries, without being very directly guided by them.

A last foreign influence, and one more immediate than either of the others, were the romances and *fabliaux* of the Normans. The *fabliaux* were of a popular cast, briefer than the romances, and more diversified in their subjects. They had the ease, humor, and variety of the story, and were keyed to minor occasions. The romances were fitted to the intellectual palate of the gentry, were narrative and heroic, and required for their rehearsal a more select occasion. The minstrels of northern and southern France divided the sentiments of chivalry between them. The valor and daring of the true cavalier were magnified by the Trouvère; while the amatory song of the Troubadour dwelt on the devotion of the knight to his lady-love. Petrarch stood in much the same relation to the lyric poetry of the south as Chaucer did to the epic verse of the north. Each form degenerated, though the degeneracy of erotic song is ever more fatal than that of heroic verse. The sentiment of love had, at best, in chivalry but an artificial and forced development, and was ready for an easy decline into lasciviousness. The courage and valor of chivalry were more simple, sincere, normal to the condition of society; and though liable to become hair-brained and extravagant in the exploits undertaken, yet retained some sound and wholesome quality.

The romances deserve attention because of the influence they exerted on our Norman ancestry, and the social character of western Europe; because a first and chief literary service to which the early English was put was the reception, and circulation, in prose and metrical form, of these narratives, as translated from the French; and because the character of English poetry has all along been affected by them, and that too strongly in its later periods. The chief subjects of these romances were Arthur and his knights, Charlemagne and his followers. Later were added warriors of the Crusades, and Grecian heroes. The story of Arthur and his knights of the round table offers a good illustration of the growth of poetic fiction, its steady enlargement, the transmission of its resources, the currency and increasing interest it gives to its inventions. As chivalry was an institution of rigid and overstrained sentiments, this, its literary side, was very requisite to it, both as expressing and enforcing its views of character, as stimulating and rewarding its heroes. The minstrel was essential to the knightly pageant, as giving body, form and circulation to those fine-spun sentiments of life, of love, and of loyalty; making them felt and operative in the rough, lawless impulses of the age. Without the minstrel to rehearse, in hours of leisure and festivity, warlike achievements; and make positive, frequent and pungent their stimulus, chivalry could scarcely have gained or retained the influence it exerted. It is not surprising that the minstrel became a sort of sacred character with claims of ingress and entertainment everywhere. The minstrel put the experience and exploits of the knight in their most transfigured and poetic form, and rehearsed them to his flattered and delighted senses. He became to the knight his idealizing spirit, holding before him a magic mirror, in which his deeds found the liveliest and most fascinating reflection. The knight thus learned how nobly he acted, how tenderly he felt, and with what enchantment he was invested. When these romances became more extravagant, and were, moreover, in the decay of chivalry, increasingly divorced from the actual temper and wants of men, it was a most serviceable task which Cervantes undertook in Don Quixote, that of turn ing into ridicule the notion of knight errantry. We shall scarcely understand the value and success of this work, except as we see in it a last blow given to a proud and mischievous sentiment lingering beyond its time.

The Normans, famous cavaliers, haughty and irritable, had embodied their social feelings in this Romance literature, and could scarcely unite themselves to a new language and nationality without a transfer of these, their favorite literary recreations. Thus the fourteenth century beheld a large reproduction in English of these works, so essential to an adventurous and chivalrous gentry. Thus were they able to wont themselves to their new home with a reduced sense of loss.

We have now spoken of the essential constituents of literature, urging two points, that the æsthetical impulse, or the element of form, is predominant in literature, and the more so as long periods are taken into consideration; and that a controlling force, giving character to the literary effort of any period, is found in the ethical nature. This is the light which imparts depth and coloring to our spiritual heavens, and, negatively or positively, determines the tone of the passing hour. We have spoken of the sluggish strength of the Saxons, the flexible enterprise of the Normans, slowly uniting to form English character on a type of unrivalled, patient, practical and aspiring sagacity. We then passed to the foreign influences at work in England in the fourteenth century, the initiative period of its literature. In common with western Europe, the germs which began to reclothe the earth, when the flood of barbaric invasion had passed by, and the sedimentary deposit had become fixed, were found in Christianity, modified and sustained by Latin civilization. The classical influence on popular literature showed itself chiefly in a fund of stories, wrought and rewrought by the minstrelsy of different nations. Italy, as at the very centre of these civilizing forces, yielded the earliest growth, and became a source of art and literary cultivation to the Western nations. A third force felt in England was the native Norman poetry, indigenous to the times, peculiarly vigorous, and closely connected with their chivalrous character and customs.

Such were the more remote fountains that fed the streams of English thought. We shall next turn to those which at home more directly and copiously maintained it. Many are the forces, near at hand and afar off, that are at work in national character and national life. If the future lies an open field before us, we march to take possession of it with our flocks and herds and household stuff. The good and the evil travel on together, and renew their conflict at each successive stage. We have sketched the leading conditions under which the English nation, newly compacted in its elements, occupied the fourteenth century, and made ready to work out the national history. As this evolves itself, we shall see the old taking up the new, and the new uniting itself to the old, with the organic freedom of forces, that hold within themselves their own law of life.

2

LECTURE II.

WE have now to speak of those home or domestic influences which in England gathered about and helped to shape the literature of the fourteenth century.

They drop into four classes; religious or ethical forces, social forces, language, and the directions or divisions of literature. These lie like concentric circles around the germinant points of growth, each succeeding one approaching more nearly, and affecting more definitely, the literary product of the time ; yet falling off in the scope and breadth of its influence.

The outer, or ethical circle, when it fails to determine the immediate form and spirit of a production, constitutes none the less the atmosphere, the climate, under which it grows up, and thus decides the vigor of its life. Ethical influences so pervade our national life, that, positively or negatively, they set limits to all that is said or done in it. Like the rarity or density of the air, they settle the flight that is open to a given stroke of wing, how high it shall bear the spirit upward.

In the fourteenth century, religion inter-penetrated society, visibly touching and modifying it at

(26)

all points.   Its apparent power was much greater
than now, its actual power much less.   In proportion as faith forsakes the heart, and therefore ceases
to rule in its own hidden and spiritual realm, does
it strive, by compensation, in an external, solemn
and ceremonial way, to show its presence, and secure authority over a portion of the actions of men.
When men make a compromise with religion, withholding a part and giving a part, their religious acts
become at once exacting in form and ostentatious
in fulfilment.   They are the purchase-money, the
exemption payment, good only as they are clearly
and abundantly certified.   Forms and superstitions
are surface eruptions; the blood clearing itself by
cutaneous disease.   The national life, failing to
absorb and healthily to use the spiritual element,
casts it to the surface in fears, credulities, and
frivolous observances.

In this and adjunct centuries, court, castle,
cloister and cottage were equally infested with religion, and almost equally destitute of it.   The corruption of the theory and practice of religion, was
preparing the way for the reformation.   The sources
of religious authority had become the sources of
evil, and virtue had been compelled to find a refuge
in the individual heart alone.   This is the description of Avignon while the seat of the papacy, as
given by Petrarch.   " You imagine that the city of
Avignon is the same now that it was when you re-
sided in it ; it is very different.   It was then, it is
true, the worst and vilest place on earth, but it has
now become a terrestrial hell, a residence of fiends

and devils, a receptacle of all that is most wicked and abominable. In this city there is no piety, no reverence or fear of God, no faith or charity, nothing that is holy, just, equitable or humane. Why should I speak of truth when not only the houses, palaces, courts, churches and the thrones of popes and cardinals, but the very earth and air seem to teem with lies. Good men have of late been treated with so much contempt and scorn, that there is not one left amongst them to be an object of their laughter." *

This corruption was unequal in different branches of the church. The higher clergy had more incentives to vice than the inferior clergy, and among these were to be found many devout men. The mendicant orders also, existing under a peculiarly distorted and vagrant form of life, became correspondingly vicious and worthless. In the gallery of the Canterbury Tales, we have portraits of various religious personages. Let us glance at them.

First, there is a well-to-do monk, with gown lined with the finest fur, a lover of good horses and good living, and fond of the chase.

> His hed was balled, and shone as any glass,
> And eke his face, as it hadde ben anoint,
> He was a lord ful fat and in good point.
> His eyen stepe, and rolling in his head,
>
>   *   *   *   *   *   *   *   *
>
> He was not pale as a forpined gost,
> A fat swan loved he best of any rost.

He cares little about the rules of his order, and is bent on having a good time.

* Henry's "History of Great Britain," vol. viii. p. 366.

> This ilke monk lette olde thinges pace.
> And held after the newe world the trace.
> He yave not of the text a pulled hen,
> That saith, that hunters ben not holy men:

Next comes a friar, a mendicant, full of dalliance and fair language.

> He was an esy man to give penance,
> Ther as he wiste to han a good pitance:

*　　*　　*　　*　　*　　*　　*　　*

> Therto he strong was as a champioun,
> And knew wel the tavernes in every toun,
> And every hosteler and gay tapstere.

He shirked beggars, was familiar with prosperous farmers, pleased the housewives, and had more skill than any one in his cloister in securing, by means of soft, lisping English, a merry song, a twinkling eye, even from the poorest widow, a farthing before he left.

Then comes the clerk of Oxford, as yet without a benefice.

> As lene was his hors as is a rake,
> And he was not right fat, I undertake.

He had in him the spirit of scholarship, however, and preferred to have at his bed's head, twenty books of Aristotle than rich robes or fiddle.

> Of studie toke he moste cure and hede,
> Not a word spake he more than was nede;
> And that was said in forme and reverence,
> And short and quike, and ful of high sentence.

On the parish parson, Chaucer bestows a rich dowry of graces. He is learned, devout, diligent, self-denying; watching over his flock with tenderness, and guiding them equaliy by example and precept. He withholds nothing necessary to complete the character of a faithful and loving teacher.

> That Christes gospel trewely wolde preche,
>
> *   *   *   *   *   *   *   *
>
> A better preest I trowe that nowher non is,
> He waited after no pompe ne reverence,
> Ne maked him no spiced conscience,
> But Christes lore, and his apostles twelve,
> He taught, but first he folwed it himselve.

Quite another person is the sompnour, or summoner, whose office it was to call any person who had broken the laws of Holy Church. He had a fire-red face, narrow eyes, scald brows, a beard thin and scurvy, and warts and freckles, that no ointment could mollify. He liked leeks, onions and strong wine, and when tipsy, shouted his law Latin as one mad. He was a terror to children, commuted the sentences of the arch-deacon for a fine, and sought everywhere his vicious and lecherous pleasures, yielding like indulgences to others on terms of a bribe.

One other religious character appears in the pardoner. His yellow hair flowed loosely down his shoulders.

> His wallet lay beforne him in his lappe,
> Bret-ful of pardon come from Rome al hote,
>
> *   *   *   *   *   *   *   *
>
> And in a glas he hadde pigges bones,

which he sold as those of saints.

> But with these relikes, whanne that he fond
> A poure persone dwelling up on lond,
> Upon a day, he gat him more moneie
> Than that the persone gat in monethes tweie.

He performed his services in a loud commanding voice, denounced habitually the love of money
as the root of all evil, produced his bulls from Rome,
spoke a few words in Latin to season his discourse,
and admonished his hearers,

> That no man be so bold, ne preest ne clerk,
> Me to disturbe of Christes holy werk.

He then produced his relics, informed the rustics of
the various cures they would work on man and
beast, and their power to remove jealousy. He
unblushingly announces, to his fellow-travellers, his
temper of mind.

> For I wol preche and beg in sondry londes,
> I wol not do no labour with min hondes,
> Ne make baskettes for to live therby,
> Because I wol not beggen idelly,
> I wol non of the apostles contrefete:
> I wol have money, wolle, chese and whete,
> Al were it yeven of the pourest page,
> Or of the pourest widewe in a village:
> Al shulde hire children sterven for famine.

Such are the strong contradictions of character
that the religious world presented in the time of
Chaucer, and such the preponderance of evil.
Over against the devout parson, appear the sleek,
luxurious, self-indulgent monk, with strong physical
appetites; the meddlesome friar, full of low cunning, importunate and unscrupulous; the summoner,
or go-between in ecclesiastical courts, persecuting
the innocent, sheltering offenders, commuting penalties, loathsome in the personal fruits of sin, and
full of effrontery; the pardoner, bent on gain,
plausible in appearance, sacrilegious in speech,

unconscientious in method, with a joint stock of
falsehood and cunning, working as an inexhaustible
vein of wealth, the ignorance and superstition of
the lower classes ; and a canon, introduced later,
who is deeply involved in the delusions and frauds
of alchemy.

There are in this picture of the religious life of
the times, the sharpest contradictions and the
highest irritations, These are of two kinds, both
of which strongly affected the literature of the century ; the irritation of the ethical sense of a few, the
irritation of the common-sense of many. The one
result finds representation in Wicliffe, the other in
Chaucer. The spirit of Christianity has never been
so smothered under those rank overgrowths of superstition that have shot above it, as not, from time
to time, to make new points of disclosure. This
has never been merely a fallen and decaying trunk,
nourishing lichen, moss and fern, but has some-
where sent up a fresh growth, wherewith to replace
and continue the primitive stock. Early and significant among those movements of sturdy resistance,
which at length resulted in the Reformation, was
that of Wicliffe, a rejection on moral grounds of
that perverted, religious life expressed in the eccle-
siasticism of the time. Christianity indicates its
independent, spiritual power, shows itself to be
rooted in the constitution of man and the world, by
the vigorous way in which it has ever opened a new
conflict within its own household, rejected the devel-
opments which oppressing, perverting circumstances
have fastened upon it, and, returning to initial prin-

ciples, has once more forced its way outward in renewed, regenerated activity. One of the purest and
most influential of these efforts of restoration found
its origin in this antagonism of the religious life of
England.

The second irritation was more general, but less
powerful than this of the religious sense. It sprang
from the exacting, dishonest and openly corrupt form
which religious action had assumed. It rejected
the monk, not because he was a monk, but because
he despised and laughed at the rules of his order.
It rejected the friar, not because he imposed con-
fession and penance, but because he did it in his own
behoof; the summoner, not as an officer of justice,
but for his ribaldry and extortion; and the seller of
indulgences, not on account of his traffic, but because he dealt in sham relics.

> And thus with fained flattering and japes,
> He made the persone and the peple, his apes.

The summoner and mendicant friar were especially distasteful to the English. They each, in the
Canterbury Tales, expose the misdeeds of the other,
and, in a conflict of mutual abuse, are drawn out
and set apart for our equal and hearty detestation.
They both sinned against strong English feelings,
the one against fair dealing, and honesty between
man and man; and the other against the privacy and
purity of the home. The mendicant was held in
detestation as an unmanly, impertinent beggar, who
pretended to pay for his keep and clothing in
prayers, and then shirked even this return. His
habitual and unforgiven sin was that,

2*

> In every hous he gan to pore and prie,

and thus left no place free from his meddling and mischief, his sales and pious pilfer.

The offence of the summoner, though less irritating and constant, was not less grave. In the tales to which reference has been made, one of the class serves a false notice on a widow, and then professes himself willing to hush up the matter for twelve pence. Failing of this, he lays claim to her new pan. The upshot is, that the devil, who has been the travelling companion in disguise of the summoner, puts in an appearance, and claims his own in this wise,

> Now brother, quod the devil, be not wroth;
> Thy body and this panne ben min by right,
> Thou shalt with me to helle yet to-night.
> Wher thou shalt knowen of our privatee
> More than a maister of divinitee.

While, therefore, these pertinacious, multiplied, omnipresent abuses of the religious impulse found a strong support in the ignorance and superstition of the masses, they were also at war with stubborn English instincts, a love of home, industry and justice; and were a perpetual irritant to the common-sense and good-will of the more intelligent. The religious influence of the time, therefore, was one of general restlessness, provoking satire and stern attack.

The social phase of life, the second circle of force that gathered about our literature, was of an equally declared and extreme cast. Its prevailing spirit was that of chivalry. However, the poet may idealize this institution, the philanthropist can only regard it as casting a slight glow over a very dark and discouraging period. It grew out of incessant warfare, and this under the unendurable form of public and private feud, of contagious, universal and interminable strife ; a state of things which a lingering sentiment of humanity sought feebly to remedy by the Truce of God, rescuing, under the sanction of religious sentiments, a portion of each week from acts of violence. The mailed knight fills the historic, as well as the poetic, page ; and the gentry of France, cutting down and riding over their own foot-soldiers at the battle of Cressy, the more quickly to reach the enemy, reveals the spirit of the age. The soldier came to receive much larger pay than the artisan ; and gentility honored or won its rank in the tournament and on the battle-field. The literature, like the life of the time, was imbued with an extravagant martial spirit. A large amount of composition in Western Europe gave itself to inflaming the sentiments of chivalry, and resulted in incalculable mischief, so far as all peaceful and just life was concerned.

No permanent, civil, commercial or social good could grow out of this martial mania, or bless a people cursed by it. The fictions of poetry may make a glowing dream of it, but the facts of history can only show it to have been a waking, widespread horror ; a perpetual disruption of society, and overthrow of its peaceful virtues and fruitful arts.

The courtly qualities into which chivalry was baptized, were courage, loyalty, courtesy, munifi-

cence. Its sentiment was honor; its reward, love.
Exalted as these incentives may seem, they were
so divorced from sober, substantial, retiring virtues;
so overleaped the bounds of common-sense and
common honesty, as often to make their possessors
more implacable and infuriate than simple, native
savageness would have rendered them. The honor
of knights was one that wrought irritation among
themselves, and contempt toward all others; their
love and courtesy were fanciful, exaggerated sentiments, ready to overstep the limits of marital obligation and domestic virtue. Their courage and loyalty
were merely the breath of praise, with which they
blew their own passions into an intolerable heat;
and their munificence, the free, careless hand which
goes with rapine and tyranny. Such virtues, like
polished armor, may dazzle the vagrant eye, but so
far as they conceal, adorn and quicken the demoni-
ac spirit of war, they are all the worse for the brilliancy of the disguise. Prodigal splendor, thought-
less courage, and that magnanimity which, punctili-
ous to equals, makes little of the safety and the
happiness and the rights of inferiors that chance to
lie in its path, have not much to commend them
to humanity. They are born of selfishness and tyranny, and, therefore, in their ultimate elements
are most mean and base and worthless.

We are wont to think that women were especially indebted to the courtesy of chivalry, and this, in
a measure, is true, if we consider the violence and
rude passion of the times. Man as against man,
enforced certain restraints under this sentiment.

It was a reduction and softening down of a rough and lawless period. Yet it, itself, often rose to a foolish fanaticism, or sank to gross impurity. It had its "love fraternities," "love courts," leading to absurdities only less than those of the religious sentiment; and instituting obligations quite in oversight of the duties of domestic life. If we were to go back to the darkness of those dark days, we might be glad to cheer it with the light of chivalry, but fortunately we are rid of both.

Yet if men are to be brutish, we would certainly desire that they might also be courageous; if they are to be proud, we would wish to temper pride with courtesy; if they are to fight, it is better they should do it in fellowship, for this is partial peace; if they are to revel, that their indulgences should come with social sentiments and jollity. Chivalry was the deceptive bloom of unripe fruit; those who set their teeth in it, found it sharp and indigestible. Chivalry gave a tint of amethyst to a bitter winter's day. Those who looked out from castle windows, found their delight in it, but God's poor were frozen none the less. Later, as the expression of a sweet and gentle heart, as the dream of poetry, it has become quite another thing, a prodigality of nature that at once satisfies the mind and feeds the senses.

Pride, in a violent and offensive form, is closely connected with the ascendancy of the military spirit.

Says Froissart: "When I was at Bordeaux, a little before the departure of the Prince of Wales on his expedition into Spain, I observed that the

English were so proud and haughty, that they could not behave to the people of other nations with any appearance of civility."

Says William of Malmsbury : "Every one swelling with pride and rancor scorns to cast a look on his inferiors, disclaims his equals, and proudly rivals his superiors." A Venetian traveller gives this description of the English : "They think that there are no other men than themselves, and no other world but England ; and whenever they see a handsome foreigner, they say that he looks like an Englishman." This pride, enhanced, doubtless, by the superiority of the Norman to the Saxon, was also greatly strengthened by the personal superiority of the knight, encased in armor, to soldiers of inferior grade. To the inevitable arrogance of military authority, was thus added almost complete personal impunity. The musket-ball, when it came, was a great leveller, and powder has been the most democratic of inventions. Modern society, though in fact widening the real differences in character and advantages between the high and low, has greatly reduced the pride that attends upon these distinctions. The knight, scarcely superior to his followers in cultivation, was thrown by the conditions of his life on terms of familiar intercourse, almost intimacy, with them. With all his haughtiness, he mingled habitually with his servants, and accepted close personal service from them. He combined, in one character, the arrogant leader and jovial companion, drawing near to his retainers in tastes and sentiments, while he stood apart from them in rank.

Thus the rough leader both swears with and swears at his comrades.

The luxury of the nobility showed itself chiefly in food and dress. Their castles, constructed for defense, were, in most cases, but narrow and cheerless abodes. Their feasts were of a hearty and rollicking, rather than of a refined and luxurious, character. Sixty fat oxen are mentioned as an item in one of them. A love of hospitality early belonged to the English. Says the same Italian traveller, "They think that no greater honor can be conferred or received, than to invite others to eat with them ; and they would sooner give five or six ducats to provide an entertainment for a person, than a groat to assist him in any distress." *   Over against this luxury of the few, we have to put very general poverty and a low grade of life, especially in the country and villages. The laws were very inadequately administered, and property was insecure. The peasantry in their houses of " mud and sticks " were often at the mercy of depredators, and agriculture was greatly depressed. This is shown by the frequent and severe famines, and the various forms of pestilence, the plague, the sweating sickness, the black tongue, that swept through the country, at times almost depopulating it. Discouragement, poverty and extreme ignorance hovered over the masses. Debased by superstition, and familiar with injury, they had too little to hope for, and too little to lose, to offer much resistance. In the open country, so weak were the laws, there was little pro-

* Knight's " History of England," vol. ii. p. 254.

tection for industry, and hence little motive to it. The home of the peasant was open to plunder, without hope of redress. The coat of arms of one of these marauders bore this inscription, " I am Captain Warner, commander of a troop of robbers, an enemy to God, without pity and without mercy."* In the cities, especially in London, the middle classes first learned their power, and by commerce and the arts climbed into strength. The domestic virtues had yet secured but a slight foothold, and the homes of the nobles with their heavy, cheerless walls, and large dining-halls, pushed into the foreground the ideas of feasting and defense. War stood on the right side, and riot on the left.

The character of woman always goes far to define social influences, as she, above all, is subject to them, and they in turn are, in large part, in her keeping. There are two types of female character that appear in Chaucer, the fruits, on opposite sides, of the spirit of the age. The first is represented by the prioress, simple, pleasing, and dainty, winning in manners, gentle and pitiful in disposition.

> " At mete was she wel ytaughte withalle ;
> She lette no morsel from hire lippes falle,
> Ne wette hire fingres in hire sauce depe.
> Wel coude she carie a morsel, and wel kepe,
> Thatte no drope ne fell upon hire brest."

Pretty and agreeable accomplishments were these, when one without forks shared his trencher with his companion. Forks, needful instruments as they are of refinement, seem to have fallen earlier to

---

* Henry's History, vol. viii. p. 386.

the Fiji than to Englishmen. It is probable, therefore, that human flesh was one of the first morsels held in dainty contemplation at a fork's end.*

Quite opposite to her, is the type seen in the wife of Bath, skilled in weaving and domestic manufacture, bold in bearing, and, withal, a woman of large travel.

"Thrice had she been at Jerusalem." She was loud in laughter and in talk.

> " Bold was hire face, and fayre and rede of hew.
> Housbondes at the chirche dore had she had five."

Jaunty, thrifty, and fearless, careful neither in speech nor act, she made herself formidable either as a spouse or a companion. Her latest and best conjugal adjustment was this:

> " And whan that I had getten unto me
> By maistrie all the soverainetee,
> And that he sayd, min owen trewe wif,
> Do as thee list, the terme of all thy lif,
> Kepe thin honour, and kepe eke min estat ;
> After that day we never had debat."

A like and stronger contrast is there between such a character as Grisilde and the hostess of the Tabard ; the one softening the harsh, extreme tyranny of her lord by patient submission and unconquerable affection ; the other striving perpetually to goad and exasperate her husband into an ill-nature equal to her own.

> " By Goddes bones, whan I bete my knaves,
> She bringeth me the grete clobbed staves,
> And cryeth ; slee the dogges everich on,
> And breke hem bothe bak and every bon."

---

* Pre-Historic Times, p. 454.

These contrasts belong to a period of rude domination, where the only choice for woman lay between the extremes of submission and resistance; between coarse strength, lawless, unlovely and invulnerable force; and meek endurance, the persuasion of patience, the gentle, admirable graces of weakness. One may love these virtues, though he hates the violence that evokes them. English society in the time of Chaucer was still in that savage state in which woman must either shy and dodge the brutality about her, making such a show as she was able of the mild and submissive traits of character; or, bursting the bonds of slavery and nature at once, become formidable by becoming unendurable, setting up her safeguards in the violence of vituperation. Thus we have the shrew; a character so familiar in the early drama. The virtues and vices of bondage partake alike of its taint.

The church sinned against woman in two respects. While it made of marriage a sacrament, it, nevertheless, by insisting on the celibacy of the clergy, and constructing its religious orders on the same principle, gave an inferior, an impure character to this relation, especially fitted to reflect discredit upon woman. Far worse than this: by the licentiousness of its chosen servants it invaded the household, and established, as vicious connections, those relations which it scorned to accept in good faith. Thus the religious corps became as numerous, as searching, and as unclean as the frogs of Egypt, which penetrated into all quarters, into the ovens and kneading-troughs, leaving their filthy trail wherever they went. Henry, Bishop of Liege, could unblushingly boast the birth of twenty-two children in fourteen years.

Chaucer says, that many hundred years ago, England was full of fairies and elfs, but now every field and every stream so swarms with friars, thick as motes in a sunbeam, that the jolly crew have altogether fled. He delivers the last telling blow of his irony in the words:

> " Women may now go safely up and doun,
>   In every bush, and under every tree,
>   Ther is non other incubus but he,
>   And he ne will don hem no dishonour."

Such is the gain the poetic satire tosses to view, the presence of scrupulous, meek-eyed friars, in the place of wanton, mischief-making fairies, in the groves and along the by-paths.

One of the most undeniable social features of the time, showing their half-barbaric cast, was that sensuality of language which is the cheap dye of vulgar wit. The taint of it is especially strong in Chaucer, frequently quite overpowering the poetic aroma. One wonders what evil beast has strayed among these flowers. I confess to a certain shame in speaking of Chaucer to the healthy and pure, so far is he from wholesome companionship. As mirrored in the Canterbury Tales, English speech was at once gross and licentious. The offence is palpable to the very senses, and not to the moral instincts simply. Startled by the sudden burden of the air, we hasten on, nor care to know all the grounds of the wrong done us. Distance is our instant and only remedy. Those superior instincts of our nature, by which we lift the eye and thought from the animal portions and gross functions of our being, by which we move amid contamination as light unstained of evil things, were all forgotten; and men, as swine, rooted for food where food chanced to be. There is no apology for this; it is the personal impurity, the filth unwashed away, that remain from a savage life. There is only one point of reduction we have to make. Language, before it is cleansed of a given license, does not, to those who then use it, bring the same gross imagery and rank offence, that it necessarily does to those, who, from an advanced position, for a moment, return to it. Though it is not true, that language and life, the exterior form and interior fact of virtue, are independent of each other; that ribaldry does not taint the blood, and burn as fire in the bones, it is true, that coarseness of speech and grossness of action, owing a portion of their startling effect upon us to the want of familiarity, are more consistent with substantial purity in those who are habituated to them, than they at first sight seem to be. Enough; we thank God there are five centuries between us and this surface sewerage of early English society. Vice is buried deeper, and by so much leaves the atmosphere purer, now than then.

Our third topic is that of language. For the first two hundred years following the Conquest, the divisions of speech seem to have been strongly de-

fined. Latin, the language of the church, was the
universal tongue, the medium of communication on
topics of religion and philosophy. French was the
speech of the court and nobles; and Saxon, of the
mass of the nation. Layamon's Chronicle, a work
of thirty-two thousand lines, written in Saxon, a
century and a half after the Conquest, contains
scarcely fifty French words. All of these languages were used carelessly, and, with the excep-
tion of Latin, chiefly in speech. They, therefore,
underwent rapid changes. Latin was saved from
permanent debasement by possessing a fixed point
of reversion and revision in classical literature, in a
standard previously set up, and which none could
abrogate or permanently modify. We may well
believe, however, that Latin suffered much perversion in its ordinary use. This is shown in what is
termed Leonine Verse, usually devoted to satire,
and constructed on accent and rhyme in neglect of
quantity; also in Macaronic Poetry, an amalgam of
different languages. Two archbishops in succession cautioned the universities against such forms
as; ego curret, tu curret, curens est ego, pressing
the point that they were not correct. Some have
supposed from the constancy with which Latin was
used in accounts, that there was a very general
familiarity with it. When, however, we look at
those accounts, we see that very little knowledge of
Latin was required for their composition. A few
connecting phrases were sufficient, and rendered
the same exhaustive service as a half-dozen words
to a court crier. We give an abridged example:

" Et pro uno seedcod empto III l,
  Et pro factura de drawgere IIId.
  Et pro uno dongecart empto XIVd."*

The Norman French, in the latter stages of change, as the nobles were slowly adopting the English, must, as a spoken language, have had a very shifting, careless law of use. This change seems to have occurred mainly in the fourteenth century. It was accompanied by the consolidation of the nation to which reference has been made; by a larger transfer of French romances to the English; and by that new national character shown in the works of Chaucer, marked though they are with French idioms and filled with French words. The Saxon, the neglected tongue of the common people, losing its organic force, first confounded and then dropped its grammatical inflexions. It thus passed into the simple and hospitable English, which, almost devoid of inflexions, could receive all the words of other languages that any chose to bring to it. The Saxon gave the bulk of its vocabulary to the English, left behind its distinctive and exacting features of grammar, and with the simplest possible construction, passed over as a new language to new-comers. That English pronunciation, under such a derivation, should be a network of perplexities and anomalies, is not surprising.

The English, in its very limited and fragmentary grammar, and comprehensive vocabulary, arose from social exigencies, which the nation inevitably

---

* Henry's History of Great Britain, vol. viii. p. 271.

and unconsciously strove to meet; and from the
fresh nationality which all parties were combining
to develop. In the fourteenth century, the uniting, constructive forces, had so far come to prevail,
that a new language, open for all uses, and ready
for a great career, was the result. Chaucer laid
hold of this germinant speech, disclosed its power
helped farther to determine the proportion of elements which should belong to it, and passed it on,
accelerated in growth and enriched by his handling.
He justified the language to itself and to others by
showing what it could do. He strengthened and
honored it by great literary works, and thus commended it to public favor. It has been observed,
that the English has changed less than other European languages in the years that have intervened
between the present and the fourteenth century.
For this fact, several reasons may be given. The
excellence and eminence of Chaucer served to set
up a standard, to establish early an authority in
the language. This conservative tendency was
greatly strengthened later by the translations of
the Bible, intimately connected with each other,
generally circulated, and closely united to popular
speech. Moreover, our chief literary period, that
of Elizabeth, lies relatively well back in our history, and thus early stamped on the language its
character. The linguistic fact of most significance
in the fourteenth century, is the junction then
effected in the elements of our vocabulary. We
may represent this union as the flowing of the
Norman into the Saxon, receiving from it a new

law and direction, and passing on with it as English. While, however, there was an influx in volume of French words in the fourteenth century, many smaller tributaries from it and the Latin, earlier and later, passed without observation into the new tongue, the great river of English speech.

The fourth and last circle of influence which gathered about our early literature, were the forms it assumed. It was almost exclusively a literature of poetry. The prose works of the time have an archaic and moral interest for us, rather than an artistic one. Poetry, not only comes first in literature proper, it is likely long to remain the almost exclusive feature of literary art, and is sure to retain the first position in all creative periods. Poetry owes so much to form, is so far the best expression of a shaping artistic force, as at once to imply its presence, and to invite its labor. Nor is it strange that we have poetry before we have prose, any more than it is strange that we have cathedrals, while those who build them still live in hovels. The strongest, most universal, most elevating impulse will be the first to command art. This in architecture is religion; and in literature is imaginative sentiment. Not till men have settled down to a faithful, thorough view of life, will they value prose as a vehicle of truth, a thesaurus of facts; and not till art has so diffused itself as to give grace and expression to the familiar, homely things of daily life, will prose become artistic, and pass up into literature.

Moreover, poetry has a definite form, a sensible impression, which allows its oral transfer without change, its rehearsal without shifting, aimless modifications. While language lives chiefly on the tongue and in the ear, the rhythm of poetry is the first luxury of speech, and takes to its service, the universal, easily aroused love of music, The minstrel blends in his rehearsal two arts, and draws the heart after him with double bonds. The changes also which rhythm calls for are readily made in these flexible periods of speech, and themselves become controlling, formative laws.

Prose, on the other hand, in its typical service, instruction,—for it is not till later, it furnishes the novel stealing in part the purposes of poetry,—belongs to written language, and periods of patient thought ; and implies, therefore, that the useful is holding even sway with the beautiful, reflection with imagination. Art, in the fourteenth century, rested as yet with poetry. We have, indeed, prose in two most diverse forms, but prose that serves rather to fix a date than to illuminate it.

Sir John Mandeville, in the middle of the century, gives us his gossipy, fugacious travels that stint at no marvels, and grant to myths as easy admittance as if the author were at a fairy tale. There are thus huddled together, fancies for the poet and a few facts for the historian ; as first reapers, on the margin of a great field, may gather and bind in one sheaf, grass and flowers and scattered heads of grain. The only other prose author requiring mention is Wicliffe. His was a simple,

3

sturdy, moral purpose; a translation of the Bible into the vernacular, the English of common life. In this he was aided by others. The simplicity and spirituality of their motive, and the direct, colloquial force of the current language, gave to this version a character like that which still belongs to our English Bible. This translation, appearing in 1480, had a wide circulation, though unaided by printing, and passed from hand to hand with danger.

It wrought secretly in the English mind for a century and a half, waiting for that second and more fortunate initiation of a like work under Tyndale, which gives the leading date to our present version.

These, then, are the domestic influences, the coarse and conflicting forces which joined hands, and gathered close around the growth of our literary art: a religion overlying offensively the surface of society, at war equally with the honest instincts of the human heart, and with the seeds of life hidden under its own corruptions; a social temper, extravagant and absurd in its fanciful virtues, gross in its real vices, fighting the deadliest sins with a poetic, fictitious sentiment; a language gorged with wayward, unorganized material, and waiting for some mastery of mind, some fire of the spirit to lift, consolidate and temper it; and a literature of poetry, that, with careless, uncritical strength, used or abused, as happened, whatever came to hand, that grew and flourished with native vigor, on the elements about it, rank as these sometimes were.

LECTURE III.

WE have now spoken of both the foreign and
domestic influences that gathered about the fourteenth century, the initiative period of English literature. There was but one man of such power
that we need to consider him separately; to mark
the control of his genius as itself a distinct element
of growth. That man was Chaucer. Though the
times in a measure circumscribe genius, genius
gives to the times the brightest light that is in
them. The position and material of the illumina-
tion are found in the age; but how far its pointed
flame shall ascend is determined by him who feeds
it. Without Chaucer, the fourteenth century would
flicker and glimmer in our literary history with a
light but little greater than that of antecedent years.
If the dreary, tedious Gower, for a time at least the
friend of Chaucer, remained as the chief representative of early English poetry, few indeed would
seek those pale rays, or much value them when
found. It was the task of genius to lift the period

(51)

into permanent distinction, and shed upon it its serene glory. Gower, ambling his Pegasus with placid indifference along a way of Latin or French or English verse, as it chanced, alike plodding in all, established the average grade of the time, spreads out, in his multitudinous verse, the Egyptian plain, above which towers in strength Chaucer, a sphynx that renders conspicuous and memorable through the silent repose of many centuries the entrance of that way, which leads in literature to our great national labors.

Chaucer was of moderate stature, full form, of somewhat retiring manners, with a sharp, humorous and downcast eye; a lover of books, and good living; of large experience, and varied intercourse with men. His life was not merely one of literary activity, but of extensive public service. He was directly attached to the court, and assigned missions of trust at home and abroad.

In quality of manhood he was thoroughly English. English in the outward, observant cast of his mind; in his honest handling of facts without gloss or concealment; in his humor, his good-fellowship, his love of men and their doings. Says Browne, in his enforcement of this point, "The national character is a root of bravery rising to a stem of strong, social feeling, gnarled and twisted just above the ground with genuine fun. Said to be slow to talk, the English are good fellows through it all. To put it differently, they are before all things human and sociable. In this sense, who is an Englishman more English than Chaucer. He loves the haunts of men, the places where they dwell, the episodes of mutual need that bring and keep them together; meat and drink; industry and play; the uprisings and downsittings, the incomings and outgoings of men and women." *

Thus English in character, Chaucer is the first national poet. This national force of the man is seen in many directions. His composition was fitted to interest all classes. Unlike the ballad or the romance or the treatise, it was directed to no one division of society, but brought amusement to all. It broke away from the literary traditions and restricted tastes of ranks and classes, and gave itself to general themes. This is especially true of his later and greater production, the Canterbury Tales Nothing could be more broad and catholic than these, open to the Englishman as English, and to man as man.

This nationality of taste is also seen in his uniform choice of the English language. He early translated the Romaunt of the Rose, one of the most popular of French poems, by way of adding interest and grace to his mother tongue. He acquired that mastery over the English, that ease of versification and aptness of expression in it, which bespeak one in love with his language, aiding it and aided by it in equal proportion. This clinging to the national speech, the coarse vernacular, and building it up in literary beauty and strength, disclose the truly national bent of his feelings and tastes. This, too, was at a time when the English

* Chaucer's England, vol. i. p. 47.

had hardly emerged from the disgrace of its servitude, and when unimpassioned poets, like Gower,
wandered far from the popular heart in Latin and
in French. There was a national vindication and
national service in this action of Chaucer ; and a
flavor, therefore, of national gratitude should mingle with our admiration of him.

Again, Chaucer was a progressive poet ; not a
radical reformatory poet, but one who always and
easily perceived the line of improvement, and had a
predilection for it ; chose to walk along it, at least
so far as good fellowship would allow him. Thus,
though by no means a reformer in the sense in
which Wicliffe was one, and ready doubtless to
render a general assent to the doctrines and even
the superstitions of the church, he had a keen
discernment of its many abuses in practice, and
lashes the delinquents with unsparing satire. It
is thought that he owed some of his predilection
for English, and vigor in it, to an acquaintance with
Wicliffe, and to the Piers Ploughman of Lang-
lande. This poem, of a religious, satirical, allegorical and erratic character, fitted for popular circulation, was more vigorous and of sharper insight
than any other production of the period save the
works of Chaucer. " It was written with as intense
an earnestness, and as untiring a search after truth
as any production in the English language." * Its
occasional felicity of expression and popular cast,
its satirical and social features, constituted it a
fitting study for the author of the Canterbury

* Introduction of the Early English Text Society.

Tales. It has also about the same measure of the reformatory spirit as that which fell to the works of Chaucer, though it is certainly written in a much sterner mood. While Chaucer fits his satire to his easy and ethically indolent temper, it is nevertheless directed with unerring instinct to the right mark.

He was equally progressive in his political spirit. The son of a trader of the city of London, he entered earnestly into the conflict of the mayoralty of the city in behalf of John of Northampton, the candidate of municipal rights and reform. The proximity of London to Westminster, and its growing commercial strength, made it jealous of court influences, progressive and liberal in its sentiments. For his participation in this contest, Chaucer fell under the displeasure of the court. His democratic sentiments appear also in his writings, in the cast of his characters, and in the words he puts into their mouths. " Straw for your gentillesse," exclaims the host of the Tabard, and we feel that it is Chaucer, speaking out of a healthy English heart. He repeatedly expresses in full his estimate of rank ; as in the wife of Bath's tale :

" But for ye speken of swiche gentillesse,
　As is descended out of old richesse,
　That therefore shullen ye be gentilmen ;
　Swiche arrogance n'is not worth an hen.

And he that wol han pris of his genterie,
　For he was boren of a gentil hous,
　And had his elders noble and vertuous,
　And n'ill himselven do no gentil dedes,

Ne folwe his gentil auncestrie, that ded is,
He n'is not gentil, be he duk or erl;
For vilains sinful dedes make a cherl.
For gentillesse n'is but the renomee
Of thin auncestres, for hir high bountee,
Which is a strange thing to thy persone:
Thy gentillesse cometh fro God alone.
Than cometh our veray gentillesse of grace,
It was no thing bequethed us with our place."

The fundamental principle of human liberty is not merely set forth in this passage, but the grounds of it are vigorously urged. Thus, in the birth of the English nation, in the obscure beginnings of that great controversy, which, ripening from generation to generation, has given form and character to English history, and achieved the liberty of the freest and most peaceful of the nations of the earth, a voice was found, the voice of her first great poet, to ring forth the rights of manhood and virtue.

In his own art, poetry, Chaucer was equally progressive, though he reaches his highest results by a growth rather than by a leap. The poetry of his time was made narrow and puerile by the extravagant and artificial sentiment of chivalry; and by a tendency to obscure, trivial allegory. Both of these restraints Chaucer cast off, and at length reached a form of composition as direct, natural and entertaining as that of any of his successors. Godwin says very strongly of him, "While the romantic writers of the twelfth and thirteenth centuries are not less exuberant than Homer in the description of blows and wounds and fighting fields, Chaucer has not prostituted one line to the fashionable pursuit."* We owe much to this better, broader tendency of Chaucer. His works helped quietly to displace the literature of chivalry, and to breathe into English letters a more serene and comprehensive spirit. We thus had no need of a Cervantes to arrest with satire the extravagance and feebleness of an effeté system. This early acceptance of real, common life as his subject shows the humanity of Chaucer, and the penetrative, commanding character of his mind.

. The taste for allegory was inwoven with that of chivalry, and resulted in conceits still more remote and fanciful. It was also united with a belief in enchantments, and a constant intervention of supernatural agents in the absorbing affairs of knighthood. Acceptable allegory, from the artificial form of its composition, can occur but rarely in literature. It belongs, on the whole, to rude periods and uncultivated minds. Device, cunning contrivance, a spirit of riddles accompany a state of semi-enlightenment, in which the mind delights in its own gymnastic feats; not yet sobered by a clear, direct view of outward beauty, or brought down to a quiet search into the increasing wonders of knowledge Early English literature is full of allegory, the rude mind being pleased with the play and illusion of a double meaning, when it cared little for the sentiments involved. Moreover a predominant imagination gave easy and perfect personification to abstract qualities, and Messrs. Do-well, Do-better and Do-best became an effective, substantial oligar-

* Life of Chaucer, vol. ii. p. 220.

3*

chy in the kingdom of virtue. It was only when these and like conceptions came forth from the world of ideas as visible figures, ready, with extended hands, to take partners, and become com panions in the sports and labors of men, that allegory, freely entering the thoughts by the door of a vigorous fancy, exerted a controlling influence over the ordinary mind. Thus religion has never been able in illiterate periods to keep sufficiently in the background the tendency to personification, and angels and demons, swarming in on either hand, have overpowered the rational, voluntary life of man. This extravagance of allegory easily united itself to that of chivalry, and gave rise to productions fanciful and puerile. The earlier works of Chaucer, The Court of Love, The Assembly of Fowls, The Flower and the Leaf, Chaucer's Dream were constructed under the influence of this prevalent taste. The House of Fame is in the best vein of allegory, and the great poet is less hampered than another by the artificial and the false. It is plainly to be seen, that not till his later works did Chaucer win his entire liberty, and give himself fearlessly to the simple, native force of his theme. In the Canterbury Tales, allegory disappears, and we have once more the plain, pleasing conditions of daily life.

In language we have already marked the progressive spirit of Chaucer. He had the insight to see, and the feeling to greet, the strength of the new-born tongue; and by this sympathy with rising greatness, and coming times, exerted an influence incalculably more than would otherwise have fallen to him. His works in Latin would have been as seed stored under lock and key; in English, they fell into a virgin soil, and with them, and under their shadow, have arisen the trees, shrubs and flowers of a broad, prolific land.

We have thus far spoken of those general characteristics of the works of Chaucer which made them at the time especially significant; we now turn to their more intrinsic and peculiar qualities. Without central, creative force, these radiating influences would have speedily fallen off.

As the great work of Chaucer is the Canterbury Tales, it is common, resting his merits on this, to speak of him as possessed of high dramatic power. Its general prologue contains a series of characters introduced with sharp delineation; while the connecting prologues of the several stories present brief, but spirited, dialogue. These portions fall sensibly short of dramatic composition in its pure form, yet imply something of the same power. The dramatic writer is creative rather than descriptive, works from within, causes character to grow up before us from its living constituents in words and actions. The narrator, the novelist is as often descriptive as creative; works by observation, and is more exterior to the circumstances and parties he delineates. Yet he cannot, though more aided by description, prosper by it alone. With true dramatic force he must set his characters in action, and from time to time give them the play of lifelike dialogue. The dramatist moves exclusively in the vigorous elements of speech and action; the narrator supports his personages and unites his events with the lighter, more facile resources of description. It may well happen, therefore, that one, like Fielding, should prosper as a novelist, and fail as a dramatist. Keen observation goes far to give success in the one undertaking; while, in the other, this must have passed over into intuitive insight, and easy instinctive development. If, therefore, we withhold the term dramatic from Chaucer in its full, precise form, we must concede it in its rudiments, as expressing that pictorial power which deals in a living way with men and their actions; and finds the characters whom it calls up proportionate, natural and pliant to its purposes. This power Chaucer possessed in a high degree, and the people of his tales come before us as a veritable troop of pilgrims, each with the mark of an individual character and of a peculiar calling strongly on him. We come at the life of the century through this motley company, as they file out of the courtyard of the inn; we reach its temper, and catch the flavor of its sentiments, as certainly as we do those of our own society in the streets of our cities. When the artist sketches them, trotting leisurely on, in loose array, marshalled by my host of the Tabard, we know them each and all; they are as familiar to us in garb and carriage as the persons who, in apt illustration, face a descriptive page in Dickens.

Chaucer, like all who excel in the delineation of character, was a master of humor and pathos. These are the light and shade of every human pic-

ture, and must everywhere inter-penetrate each
other in shifting proportions. They give to each
other by contrast and by change intensity and relief. As light and darkness are expressed in degrees, turn upon the diverse state of one element,
so pathos and humor, the sober and the sportive,
are one living, sympathetic impulse differently act
ed on, met by diverse forces in the outside world.
The transition from one to the other is safe and
easy, when the artist feels alike the force of both,
and floats on an emotional current, that gathers, of
its own bias, deep and sombre shadows under the
overhanging bank, or glides gayly, noisily down the
steep incline.

Chaucer was strongly predisposed to humor.
His serenity and good-nature led him into the sun
shine. He loved to take things lightly, occupied
with their surface play, with only such brief glances
into their mysteries and woes as would allow him
to return with unbroken spirits. His humor is a
well-meaning, pleasant sprite, that can only be sad-
dened for a moment by the flying shadow of grief,
and, easily shirking the burden, comes back with
wonted good-nature and relish to the trifles, the
haps and mishaps of intercourse.

Closely allied to this sportive vein of Chaucer is
his vulgarity. He has the sensual vulgarity of
grossness, up to, or very nearly up to, his times.
Yet it is not the sin, the filth, but the fun of the
thing that he is after; and so manifest is this, that
we laugh away in part our irritation and shame. We
feel that we have been caught, yet so fairly caught,

that we are unwilling to be angry. Laughter is
wholesome, and the malignant spirits of irreverence,
the impure spirits of unseemly jesting, are in a
measure exorcised by it. As malarious vapor rapidly
disappears under the open sky, and requires to be
confined in a chamber, or shut up in a close court,
to become deadly, so vice, held within a vicious
heart, is tenfold pestilential, and shoots out through
the bitter word, like a scalding jet of steam. With
Chaucer, vulgarity lay under the broad heavens, an
offensive fact indeed, but one with which he had
no more to do than another. He chose to laugh,
others might run away and hide, if they pleased.
So much perhaps may be fairly said in extenuation;
yet these low, sensual features remain, a thing of
bad significance. One needs to know the moral
constitution of the recipient, or he may breathe pestilence in this atmosphere. If one goes to Chaucer
for pleasure, he eats honey from the carcase of a
lion; while he feeds one sense, he may have occasion to close others. Yet with all we acquit him of
the lasciviousness of later periods.

While society is the chosen theme of Chaucer,
he has a kindly love of nature. He treats of it
without analysis and without interpretation; but
with a quick perception of its pleasant, cheerful,
aspects. Thus he speaks of the morning in the
Squiere's Tale:

> Up riseth freshe Canace hireselve,
> As rody and bright, as the yonge sonne,
> That in the ram is foure degrees yronne;
>
> *　　*　　*　　*　　*　　*　　*　　*

The vapour, which that fro the erthe glode,
Maketh the sonne to seme rody and brode :
But natheles, it was so faire a sight,
That it made all hir hertes for to light,
What for the seson, and the morwening,
And for the foules that she herde sing.
For right anon she wiste what they ment,
Right by hir song, and knew al hir intent.

An exterior appreciation of the good and beauty of the world is the first spontaneous tribute of the poetic spirit to nature; an analytic, penetrative and spiritual interpretation of it belongs to a period of more reflection.

From these characteristics of Chaucer, his national and progressive temper, his strong sympathies with men, his sense of the abuses under which they suffered, and his good-will to them, we see that he felt appreciatively the moral forces of his age, and that his genius ripened under them, both in the direction and form of his labors. He was not, it is true, a reformer; artists as artists are rarely, if ever so. An urgent, cogent, ethical sentiment eats a man up, gives the soul an intensity and velocity that are sublime, perhaps, but not beautiful. The true poet of a period feels the moral elements at work about him, but is not driven by them. He is left sufficiently free to treat them artistically, æsthetically, appreciatively, with something of the patience and sufferance we find in nature, in the imperturbable tarrying of Divine Providence till events ripen. He has little of the haste, struggle, fierceness, over-estimates of reform. There is an affection in him for the present and the past, a catholic appreciation of their beauties, an eye for their inner embryonic forces, which make him less headstrong in change, less confident of its results. He uses the ethical light that is in him not so much to cast deep shadows on the sins of the hour, as to bring out in bright relief its virtues, and to make each declining sun shed long beams of promise on the horizon, assuring us that the days hold each other and unfold each other with one continuous, triumphant force. The great poet feels the ethical temper and working of his time, as one who tarries in the sunlight, not as one who works in it; as one who enjoys it, rather than as one who is put to speed under it. Without a wakeful consciousness to moral elements, the mind is left opaque and feeble; fiercely stimulated by them, it is thrown into discipleship, and achieves an epic, rather than writes one; simply translucent and receptive under them, it breaks their solid beams into brilliant lines of color.

Chaucer, like most men of unusual powers, gained the appreciation that has fallen to him somewhat slowly. It is by some thought that in the esteem of his own times, and of those immediately subsequent, he scarcely surpassed Gower, of whom Lowell has said, " Our literature had to lie by and recruit for more than four centuries ere it could give us an equal vacuity in Tupper, so persistent a uniformity of commonplace in the Recreations of a Country Parson."*

Having thus presented the forces at work in the last half of the fourteenth century, and the

* My Study Windows, p. 260.

height to which genius carried them, we turn to the interregnum of English literature, the fifteenth century and the earlier portion of the sixteenth. This may be called the retrogressive period, and so separated the times which preceded from those which followed it, that the problem of progress was taken up almost anew at a later date. Not only was nothing added to the ground gained in the fourteenth century, the genius of that period suffered eclipse, and was not disclosed again for two centuries. In Scotland, indeed, a literature more nearly corresponding to that of the fourteenth century in England found place in the fifteenth, and the deferred dawn of letters appeared in the north, with less brilliancy, under Dunbar and his associates.

A chief reason for this barrenness of the fifteenth century was the stern repression which met all free inquiry. "The University of Oxford chose twelve of its members to examine the writings of Wicliffe, and the report made presented two hundred and sixty-seven opinions which were described as worthy of fire."[*] So voluminous and hot a censure did this university, and with it all England, pass on him who first brought to it bold, free thought, and religious emancipation. Severe measures were set on foot; the reformation, as a forest conflagration, was extinguished. It was not, however, completely trampled out; it sank into the soil, ran along the low ground, and smouldered in various places as the intelligence or independence of the common people gave it opportunity. The

* Revolutions in English History, vol. i. p 590.

hold which the new doctrines maintained on the popular mind is shown in a work entitled, The Lantern of Light, a fearless exposure of religious corruption; and in the martyrdom of Claydon at Smithfield. The reaction in the church, however, was so complete, that its upper orders became more than ever luxurious and licentious, its lower orders increasingly dissolute; both uniting to suppress the present movement, and to provoke a new one more thorough and irresistible.

The cause of religious liberty was identified, as it always must be, with that of intellectual freedom. Learning declined, especially at Oxford, and her scholars, through the poverty of her foundations, became "travelling mendicants," treated, at times, with the utmost indignity. Herein is a first and sufficient reason for the literary feebleness of the period. The bold proffer of life that was made it had been rejected, and the reactionary influences of vice, ignorance and superstition were in the ascendant.

A second, confirmatory force were the civil wars, which raged in the latter portion of the century. They involved little or no principle, were ambitious struggles for power, carried lawless violence everywhere, and were thus thoroughly opposed to the peaceful and enlightened arts. The immediate influence of these wars of succession was almost wholly evil, though they tended at length to consolidate and strengthen society and government. This civil strife was greatly aided by the comparative independence and power of the nobles. Many of these perished on the battle-field, or on the scaffold. They mutually broke each other in pieces, and when the succession was finally established in the strong hand of Henry VII. they were prepared to render an obedience more complete, and to fall into a position more subordinate, than ever before. The government was established on stronger foundations; and later insurrections, like those of Suffolk and of the Commonwealth, were in the interests of the people rather than of the nobles. The law of Henry the VII. forbidding to the nobles the maintenance of retainers, other than domestic servants, shows at once how thoroughly the power of the aristocracy was broken. This pulverizing afresh of society, making way for a new, national aggregation, was the chief beneficial result of the Wars of the Roses, and was ultimately, therefore, favorable to the more truly national life which belonged to the reign of Elizabeth. These wars helped to do, in the political world, what reform, at a later period, accomplished in the religious world; and an arrogant nobility and a haughty clergy slowly sank to a level more consistent with national unity and national liberty. Separate centres of influence and intrigue were broken up, and all power began to go forth from the court, the government, the nation, the popular heart.

The latter portion of the fifteenth century, 1474, was marked by the introduction of printing into England. This art, however, unfolded its vast resources very slowly. It offers means only, and demands a great and noble spirit for their use. For the first fifty years of its existence, it was waiting for the power, that should lay hold of it, as a ready weapon, and smite with it the intellectual tyranny of the times. Its first labors were inspired by no great purpose, and were in part unfavorable to scholarship. Manuscripts were negligently reproduced, and, displaced by their printed rivals, disappeared, rendering more difficult the careful editing of later critical periods. There was, none the less, slumbering in the press another of those powers which were to make the next struggle for intellectual liberty so different in its results from those that had preceded. The bullet was not more fatal to the sway of the mailed knight than were the swift, prolific messengers of the press to the dominion of the religious and philosophical bigot. Invention, which has always found its home with the people, furnished the two weapons, which, more than all others, have levelled aristocracy and hierarchy, and put men in possession of their civil and religious birthright. The people have wrought most effectively in their own cause by that inventive power which is the best development of their strength.

This period of subsidence, in which every repressive influence rushed in to submerge the germinant seeds of progress, presents as much to interest us in its prose as in its poetry, and offers but very little in either direction. On the one side are Pecock, Fortescue, Malory; on the other Occleve, Lydgate, Skelton. We pass them all, merely mentioning them that they may give a little distention to a period that would otherwise collapse, and be lost to our literature; a dreary one hundred and fifty years whose consolation is, that the downward here touched the upward movement, and passed into it. Out of this darkness leaped the day we hail with double delight. As this period drew to a close, in the vigorous reign of Henry VIII., those forces were active, which were to shape the coming years of progress, and began to show in such men as Tyndale, Coverdale, More, Ascham, Surrey, the strength and diversity of later years.

We now pass to the period designated as Elizabethan; the first creative period of English letters. Times, like colors on the clouds, have no definite outlines; they have centres, surfaces, directions, not margins. We gather into this period the antecedent causes which gave rise to it, and its own fruits ripening in times immediately subsequent. It is the period of Spenser, Shakespeare and Milton. It is clearly defined in the first, reaches its zenith in the second, and passes away in the third. As this is the great era of our literary history, and also the first of its stages of consecutive, derivative growth, we must study carefully its productive forces; those in which it had its origin.

As we attribute very much of the superiority of this period to the ethical activity called out by the Reformation, we wish to inquire into the real value in progress of the ethical power. Some, like Buckle, have assiduously disparaged its influence in civilization. His view owes whatever of plausibility belongs to it to the limited meaning attached to the word moral. It is often restricted to religious activity, and even at that, to a dogmatic, formal and preceptive one. If we give to the word ethical, the compass which falls to it from the depth and activity of the ethical sentiment in our constitution, we shall hardly afterward deny the important part played by this impulse in all periods of progress. Religious activity is but the more intense play of the moral nature, its movement under the leading facts of our spiritual relations in life. A false religion is the most fatal of anodynes to the conscientious insight of the mind, and times of quiet submission to this external tyranny of priest, ritual and creed, should be instanced, not as examples of the activity of the moral sentiments, but of their repression and perversion. The fungi that feed upon a tree, consuming its native quality, are no measure of its own vital force. The moral nature is never so thoroughly put to sleep, and never so truly impotent, as in periods of corrupt sacerdotal rule ; in which external authority is substituted for internal conviction, submission for virtue, and a ritual service for the guidance of a quickened conscience. If we were in search of specimen periods, showing what is possible in art and literature aside from the moral nature, we should bring forward these moments of paralysis, of torpid and benumbed sensibility. On the other hand, reform in religion, a reasserting of individual rights, a resurrection of private thought, interpretation, conviction, constitute the spring-time of ethical sentiment. Though the movement may be partial, so far as it goes, it is a rebellion of con-

science against usurped authority.   Civil liberty
and the love of liberty are to be pronounced upon,
not during the stretches of despotism, but in those
halcyon days in which every man's blood tingles with
hope, desire, achievement ; nor in those only, save
as the end is wisely proposed, the labor successfully
consummated.

All that activity, then, within the field of religion
by which truth has struggled to cast off error, the
better to abolish the worse tendency, the freer the
more servile one, appeal being taken to the moral
nature of man, to his own convictions, is the product
of ethical force, whose seeds are always in the soil,
and sure, when the reign of winter relaxes, to find
their way to the light.   This appeal, to the individual life may not always be direct ; it may be made,
in the first instance to history, or to the Bible, or, as
by Voltaire, to practical intelligence ; but it underlies
none the less every other appeal, since history and
the Bible and practical intelligence must have interpretation ; and this can only be given by the individual to the individual.   Even if we abrogate our
own powers in behalf of those of another, or those
of a set of men, this new bill of disfranchisement
we must first consider, and put to it our own seal ;
we catch at least a gleam of light, though we see fit
to quench it again.

Hence periods of struggle in belief are pre-eminently ethical periods, and also periods of intense
individuality and personal activity, accompanied
with an exalted sense of power and responsibility.
The whole nature of man is lifted by this inspira-

tion of independent guidance and government, this walking alone with truth, this gathering, under the eye and favor of God, into his own hand the lines of control, and going forth to achieve a life that shall fulfil a private, and thus a general, purpose. If there are possibilities in men, these periods of liberty, of ethical strength, of a central movement forward, can not fail to develop them.

Nor do the infidelity and unbelief which are sure to belong to these eras of progress at all militate with this view of the force of the moral sentiment, they rather confirm it. Unbelief that is positive, that is asserted as a right, that passes into a crusade, does so by virtue of the moral nature, directly and indirectly. Liberty is a claim and a passion with it. The mind, irritated by a perpetual, persecuting tyranny, wanders in mere wantonness, for a little, before it will accept any principle that may become to it a fresh yoke in the school of enforced belief. The licenses of skepticism are often reactions against imperious faith; as are those of liberty the resentments which have sprung up under the maddening hand of irresponsible power. The effervescence of thought is due to the revolt and ferment of the moral nature, the nature which resents wrongs and claims rights, the nature that thinks of the fitness of thought, and with indignation of any opinion, creed or custom that would smother thought. Whether the mind of the devout reformer is primarily delighted with the truth ; or, less devout, but not less free, is pleased with its own exhilarating search for it, the fact is the same ; it is the return of the mind to its powers, its liberties, its responsibilities; and this is an ethical victory.

Even if the point of advance is one of science, of mere knowledge, the opposition it meets with, if any, is likely to come from the moral world, to be a religious anathema; and the counter assertion, therefore, will necessarily be one resting on a moral basis, the mind's right to the truth, its right to its own powers, and to whatever God has sealed under them as its inheritance in his intellectual and spiritual kingdoms. Liberty is the starting-point of science, liberty to inquire, accept, reject; but the battles of liberty have been fought, and must be fought in connection with religious truth, that truth that involves immediate duties and dangers, and is involved in all the cogent concerns of this and another life. Hence the secondary struggle must share the fortunes of the primary one, the skirmish must go as goes the battle, and we shall only be intellectually, æsthetically free, as we are spiritually free. The ethical element finds place in every conflict because it is so pervasive, fundamental; and while it may seem merely to cover the retreat of error, it heads the advance of truth.

We have said, that those who depreciate the moral sentiment should look for excellence to periods of superstitious repose; they may also look for it to times of passive unbelief, mere negation, that cares little for what it denies, and is not even earnest in the denial. Quiet, tacit belief and unbelief fall off alike, though on opposite sides, from ethical power; and so far as there is good in either

4

of them, any invention, any bold realization of the undertakings or pleasures of life, we concede it to be the fruits of secondary impulses ; we make it over to purely intellectual action.

How can it be otherwise than that the ethical sentiment, as we understand it, should be large-minded, bold, creative ; and that all that has been creative, bold, large-minded in any art, should, at least tacitly, have claimed this liberty, and exercised this inspiration. Secondary impulses give secondary qualities, but the primary impulse of great and pervasive power is this freedom of the mind, its right to see, to judge, to act ; its sense of a destiny, and of its power to fulfil that destiny.

We are prepared, then, to put down as first, and first to consider, among those general conditions which made a great epoch out of the Elizabethan age, the unusual activity of religious, polemic thought, breaking the narrow bounds of minute dogma, and resuming its hold on principles. To this first influence we add, second, as one with it, and sustaining to it the relation both of effect and cause, the revival of learning, more especially classical learning ; third, the earlier steps toward scientific progress ; fourth, discovery ; and fifth, invention. We shall speak of each of these general conditions from which date our modern civilization, before we turn to those special causes which helped to develop our first creative period—an era so brilliant in itself, and so influential on all that have followed, that in understanding it, we start in possession of the secret springs of our consecutive, literary history.

LECTURE IV.

THE ethical forces of the sixteenth century, of whose claims to influence we have spoken, disclosed themselves in a religious struggle which affected the entire Latin Church, and resolved itself, in different places and between different parties, into every degree and every diversity of strife. It was a dissolution of old beliefs, with a reformation, under local and individual tendencies, of many new shades of faith. This, which was the reproach of the reformation in the eyes of the Catholic, was in fact its chief merit. Men were not passed from one overshadowing organization to another, but were compelled, amid endless phases of belief, to think and act with relative independence.

We have in John Morley an able and independent witness, who says, in his treatise on Voltaire, "Protestantism was indirectly the means of creating and dispersing an atmosphere of rationalism, in which there speedily sprang up philosophic, theological and political influences, all of them entirely antagonistic to the old order of thought and insti-

tution. The whole intellectual temperature underwent a permanent change, that was silently mortal
to the most flourishing tenets of all sorts."*

Whatever was the cause of the great fruitful-
ness in letters of the last portion of the sixteenth,
and of the earlier half of the seventeenth century
no other general, pervasive force, searching into all
ranks and relations of society, existed at that or
at any subsequent period like this of the Reformation. The leading events of the political world all
turned upon it for more than a century. From the
amours of Henry VIII. to the tragedy of Mary
Queen of Scots, every stirring event in English
history either drew its passion from the relig-
ous sentiment, or was strongly colored by it.
Foreign policy and domestic policy were alike inseparable from religion. The regency in Scotland; the relation of England to the Netherlands
and to Spain; the sense of power that came to
her in exerting a controlling influence on the continent, while maintaining peace in her own borders,
turned one and all on diversities of faith. The
great political names and events of the period,
both in England and on the Continent, are indis-
solubly interwoven with religious controversies,
Gustavus Adolphus, Charles V., Philip II., Henry
VIII., Mary, Elizabeth, the rise of the Netherlands,
the struggle of the Huguenots, the settlement of
the new world, the growth of constitutional liberty
in England.

Nor was the influence of religious differences in

* Voltaire, p. 86.

the domestic relations of England less manifest.
To say nothing of that perpetual strife, passing
under Mary into an extensive and bloody persecution, which pervaded English social and political relations during the sixteenth century, on the
ground of conflicting faiths and rituals, what one
change could have been more sweeping, or have
altered, in a more striking way, the face of society,
than the overthrow of the monasteries, so numerous and so venerable. A measure of this character, wholesale and sudden, was attended with
very mixed results. It greatly diminished the
popular reverence for religious orders, and rapidly
reduced their hold on the public mind, both by
the exposure of the corruption of these institutions,
of the religious tricks which had been practiced in
them on the credulity of the masses, and also by
that sudden loss of prestige, which, with the many,
attends on misfortune. The burden of a large un-
productive class was lifted from the people, and
industry and independence gained a victory over
indolence, deception and exaction. For these
gains there were compensations. Valuable manuscripts may have been lost; communities, in part
devoted to scholarship, to popular instruction, and
to charity, were broken up; and the support of
the most worthless and vagrant of the monks was
shifted, not escaped. No well rooted abuse gives
way without tearing up the soil somewhat, and involving local interests in its fall.

The direct literary influence of the Reformation
is nowhere more manifest than in England. The

history of the English Bible presents it in the
clearest light. Our present version has held un-
questioned supremacy for more than two centuries
and a half; has been found, in later periods, in
almost every English household; has received
weekly enforcement from innumerable pulpits;
and been the direct occasion of a large share of
the printed matter that has come from the English
press. It has thus exerted a literary influence,
greater in volume beyond all comparison than has
fallen to any other book. The works of Shakespeare may have affected single minds, from a
literary point of view, more strongly than the Bible,
but the style and language of our version, aside
from its religious authority, have exercised a control incalculably greater on our general literature.
We may instance Bunyan's Allegories, whose
merits have never been surpassed in their own
field, as among those productions which have
sprung directly from the Scriptures, bulblets half
inclosed in the parent bulb. No such complete
and prosperous dependence can elsewhere be found
in our literary history, as this between the Bible
and many of its literary offspring. This version,
so influential, arose with co. responding painstaking,
and under a most fortunate concurrence of influences. Tyndale, by his translation of 1525, began
the work. The masculine vigor of the man, the simplicity and earnestness of his purpose, and its popular bent, together with the prevalent Saxon features
of our speech, united to give this early and most
influential rendering of the Scriptures an idiomatic

force and directness which it helped to impart to all
the versions that followed, and the more easily as
many of these arose under kindred conditions. For
nearly a hundred years, version followed version,
with constant comparison, and with a firm hold on
previous and cotemporary work. At length with
fearless revision, yet with deserved deference to
former editions, appeared the authorized version,
the fruits of the ripest scholarship, at home and
abroad. The labors of the century were gathered
up in it. Catholics, churchmen, dissenters, men
of varying belief, had virtually labored upon it.
The hands of martyrs had wrought in it, Tyndale,
Rogers, Cranmer ; and so it prospered by violence
and by favor, till at length it came forward under
the solemn endorsement of the English Church,
and tacitly of the nation, its own work through its
most devout scholars, its varied beliefs, and the
years of its most intense religious life. It has
thus grown into a reverence and honor among
us, which lead us to draw back from change, and
to forget, when further revision is thought of, that
bold diligence to which its own merits are due.

Correspondingly did the Bible gain in general
influence. In 1543 the translations of Tyndale were
proscribed by parliament. Any portion of the
Bible, under penalty of imprisonment, was denied
to "women (except noble or gentle women), artif-
icers, apprentices, journeymen, serving men, husbandmen, and laborers." This was a remnant of
the hostility with which his work had been met at
the outset. But previously to this, the Great Bible

had been opened in the churches for public reading, and many earnest and disputatious groups had gathered about it. "Classes and households were divided. On the one side were the stern citizens of the old school, to whom change seemed to be the beginning of license ; on the other young men burning with zeal to carry to the utmost the spiritual freedom of which they had caught sight."*

The withholding of one rendering only gave occasion to another ; and that the partisans of both the Bishop's Bible and the Geneva version, representing the extremes of religious sentiment, should finally have accepted King James' version is a proof of the candor and carefulness that gathered into it the excellencies of previous work. A wider circulation of the Scriptures, a more profound interest in them, and a better understanding of them, were thus the fruits of the jealous advocacy, the earnest attack and defense of successive editions. That a kindred spirit prevailed on the continent, though in a less degree, is seen in the fact, that, in addition to Latin versions, a French, an English, an Italian, and a Spanish Bible, proceeded, in a brief period, from Geneva and Basle.

Incident to this religious activity, this earnest and critical study of the Scriptures, there was a large amount of theological composition. Writers of this class have always been numerous in England. It is true, indeed, that the productions of but very few of them have obtained an acknowledged position in our literature, but they have not

* History of the English Bible, p. 110.

for that reason failed to have a powerful hold on the national mind. Forces for the moment very efficient, frequently miss any direct mastery over later periods. They reach these in their influence only by being absorbed into earlier times, and thus swelling the stream as it flows by. Immediate and remote control turn on different principles. If one is so in sympathy with his own generation as to impress himself strongly, actively upon it, he almost necessarily passes away with it. If one, in his works, catches a prophetic forecast of coming truth, or an excellence of art that has not been reached, he naturally fails of appreciation by those about him, and waits for the opening doors of a coming century before he finds his own audience. Each man casts anchor as he may, early or later in the stream of human life, and holds fast where first, with ploughing flukes, he begins to grapple the popular mind. Most theological composition springs from a present exigency of thought, and tarries with its direct work in the times which evoke it. Nevertheless, in shaping those times, it is most efficient, most diffusive, and, above all forms of production, gives that undertone of social sentiment by which artistic work is to be controlled. What the Raphaels of the world are to paint is determined by what they find in it, in its heart, its affections, when they come. What the Miltons of the world are to sing must be settled by the themes which win men's thoughts. Theological composition, therefore, has always affected literature beyond its literary merit, since it has not been

4*

by this merit that it has acted, but by the moral tonic there has chanced to be in it for men's minds. Great waves spring up only on deep and large waters; theology deepens and broadens that intelligence whose rise and fall in art constitute the record of literature.

Polemics are not instantly favorable to literary art, but rather the reverse. It is not till the first crackling flame abates, and genial, ruddy coals remain on the hearth, that men settle down with slippered feet into that state, at once active and placid, that favors art. The headstrong impulses of reform are unfavorable, in their first expenditure, to the coy, creative play of the imagination; but, if successful, they are sure to be followed by the suitors of art, entering gayly into the larger life that has been won for them. In a general way, the nations of Europe rank in literature according as their moral life has issued in honest, searching speculation, or in blind belief and unbelief. It has been characteristic of Italy and Spain, that they have fallen, in a powerless, unfruitful way, into superstition and infidelity, each passive and hopeless like the other; and neither of these states have reached the literary life of which they gave the promise. France has had a bolder, more decisive infidelity, provoking a more critical and earnest belief, and she has ripened a correspondingly extended literature. Germany has been held, especially in modern times, in vigorous conflict by a most searching and critical belief and unbelief, and her intellectual labors have been prodigious, her literature surpass-

ingly fruitful. England, above all European nations,
has been marked by sober, thoughtful, predominant
belief, often disturbed, but never shaken, by skepticism; and she presents a literature certainly as
varied, as abundant, as continuous, as powerful as
that of any other nation. The foundations of this
ethical strength were laid in English society, just
previous to the Elizabethan period, the first creative
period in our literary art.

The traces of this theological action are also in
our language. A large accession of words of
Latin origin came to it in the sixteenth century.
The style of More and Ascham, of the early part
of the century, is purer and simpler than that of
the prose writers of the Elizabethan age. There
are in these, both an increase of Latin words, and
a more complex, involved construction. An easy
narrative style gives place to one of weighty and
complicated thought, to assertions laden, not merely
with a primary purpose, but with many secondary
and qualifying ideas. The sentences often march
with a heavy regimental tread, as if each were a
section, or a company, in itself. They drag along
formidable words, and loosely attached clauses, like
heavy guns, and are only saved from being tedious
and cumbersome by the vigor of the thought, or the
vividness of the imagery. Grammatical relations
are not simple, or closely knit, and sometimes fail
altogether. This tendency to roll up the sentence
in masses, this plethoric habit of thought, a construction crowded full of conditions and adjuncts,
with its natural accompaniment of a Latin vocabu-

lary, belonged to prose composition all through this first creative period. This style was the product of vigorous thought, of active and uncritical faculties, that delivered sentiments in the gross, waiting for a period of more leisure and art to break them up, sort and arrange them

The following passage from the Areopagitica of Milton, illustrates the swelling sentence, the fresh spring torrent of thought.

" First, when a City shall be as it were besieg'd and blockt about, her navigable river infested, in- rodes and incursions round, defiance and battell oft rumor'd to be marching up ev'n to her walls, and suburb trenches, that then the people, or the greater part, more then at other times, wholly tak'n up with the study of highest and most important matters to be reform'd, should be disputing, reason- ing, reading, inventing, discoursing, ev'n to a rarity, and admiration, things not before discourst or written of, argues first a singular good will, con- tentednesse and confidence in your prudent fore- sight and safe government, Lords and Commons; and from thence derives it self to a gallant bravery and well grounded contempt of their enemies, as if there were no small number of as great spirits among us, as his was, who when Rome was nigh besieg'd by Hanibal, being in the City, bought that peece of ground at no cheap rate, whereon Hanibal himself encampt his own regiment."

While the revival of classical learning tended to these results in style, they were in part also the fruit of polemics. Theological discussion has so

much of it taken place in Latin, that its vocabulary
is closely united to that language ; while its logical
forms of assertion and limitation, statement and ex-
ception, tend to involved and composite sentences.
Hooker, the first great prose writer of the Elizabethan age, shows the best results of the theological habit of mind. Sound, searching and liberal in
thought, he presents a style massive, semi-fluent,
pushing and formidable; yet from time to time
breaking into a more easy and animated flow. By
universal consent, he takes rank among great English writers. A tendency which could thus early
ripen an author of so much power and skill, could
get to itself such a head, vindicates easily and at
once its claims to large literary influence.

The second agency which gave the conditions of
the creative period was the revival of classical learning. Greek scholars and literature were cordially entertained in Italy early in the fifteenth
century. The overthrow of Constantinople, in
the middle of that century, merely accelerated a
movement already well under way. A progress
in classical learning followed, which, during this
and the following century, with a fluctuating movement, extended throughout Western Europe, Eng
land being among the latest to feel it. This classical
scholarship stood in diverse relations, at different
places and different times, to the spirit of reform.
It preceded and accompanied it, rather than followed it, in Europe. In Italy, the popes welcomed
this revival, and it there chiefly accelerated art, then
passing forward to its great achievements. Art felt

a double tendency, a Christian bias and a classical
one, or—in contrasted language—a pagan one.   It
gave itself, on the one side, with devout belief to
religious themes, and, on the other, to the resusci-
tation of Greek and Latin mythology.   When encountered by no strong reformatory current, classical knowledge tended to this division of effects.
Some added it as mere culture to previous character ; and others, awakened as from a dream to this
wonderful Greek and Roman world, so full of civilization and art, yet without a Christian faith, themselves lost the sense of necessity and certainty in
their creed, and became skeptical of a system that
could in so many things be taught of the past.
Classical art and classical letters, so alien to Christianity, could not win their æsthetical hold on the
sentiments without weakening the foundations of
belief already feeble, and introducing feelings quite
out of harmony both with the purity and the credulity of former faiths.   Thus there was an opportunity given for the formation of an opinion adverse to
the classics, as impure, irreligious, heathenish.

There was another, however, and very different
relation which this knowledge came to assume.   The
appeal being very universally taken by reform to
the Scriptures, a spirit of searching inquiry into
these sources of truth sprang up.   An extended
acquaintance with Latin and Greek became a necessity to the reformer, if he would master old, or
form new, versions of the Bible ; and classical
scholarship allied itself closely, in Erasmus, Luther,
Beza, Tyndale, and many others, to the Reforma-

tion. This was especially true in England, so that to call one a Greek, a lover of Greek letters, was equivalent to pronouncing him a heretic. While this was the deepest and the prevailing affinity of the new culture, it met with variable favor according to the wisdom of times and parties.

Classical learning, then, both by belief and unbelief, both as an instrument and a discovery, as giving a deeper hold on the facts of revelation and redisclosing the facts of an earlier world, wrought liberty, enthusiasm, progress. Greek and Latin letters have ever since been strongly influential on English literature, with a power varying primarily with the knowledge and tastes of the individual, and secondarily with the age to which he has belonged.

An unfavorable literary result of this revival of knowledge, were the conceits and pedantry of style to which it led. Not only was the language embarrassed and choked with its new words, remote allusions, tricks of expression, dodges of thought, became popular, and vitiated, in a measure, the composition of even the best writers. Knowledge overpowered invention, and the resources of expression its simplicity and purity. This tendency, in an earlier form, is especially traceable to Lilly, and from one of his works is named Euphuism. He himself characterizes it as a thing of "fine phrases, smooth quips, merry taunts, jesting without meane and mirth without measure." Later, assuming the form of pedantry and a play upon words, it constituted a distinguishing feature of the school of writers termed metaphysical. It evidently finds no direct support in classical composition, nor indeed in any knowledge, but was rather a fashion, springing from a pedantic and facetious play of thought, with resources not yet wholly bent to simple and worthy service.

A next general force, though as yet very feeble, were the incipient movements of science. These were felt in Italy as early as the close of the fifteenth century. Leonardo da Vinci was followed in the sixteenth century by Galileo, whose labors gave rise at the opening of the seventeenth century to a vigorous Italian school in natural philosophy. Copernicus and Tycho Brahe and Kepler were taking the first steps of progress in Germany. Natural science did not achieve large results in England till the next period; but it now found at least one great mind in sympathy with its spirit and methods, and able to expound them. All recognize the wonderful force of thought that belonged to Bacon. Craik thus chronicles the general impression:—"They who have not seen his greatness under one form have discovered it in another; there is a discordance among men's ways of looking at him, or their theories respecting him; but the mighty shadow which he projects athwart the two by-gone centuries lies there immovable, and still extending as time extends." * This commanding position was gained, not by actual discoveries, not by a sufficient, much less a final, exposition of the laws of progress; but by a thorough and large apprehension of the general character and

* English Literature and Language, vol. i. p. 613.

value of the new inductive method, which had
scarcely come into clear appreciation even with
those who were using it; was directly opposed to
prevalent modes of .nquiry; and was destined, by
its expansion in every department of science, to
rule the future, and constitute its chief glory. Inductive as opposed to deductive reasoning; observation as contrasted with speculation; a careful,
cautious inquiry into things as compared with logomachy, a loose legerdemain of words, had as yet
found no sufficient presentation. This task fell to
Bacon. He thus confirmed and hastened on the
new movement by justifying it to itself, by bringing it into the presence of a clear and well-sus-
tained theory, and by exalting its immediate and
practical value. Those who came after Bacon in
natural science, both in England and elsewhere,
were glad to recognize this statement and defense
of their method, and accept the force of this great
mind, which had made a way for them; which had
pronounced, with such insight and power, upon the
bent and value of the new philosophy. Bacon thus
practically announced, compacted and organized an
intellectual movement, the most fresh and fruitful
of any within the Christian era. It mattered little
that he unduly depreciated the deductive logic;
that he missed of seeing that it makes up with induction the double enginery of thought; that Aristotle commands a moiety of the realm of mind : it
it mattered little that he failed skilfully to use his
own system, or master its details of application; he
did conceive clearly, vigorously the new direction,

the new purpose, the new method of inquiry, and, establishing and defending it, he passed it over to others to develop and apply. In this later genera- tions have busied themselves, and, surprised anew in every decade with the abundance of their re- turns, they yield larger and larger honor to him, who, in such ringing, penetrating tones, proclaimed "fruit" as the object and test of inquiry. Bacon fell in readily with the external, practical cast of British thought; nay, he gave it the most emphatic and influential statement it has ever received. He looked upon the mastery of the physical world as a great end of knowledge, saw how careful and thorough must be the observation which should lead to this result; how cautious must be that transfer of things to thoughts, of objective realities into appropriate conceptions and language, if we would not have our reasoning illusion, a dodging from one empty form of expression to another; and how many prejudgments, the mere débris of habit, individual or social, hide the truth, and require to be cleared away before the virgin rock is again laid bare.

Bacon, indeed, failed to understand the scope of his philosophy, the varied resources, the diversi- fied ingenuity of thought, with which it was to be carried into all branches of physical knowledge; but this was a matter of course, since the centuries that have intervened have only partially revealed the subtile analysis and diversity of method requi- site in the different lines of inquiry.

While Bacon gave this positive push to physical

science, he indirectly affected less favorably intellectual and moral science. His influence tended
to the oversight of that large element of deduction,
which mental philosophy must always present; and
to fasten on ethics the utilitarian temper that pervades physical inquiry. We may look upon him as
indirectly a source of that materialistic philosophy
and those prudential morals which have found so
much acceptance with Englishmen. We would
make no unkind inference, but in Bacon's own history, utility, in the low bent of its aims, egregiously
miscarried, and a life of magnificent scope and con-
comitants fell into reproach and shameful estimate.
Bacon lacked practically, as he did theoretically,
the upward bias of pure reason; insight into tran-
scendental truths, letting drop their motives from
heaven, not gleaning them in prudent husbandry
from the earth.

The religious and the scientific spirit thus furnished to the Elizabethan age its two great prose
writers, Hooker and Bacon, and from that time
onward, the passing collisions and slow coalescence
of these two tendencies have been most fruitful in
thought. Science has been aggressive, religion has
stood on the defence, and deeper insight, sounder
opinion, more philanthropic sentiment, have sprung
from the conflict. In style, Bacon united to logical
power a vigorous imagination. Language thus com-
pounded, like transparent glass, lets in not only light,
but with it, and incidental to it, image after image
from the outside world, and makes of vision a feast
to the soul. His essays best present him as a writer

A fourth general force, rousing the national mind to activity, was the national enterprise, the geographical discoveries of the period. We can hardly appreciate the mental expansion, the breaking down of boundaries, the sudden rarity, that came to thought by the discovery of the new world; or the precision and unity imparted to geography and astronomy by the circumnavigation of the globe. The diameter of the globe, a first unit, a standard of reference in celestial calculations, was thus secured; and we might now know from what we went forth, and to what we returned. Classical learning restored the by-gone world, exploration disclosed a new world, laden with new hopes for the future; a fresh realm of romance and possibilities brought along side, moored to, the old historic continent, exhausted and wayworn. The English, in the last portion of the sixteenth century, were entering heartily into these discoveries, were full of the inquiring, adventuresome spirit they begot. They added enterprise to discovery, and, as in Drake, helped themselves to Spanish wealth, as opportunity offered, with a temper as unscrupulous as that with which the Spaniard won it. At no time has the world seen more daring and resolute navigators, mingling large and petty motives into enthusiastic, serviceable character. Drake, Frobisher, Davis, Raleigh led the nation in that maritime enterprise, which has ever since given expansion to the national character. The additions which such a temper brings to literature may not be very palpable, and in their most palpable forms are no sufficient index of the entire effect. The nautical novel has in part expressed this predilection of Englishmen, and serves to show how bold and breezy national tastes have been kept by this love of the sea. The poetry, the direct results of these sympathies, as Byron's apostrophe to the ocean, offers, in an outspoken form, what is always a latent element in Englis' character, imparting scope and strength to feeling.

A final agency we have to mention as introducing the new epoch is invention. The two early inventions, the conditions of later ones, giving general safety and general knowledge, were slowly working their effects into and transforming society. Gunpowder and the printing press, both democratic, the one lifting up the middle class in intelligence, the other tumbling down the aristocratic class from their pedestal of personal prowess, unhorsing them with utmost ease as they pranced on their mail-clad chargers, were progressing in serviceableness, adding to themselves those concomitant inventions, on which their value depends. Cannon and small arms in the one direction, paper, type, and their easy mechanical application in use in the other, grew out of these initial steps, and have again and again shifted their forms and methods of production, as these inventions have shown the power that is in them. In the Elizabethan period these secondary steps were well under way, and the blind giants of mechanical force were getting to work at those stupendous labors they have since accomplished. As warming up by their activity, they make contemptible all previous exertion by that which follows, we are ready to cry, Hold, this will ruin us; another book, another paper, and we are buried in hopeless ignorance under this multiplicity of the material of knowledge; another monitor, another needle-gun, another mitrailleuse, and we are undone, having lost all our labors thus far, and sunk the value of past production in this omnipotence of a too headlong, incautious present.

The success of the reformation was due, in large part, to the aid given it by the press. New versions of the Bible, rapidly scattered, gained and confirmed the popular mind. Persecution was far less efficient, and it became impossible to hunt out and eradicate the multiplied and inconspicuous messengers of reform. The incentives to literary labor were also slowly on the gain. Authorship ceased comparatively to be an expense, gradually became remunerative, and now may bring a princely fortune. There came to it also a compensation quite as valuable, the pleasure of wide influence, of sending out a work that should go in a silent way to unknown households, and bespeak the kind attention of strangers. The intellectual world was gathered in large assemblies by this invention, and listened with redoubled interest to the rapid responses drawn out.

Gunpowder brought to an end barbaric inundations; gave the civilized nations a vast superiority over the uncivilized; put them in easy immediate possession of the world, as the Spaniards and English on this continent; between themselves lodged power with those most progressive, and inventive; transferred the arts of war yet more from the body to the mind; and, without exorcising the savage fiend of strife, put restraint upon it, and made it more just in its awards. Not only was the civilized world made impregnable to barbarism, and barbarism surrendered everywhere to civilization; not only did invention become the basis of power; the physically weak were armed with weapons that made them formidable, and mere bullying became comparatively impracticable. Invention, the best product of the laboring mind, took increasing possession of that mind, gave it thoughtfulness, and weight in the councils of men, and made it heedful of the intellectual life about it. Invention, committing the implements of war to the hands of industry, rendered national wealth an essential feature of national power. War became a question of finance; and the manufacturer, merchant, broker, citizen, proportionately gained power in its decisions. Those who created, and those who held, wealth, were prime factors in the product of national greatness; a city, a seat of industry, became a centre of strength; and the productive, economic forces, gaining their true position, lifted up with them the popular element.

No later inventions are comparable with these initial ones, in their transforming character, unless it be that of the application of steam as a motive power. This has wonderfully compacted the world; shifted its centres and methods; and permeated it everywhere with the most rapid, interlaced and composite circulations. But these gains, marvellous as they are, would have been utterly impossible without the previous safety, science and civilization due to gunpowder and the printing press.

Such were the general and growing conditions of activity in this creative period. A wakeful attention had come to men in all departments, and while in religion they were claiming the rule of their own spirits; in science, discovery, invention, they had entered on the rule of the world.

We have now occasion to speak but briefly of the foreign and domestic influences which acted in a more limited way on the Elizabethan age. Chief among the first was classical scholarship. The most vigorous translation of Homer, that of Chapman, belongs to this period. The great poets were either thoroughly permeated with the classical spirit, and laden with its poetical images and myths, like Milton; or were, like Shakespeare, cognizant of these works of the past as standards of taste, and an unfailing source of material. No poet was so independent as not to feel somewhat this restored life, and the most commanding drew on its wealth with the utmost freedom. The nearer and freer legends of mediæval and chivalrous life, however, mingled with the classical story, and were often the weightier element of the two.

The second foreign influence was Italian literature. This was more controlling than in any previous or subsequent period. It disclosed itself in translations of Tasso and Ariosto; in constantly returning Italian themes in the English drama, as in Romeo and Juliet; in poetical measures, as in that

of Spenser; and in the kinds of poetry. Surrey
was most immediately the medium through which
Italian poetry affected our literature.   A translation
of two books of Virgil by him gave the first example of English blank verse, a form taken from Italy.
He also introduced under the same influence sonnets, so long a favorite variety with our poets, and
gave a beginning to our lyrical poetry.   Lyrical
poetry, as the product of subtile, refined sentiment,
falls to a somewhat late period in national development.   Its origin in Southern France, and cultivation in Italy had been the result of the extreme
development of chivalry, and the languid refinement of Southern tastes.   These chivalrous sentiments belonged in a high degree to Surrey, and
united him, on his visit to Italy, with an easy natural affinity to its literature.   Yet an English temper so far aided him, that his composition showed
more simplicity and sobriety than his models, and
we have in him the lyric spirit with little of that
extreme vaporing tenderness which had begun to
attach to it in Italy.   He was followed and aided
in this branch of poetry by Wyatt.   Thus Italy
gave us, through one in whom the rough English
character was subdued to utmost courtesy, our
earliest lyric strains, single notes from its sunny
vineyards and olive groves, floating northward to
our more rugged climate, dropping as they came
their heat of passion, and taking in its place the
glow of manlier sentiments; as coals that ceasing
to smoulder burn again in the draught of strong
winds.

5

Most noticeable of the domestic forces that affected the period was the firm, peaceful, conservative government that fell to the long reign of Elizabeth. As advanced as any English rule had yet been, unless it be the brief reign of Edward VI., in religious liberty, and in its general policy, it nevertheless held firmly to its own ground, checking rather than quickening progressive elements. Though the new, in Protestantism, as opposed to the old, in Catholicism, was accepted, that division of elements which resulted in Puritans and royalists was still incipient, and thrust back by an authority at once strong and popular. Peace at home, with a sense of power and responsibility abroad, prevailed, and kept the national mind alert in the midst of leisure. An intense antagonism to Spain, and the faith represented by it, animated and consolidated the national sentiments.

Another marked feature of this reign, enhanced by the sex, position and character of Elizabeth, was the chivalrous spirit which belonged to the court and nobility. Sir Philip Sidney, Sir Walter Raleigh were men of a fascinating character, and one which attached to this particular period in history. That which was most truly refined and just in chivalry lingered longest; as a perfume, overpowering at first, becomes sweetest as it is ready to pass away. A gentle courtesy and subdued undertone of admiration gave a color and flavor to society not otherwise obtainable, and tinctured strongly poetic sentiment. Chivalry, as a controlling institution, omnipresent, imperious, smothered as much virtue as it called forth. It lay a damp, heavy cloud on the landscape ; when it lifted here and there, if it revealed glittering surfaces, they were decked with cunning frost-work, rather than with healthful, spontaneous life. But now, when the sun had been for some time up, when these exhalations of the night were about to pass away, they softened down into a warm, roseate mist, casting the lightest shadows, and giving the most unspeakable charms.

Literature still belonged almost exclusively to the upper classes, but these had been increased in the cities by many rich citizens, into whose hands power was daily falling. They were growing up to be that body of the nation, to which nobility is as secondary as pauperism. Dramatic literature was far more comprehensive than romance literature, and gathered a more promiscuous audience. In the reign of Elizabeth, remnants of slavery were still found, and husbandmen led a coarse and brutish life; vagrancy and crime were inadequately suppressed by severe laws, unequally administered. Sixteen hundred executions are put down as the yearly average in England alone, and seventy-two thousand fell to the entire reign of Elizabeth. While, therefore, the wealthier classes were numerous enough to call forth and reward the genius of Shakespeare, they were still in close contact with an unkempt population, the coarsest staple of human kind. Amid the losses of such a state, there was this gain, that thought and speech preserved a straightforward, vigorous, idiomatic tone, ready to do rough service in rough places.

This fact served to hold in check those changes incident to the revival of learning. Latin words spread more slowly into the body of speech, and popular forms of composition, as the drama, were less choked by them. The dramatic writers of the period were usually graduates of the universities, and also men of the world; they united two vocabularies, a classical and a popular one, and thus had power above and below.

This period presents both branches of literature, poetry and prose; though the former has a decided ascendancy in quantity and quality. We have abundant prose, however, faithful to its own function, a presentation of truth; and this with an excellency of manner which gives it a place in literature. Prose, more earnest and less artistic than poetry, more single and less popular in its purpose, born of thought rather than of feeling, necessarily reaches literary excellence later. Thus during this entire period, while poetry was mounting to a point which it has hardly since transcended, prose remained more or less embarrassed by its own resources, and labored through unwieldy sentences, not native to the vigor of our tongue. It did its work by strength rather than by skill, and reached by power what it missed in grace. Prose had come to a manly birth, but was waiting to be bred by the repose and cultivation of later times.

Poetry, vigorous and creative though it was, had not fully recognized its own province. Many subjects were treated by it more appropriate to prose, and giving no sufficient play to the imagination

The form of poetry should co-exist with a poetical substance, and if the theme be essentially didactic, it is in vain that it is loaded with the imagery of the fancy. Stone good for a wall may be too coarse for statuary; topics, admirable in prose, yield insufficient feeling to poetry. Examples of these unpoetical themes are, The History of the Civil Wars, a poem by Daniel; Nosce Teipsum, a Proof of Immortality, by Davies. In so vigorous a period it was natural that plants should spring up at points that could not finally afford them nourishment. The just division of the field of literature, giving to each portion its own products, was a later growth of **judgment and** taste, one not yet quite complete.

LECTURE V.

So many are the causes involved in any com-plex effect, that an oversight of a portion of them is inevitable. It is also natural, that once made aware, in a particular direction, of this neglect, we should forthwith give the newly discovered agent more than its share of weight. The same partial, the same limited power of the mind, is shown alike in its too restricted and its too intense appreciation. Thus, having waked up to the fact that soil and climate have something to do with national charac-ter, we hasten to the conclusion, that these are the chief and controlling forces in its formation ; and that the families of men are but a higher flora, a more varied fauna, whose tendencies and capacities are impressed upon them by their environment; taking care to include in this, not merely the miner-alogy of the earth, the meteorology of the heavens, the make of the land,—its mountain fastnesses, or open plains, its secluded position or commercial ad-vantages—but also the accumulated results of these forces long since wrought into the national stock. Thus the serious and sombre phases of English character, its stern purpose and stolid animality, its severe restraints and brutal outbursts, its vigorous moral conflicts with itself and with others, are ascribed to the climate of England, damp and dejected, often driving the inhabitants into indoor life, putting them to effort in their pleasures ; and to its soil, low-lying, fertile, penetrated and close bound by the sea, yielding no hilarity, no exhilaration of sunshine and upland to the spirits, yet rewarding labor with plentiful food ; more generous to digestion than to imagination, more liberal in utilities than beauties. We are not disposed to deny, and we strive not to underrate, these physical influences ; but they are far from sufficient to explain fully any type of national character. We find no reason for this entire transfer of causation to the physical world, as if mind went for nothing among primitive forces. Lands do not yield given nations as they do given fruits, under defined qualities of soil and limits of temperature ; and if they did, in this correlation of conditions and products, there would still be included the inscrutable living agency. Irish character, ripened under much the same physical conditions with English character, is yet very unlike it. Races have varied and independent endowments, and by constitutional and acquired bias either control or greatly modify the effects that reach them from the external world.

The ethical quality which undoubtedly belongs to English as contrasted with French character is not a result of climate. It exists in very different degrees in the three political divisions of the empire, Ireland, Scotland, England; and the explanation of this varying intensity is to be found in the religious history of each of these sections. The force of religious ideas, their form of manifestation, have been very distinct for centuries in England and in France; and this fact, on which the character of each nation to-day hinges, has not been the result of diversity of soils simply, but of sentiments as well, of a variety in the ingredients of manhood rather than in those of matter, in the way in which free, unique and responsible powers have been unfolded. Into this national complexity have entered many forces, but supreme among them all have ruled those pristine elements which make up character, first individual, then national, establishing themselves at points, thence enlarging, interlacing, and growing into a net-work of living and relatively homogeneous dependencies. Certainly we cannot concede a primitive power to the plant, to the material molecule, and deny it to man. So Germany, side by side with France, and so Spain, stand each contrasted with it in national traits.

National character is not something superinduced from without; is not rugged features, grim facial outlines, and a gruff bearing caught from the cold peevish air, from the warfare of man with ungenerous nature; it is not a mood of the heavens, which, by sympathy, he has gradually transferred to his own constitution, casting this in the same mould, with the same strife of tendencies; it is rooted in deep, measurably independent, constitutional forces, abiding with him as their centre; even as matter possesses a character, and is faithful to it. Thought, manners and literature receive their coloring from the way in which this national germ shows itself in the mind and heart of a people, as a distinctive, national type.

Having seen the general influences at work on and through English character in the Elizabethan period, we now turn to consider what individual creative power added to them, what it wrought beyond the range of results level to the time and period in its graded, normal activity. There are always in a great age here and there significant clusters of forces to which we can only give an individual name, whose power we cannot trace beyond those wonderful personalities in which they inhere; men who make the period as well as are made by it. In this era we dwell upon three of these, Spenser, Shakespeare and Milton. We know of no necessary causes which laid down the frame-work of powers for any one of these three men; yet through those powers came, in large part, the Elizabethan age. Without these three it might have been a high table-land, with them it adds thereto some of the noblest altitudes of the globe.

Though all working under the conditions presented by the period, these men stood in very different relations to it. The bent of his own genius decided for each the form of his works, and gave them a very diverse direction. Spenser looked steadily toward the past; was quietly conservative in his temper, and dreamy in his cast of mind. Milton turned to the future. Fiery, almost fierce in pur-

5*

pose, under the strenuous impulse of principles, he reined in thought and imagery alike to the firm march of ideas. Shakespeare's time is the present, an omnipresent present, that roots its creations anywhere, and sets them a growing under the sunshine of the hour, as easily and freely as if that place and time were all the earth.

We speak first of Spenser. The past with its imagery, its illusions, its pomp of life, and poetical dreaminess, descended upon him, and completely drank up his quiet, unpractical spirit. With restless, yet untiring importunity, he sought from queen and courtiers those means which should leave him to the free indulgence of his tastes. He congratulated himself

> "That even the greatest did not greatly scorne
>   To heare theyr names sung in his simple layes,
>   But joyed in theyr praise."

Though adulation was not a grateful task to him, he was content to prosper by it, rather than turn to those practical, commonplace labors that command subsistence.

> "Calme was the day, and through the trembling ayre
>   Sweete-breathing Zephyrus did softly play
>   A gentle spirit, that lightly did delay
>   Hot Titians beames, which then did glyster fayre;
>   When I (whom sullein care,
>   Through discontent of my long fruitlesse stay
>   In princes court, and expectation vayne
>   Of idle hopes, which still doe fly away
>   Like empty shadows, did afflict my b ayne,)
>   Walkt forth to ease my payne
>   Along the shoare of silver streaming Themmes."

Irritated by delay and ill success, he complains, in

his Teares of the Muses, of the overshadowing influence of polemical discussion. He regards it as
the creeping forth of "barbarism and ignorance,"
instead of the restlessness of a new era. The fas-
tidious poet, anxious only to set in order one more
vision of the past, had little sympathy with any discussion, however vital, "without regard or due de-
corum kept." He knew nothing of the germs of
greater centuries yet to come that were budding
under his feet. He was only in haste to participate
in the pageant of life that was passing, or to escape
to the poetic glories of the life that had already
passed.

Spenser was a poet, not a philosopher; his mind
was more fruitful of images than of judgments.
Appearances had so strong a hold upon him as to
conceal underlying principles. Such minds are slow
to leave realities, a good achieved and a like good
dreamed of, to embark on an ocean of revolutionary
ideas in quest of new worlds. There is enough in
the present, to call forth desire, enough in the past
to furnish the decoration and tinsel of their dreams.
They are forced onward by no sense of pervasive
wrong, nor pressed to labor for a future cast in a
better mould. If patriotic, they find patriotism in
loyalty; if devout, devotion attaches them to the
hoar and venerable institutions of the established
faith. They overlook its evils, and chasten and
subdue its spirit to their own quiet, trusting moods.
Such was Spenser. He asked only to dream, and
he thought it hard that men would not at once give
him the opportunity of dreaming, and share with

him his delight in the glowing imagery of his visions. This pleasure at length came to him. In the retirement of Kilcolman, Ireland, on an estate granted him by Elizabeth, he composed the larger share of his works, above all the Faëry Queen. Adown this flowing vision, as along a pure, gentle, beautiful winding stream, he floated many a long summer's day, and never reached its end. However, as the gift of the queen lost something of its grace by the strong rapacious hand which plucked it from the heart of Ireland, so the poet did not escape the retribution which clung to it. An insurrection broke out in this land of chronic violence. His house was burnt, an infant child perished in the flames, and he fled to England, where he died shortly after. Justice and repose are exotics in this unfortunate island; they neither cling as hardy shrubs to its hillsides; nor are they successfully planted by a fostering hand in its cultivated fields.

Spenser gathered up his chief strength in one poem, the Faëry Queen. This, though so far superior to the past as not to be of it, bears throughout an archaic impress. It is the genius of the writer that holds it aloof from its affinities, lifts it above its kin, and puts it among the best productions of the new epoch, while belonging in type and form to the tedious and dreary works of a retreating age. It is allegorical, a device by which so many drooping imaginations had striven to give motion to dull themes: Hawes, writing of Dame Commyte, and Lady Grammar, and Dame Logic. It seemed to be thought that by the trick of a name the life of poetry could be made to descend upon and quicken the merest rubbish of knowledge ; that a personal appellation would bring breath to the nostrils of any the rudest image of clay ; that a title, however ill bestowed, had all the charms of rank at its command ; and that Lady Grammar, born with such ease of this formal fancy, was as veritable, sympathetic and inspired a being as any of the family of poetry. Thus also a little later, Fletcher, in his Purple Island undertook the absurd task of allegorizing into poetry an anatomical description of the human body. Spenser's poem is an allegory, and great notwithstanding ; partly, perhaps, because he often strays so freely, unmindful of the perplexed, tangled and broken threads of primary, secondary and even tertiary dependencies he has left behind him. Allegory puts the steed of the muses in harness ; it must draw by hill and by valley ; descending to the ocean or mounting along the clouds its moral is ever behind it, and with a pedler's precision, it drops a precept at every door it passes, or adds it may be some new lading of didactic import. The ingenuity of the allegory is also at war with the inventions and freedom of the poet. It gives him a line along which he must move, rather than leaves him open to impulse, at liberty to choose any way and all ways. Allegory is a cunning method of getting rollers under a truth too heavy to be moved by hand, an ingenious device for sliding a forgotten, unacceptable block of preceptive lore into the way of the workmen, as they rear the building of national or private character. It is essentially didactic, and hardly of service even in instruction, where the mind of the pupil is vigorous, receptive and eager.   To be acceptable in a lengthy form it must be accompanied, as in Bunyan's Pilgrim's Progress, by vigorous personification, often sweeping into forgetfulness its indirect lessons, and swallowing up the mind with first impressions.   Apollyon makes as good a fight as Cœur de Lion.

The allegory of Spenser is at times, as in parts of the first book, quite direct ; but more frequently the poetic fancy spurs freely forward, and leaves her didactic companion to hobble on as he may, or to tarry, till taken up again on some more sober and easy excursion.

The imagery of the poem, long and varied as it is, is all drawn from chivalry.   It thus wanders through a past already becoming to the cotemporaries of Spenser remote and unreal ; an unlocated, enchanted, and vast forest, roamed over by men and women magnified in every quality, fanciful in action, extravagant in emotion. The thoroughness with which the mind of Spenser was imbued with the sentiment of chivalry is astonishing.   He is never at a loss.   He brings forward his knights and ladies in exhaustless variety, and enters upon each new combat, with fresh spirit, and lends it novel incidents.   Chivalry was not with him, as with the court of Elizabeth, a courtesy of intercourse, a gloss of manners, the lingering splendor of a bygone life ; his poetic sentiments, his virtues, his sober thoughts, all responded to it, all sprang into being under its conditions, marched forth under its banners, vanquished or suffered defeat under the guise of its heroes. A certain shadowy, unreal character necessarily falls to the personages of the poem, so wholly are they the children of the fancy, so little of realistic or historic light is there in the eye that marshals them, so much of interpretation, of persona and local rendering. They play a part to the mind so fictitious and conventional, aside entirely from allegory; are so simply its own creations, that we watch them and move with them, in a dreamy, unreal way. Moreover the whole country, the field of their exploits, is one unmapped, with no earthly whereabouts. It enlarges before us as we move into it, and, an unknown region, holds any and everything in reserve. Its surprises fail to surprise us, so evidently are its creations feats of poetic legerdemain.

Hence it is, that the Faëry Queen, though a narrative poem, is rather a panorama of visions, a series of dreams, in which old characters return to us from we know not whence, and new ones meet us, and provoke no inquiry into their origin; causal connections are lost sight of; anything and anybody are anywhere, that is where they chance to be wanted, where the fancy puts them; and we, sufficiently occupied with the light, easy interplay, as in a night vision, put no questions, and make no complaints.

One result of this, however, is, that the poem gets no movement as a whole; there is no direction in the stream; like the dragon's tail, it is "in knots and many boughtes upwound." This was inevitable. The plan of Spenser predetermined the result. Twelve virtues, headed by religion, rose before the mind of Spenser; the discipleship of private morality, to be followed by twelve others, the guardians of public faith. To each was to be devoted a book of twelve cantos, with its own champion, its own suitable adventures, and incidental relations to the Queen of Faëry Land, and to Arthur, its model knight. These virtues became indistinct in personification, features blended The adventures of their respective heroes lacked suitableness and variety, the multiplied figures in motion lost identity, whirled on in a maze of unreal achievements, and remained interesting only by the grace and novelty of their evolutions. It was impossible on this slight plan to give either progress, connection or division to the poem; the result actually reached was inevitable The labor was too great even for the strength of Spenser. Every step exhausted the imagery and interest at his disposal; the allegorical thread was often broken, even lost for long periods together; similar positions reappeared; and he was not able again to reach the elevation and consistency of the first book.

In length also this poem belonged to a past which deemed nothing tedious, felt little of the hurry of time, and waited patiently for the end of the longest and laziest action. The concentration and energy of intellect which characterize an age of achievement were scarcely known. Writers in philosophy and poetry spun, like ever patient insects, inexhaustible webs for simple and meagre ends, their work often hanging in the winds without one poor fly to grace the issue.   This gentle, yet undying motion of Spenser, in which he seems borne on by the innate vigor of the imagination, rather than by any purpose in view, any necessity of the action, situation or characters, is seen in his full and rich comparisons.   The metaphor delays, not the thought, impels it on rather; is the long, sudden, startling leap it takes in reaching its object. The classical comparison, on the other hand, rolls on in stately fashion, like a large orbed wheel; or even spins pleasantly on its axis without progress. This is with Spenser a favorite figure.

The Faëry Queen is not merely a moral, it is a religious poem.   His own words are applicable to him.

> "The noble hart, that harbours virtuous thought,
> And is with childe of glorious great intent,
> Can never rest untill it forth have brought
> Th' eternall brood of glorie excellent."

His was a devout and earnest mind, and this it was that enabled him to transfuse riotous war, and at times sensuous imagery, with a gentle and pure spirit.   His work was a dream, a panorama of dreams, an unending sport of the imagination, an easy circling flight of fancy, and his scenes lose the cruel passions of conflict, the grossness of lust, and the contamination of physical contact.   We wander with him backward and forward through his vague land of visions, as free from soil as the sunlight, glancing lightly on the clean and the unclean.

Spenser was one of those sincere, imaginative spirits who need never forsake the past, no matter how dark and evil its fashion, for they find not the mischief that is in it; they subject it to their own impressions, casting over it the indistinctness of evening light, concealing deformities, magnifying distances, and bringing even to coarse common place an undefinable harmony. Like a glorious sunset, Spenser closed a long dark day with a splendid vision. As such a sunset is said to give the promise of the hours next to open, so he borrowed the force and spirit of the Elizabethan age, that he might render the new in prediction on the fading sky of chivalry. Spenser was a poet for poets. He brings inexhaustible refreshment to the imagination. We are not compelled to read; we wander as in a beautiful garden, we rest at pleasure, at pleasure resume our walk, or, restored in spirit, leave it altogether. From this mellow light of Spenser, which is at once evening and morning, we pass to Shakespeare, who gives us the bold, clear discoveries of midday, and that a gala day, in which foreigners and citizens of every rank crowd and jostle each other in the streets, sport in the public squares, move in pomp along the thoroughfares, and make of life a grand ever varying spectacle.

Among the art forms of the Elizabethan era, one was pre-eminent, the drama. It engrossed the best talent of the time, and attained an eminence

from which later productions of the kind have
fallen rapidly off. The English drama, though
not altogether alone, is peculiar in form. Its purpose is by dialogue purely to unfold striking
phases of character, grouped in action either
about a single or several leading personages.
With careless and vanishing distinctions, it main-
tains two forms, that of comedy and that of
tragedy, both elements easily uniting in the same
play, with a general preponderance of the one,
sufficient to define and confirm the ruling sentiment. The English drama is quite unlike the
classical, and also unlike the French drama. The
latter occupies a position somewhat between the
other two, lays more stress than the English play
on the elegant, easy evolution of the dialogue,
the intellectual tournament of thought and sentiment; cares less for variety and force of incidents, and for the vigor of character which these
express; clings far more closely to the forms
and rules of the art as shaped under classical
models; and is intolerant of the broad, bold,
easy, careless sweep of events found in the works
of Shakespeare and of his cotemporaries. The
classical drama rests on another idea, and occupies the other extreme from that which falls to the
English. The chorus, stationary in the centre of
the stage, rehearsing many events, giving lyrical
utterance and interpretation to the restricted
action as it progressed, was the formal, the controlling, external feature of the Greek drama, and
led to a limitation in time and place, and in the

number of actors, quite foreign to the spirit of our stage. The force or inner power of the Greek tragedy is as peculiar as its form; it is a rapid, mental change under a sudden accumulation of events, the quick rending of a soul by a final Nemesis, its struggle with forces gathering at once with fearful intensity. This gives it the nature of a catastrophe; the spirit being searched, Job-wise, through and through by the din and reverberation of multiplied calamity, by the sharp, lightning strokes of judgment.

The English drama owes its form to its historical origin. It was not the product of a pure and critical æsthetical sentiment; a keen relish of a complete, concise and symmetrical image. It moved leisurely, laughingly, with varied and protracted enjoyment, through a series of events, loosely united by ordinary causes; because it had slowly grown up by a presentation, rather than by a concentration and idealization, of facts; and enjoyed these in their native flavor and spirit. Its idealization lay rather in increasing the relish of events, making them spicy with humor and passion, than, as in the Greek tragedy, in selecting, combining, compacting them into one hungry ordeal of woe, over whose blistering ploughshares, with naked feet, the victim was to hasten on as he could.

The miracle play, dating back as far as the twelfth century, rehearsed to the populace in the monastery, or in the streets of the city, the Bible history, accompanied with the rudest caricature, the coarsest joke, the most incongruous additions.

The history was greatly humbled, but it was made real, and put within the reach of the grossest minds. If Gabriel, the messenger sent to Mary to ask her if she would be God's wife, loses all celestial complexion, and issues forth on the rude service of a feudal lord, yet the three parties are present, in vigorous presentation, to all minds. The miracle plays were accompanied and followed by the moralities, with a broader range of subjects, the lives of saints and legendary church history. These again gave occasion to the interludes, shorter and yet more secular pieces; and these by slow gradations to that comic and tragic rehearsal of events which constituted the earliest drama, and ripened into the scenes of Shakespeare. The later secular forms slowly took the place of the earlier religious ones, while, from beginning to end, the play was a free representation of events more or less remote from each other, and animated by a comic or tragic sentiment. Thus the English drama owes its final form to its free and historic development, and its real spirit and power to those great artists who laid hold of it as it was, and unfolded it according to its inherent character and tendencies. A verdict, growing in unanimity with each advancing year, has placed Shakespeare first among dramatic writers. Though honored by his cotemporaries, this position certainly was not by them granted to him. Beaumont and Fletcher were more sought after. Webster includes him, yet with secondary commendation, among those of whom he cherished a good opinion. Shakespeare is not merely in advance of the play-writers of his own and of subsequent times, but so far in advance as to leave a long unoccupied stretch behind him.   The galaxy of writers associated with him, clustering thick, with varied and brilliant powers, about him, owe their supreme impression to his over-balancing light.   No one of them can stand comparison with him, and each of them fades before the eye, when singled out for the purpose.   The plays, for instance, of Jonson, all weigh light when put conjointly against one of the superior dramas of Shakespeare.

The time of Shakespeare was indeed favorable to his genius, but that time was shared by Beaumont, Fletcher, Massinger, as well, and left the busy, fertile writers, that swarmed up into the warm, creative sunshine of that day, to drop into comparative oblivion.   One light only burns clear for all ages through the haze of intervening years, and its pre-eminence therefore must be attributed to those independent personal powers which genius holds within itself.   The times may furnish material, may give or remove limitations, but the germ of growth is ever in the mind that harbors it.   The one inscrutable force, which no philosopher can fully explain, is Shakespeare himself.

Close communion with men, free, bold, unreserved—men of vigorous limbs, strong appetites, impetuous passions, and many of them of keen intellect ; a language receiving large additions, untrammelled by criticism, pliant and productive in the hand of masters ; society awakened by new thoughts and stirring convictions, just conscious of the life of coming centuries that was rising within it, and not as yet heated and parted by religious and political passion, nor filled with the limited and headlong bias of conflicting elements; these were the conditions under which Shakespeare, and with him many more of like occupation, grew up in strength, in London, the centre of English life; ripened their powers in the daily use of them in their chosen avocation; themselves on the stage, saw and felt constantly the conditions of success and failure; and entered into the most direct, intense, living experience of the principles of their art. These were rare circumstances, rare forces, but Shakespeare was rarer than they all. Without him, and the few who stood nearest to him, darkness would have overtaken that epoch as easily as another. It would have disappeared as the flush of one among an hundred sunsets, and been thought of no more.

What were these powers of Shakespeare, by which this age is made inextinguishable by the centuries which roll over almost all things the darkness of oblivion, brushing from the earth the life of to-day, that they may make ready for that of to-morrow; armies camping where many another has camped, yet without intrusion, collision of spears or clatter of musketry? The drama calls above every other form of composition for the rapid, varied, complete creation of character. This power, this complication of powers, Shakespeare possessed, and it was his art. Characters that are strongly

conceived, entire and living, take care of them
selves, as easily and inevitably as do the men who
are like them. It is the imbecile and the mechanical only that are in the way, either in nature
or in art. A true character contains and commands a plot; while a plot that runs before its
characters, leaves them all manakins. Whatever
rank we give this power among powers, that rank,
in a supreme degree, falls to Shakespeare. He
was able from within to raise up, and therefore
easily to work in word and action, the most diverse and varied characters; these were the abundant, living, lively offspring of his fecund imagination. They traversed the stage, and occupied it
unendingly with humorous and tragic incidents, because these passions were in them, and they were
to the manner born. This supreme command of
human nature, this ability to make it shift its form
and color every instant, as a cloud that fades or
glows in sunlight, also enabled him to treat with
equal felicity those allied, unlike forms that hover
on the bounds of the rational, yet range beyond
them, the spirit, the witch, the monster, the idiot,
the half-dazed, or one altogether insane. As caricature, if successful, must grow out of that which
is real, must be a distortion aptly put upon it, so
the supernatural and the unnatural will only obey
those who are masters of nature.

This creative power is not imagination, though
it wakes imagination to its highest efforts; nor
judgment, though judgment constantly moderates
and consolidates its work; nor sympathy, though

sympathy, in the putting forth of this strength, gives life to it and receives it from it each instant; nor memory, though memory draws for it upon the crowded recollections of active and eventful years; nor yet perception, the combined intuition of the senses and the reason, though this lies nearer the nucleus than any other one act; it is all these, in terfusing and feeding each other, till the mind becomes a fruitful field, in which a fertile soil waits on refreshing showers, and these on the seeds of tender plants, sturdy shrubs, and towering trees. Such a prolific soul was Shakespeare's, and his creations came up in like abundance, and grew with the same overshadowing strength and luxuriant ease of life. His relation to art, it is not, therefore, difficult to define. He reached it by the inevitable force of his faculties. To bind the genius of one nation, when it attains such vigor as did that of the English people in Shakespeare, to the rules of art applicable to another time and climate, is to miss utterly the freedom which belongs to every creative impulse. As the flora of one region, or the beauty of one sky, is not that of another, so the literature of each period stands by the force of the life that is in it. Influence, instruction may lead to high art, but not imitation. To insist on any absolute excellence in Grecian architecture, or sculpture, or poetry, not to be departed from, is to make over all subsequent time to mediocrity. It is the office of genius, not to fulfil another's law, but to disclose the law of its own nature, and of its own age. This Shakespeare did; he emphasized and completed the bold, free,

6

rugged drama for which English life and history had prepared the way. He thus accomplished the work centuries had been laying out for him. This energetic English temper or form he carries with him, no matter where he casts the scenes of his drama; and while it is one which grew up historically from his age and nation, and was brought to its sovereign proportions by the strength of his single nature, it is all the more that of true art, because of these native, living, consistent forces which were unfolded in it. Taine says of Shakespeare, that his master faculty is "an imagination freed from the fetters of reason and morality." Trained in a more quiet and obedient school, one less passionate and less inspired, he regards the English stage as presenting a dramatic literature of "raving exaggerations," whose "ideas all verge on the absurd;" but the catholic critic will recognize in this language the judgment of one suddenly falling upon an art too new and strong for him, and mistaking, therefore, its very vigor and life for lawlessness. He has passed from the garden to the forest, and the trees seem to him awkward and disproportioned through excessive growth, through the impress of the struggles by which they have at length overtopped their fellows, and occupied with sturdy branches the upper air. A little time, more familiarity, might lead him to discover a majesty and freedom here, quite beyond the tempered and proportionate life that he has left.

Undoubtedly Shakespeare accepts the English method and impulse, with its restrictions upon it.

with its peculiarities, its own possibilities within it; but these, when pushed to their limits by his strength, are quite sufficient for a great and complete art. This narrowness, on the one side, and vigor, on the other, may be seen in the women of Shakespeare. His ideal is the English ideal. His best creations, those in which he gathers up the beauties of his art, are full of love, patience, dependence; quick in insight, yet without mastery; incomplete in themselves, and waiting to attach themselves to some centre of manly force and life, from which, as flowers whose roots are hidden in the crevice of a rock, they may rise and blossom in fragile beauty. He knows also the termagant, that worse than masculine nature, which, breaking its close confinement, does itself every species of violence under the wayward impulse that rules it, driven far beyond its own will by the severity of a censure it cannot soften; but he knows little of woman as a self-contained and independent power, as ruling within herself, measurably complete in her own nature, and thus able to rule and thrive with others.

Falstaff, his chief humorous creation, is also very English in character, and quite opportune to the English drama. His humor is in his flesh, his blood, his action, quite as much as on his tongue. He is full of vitiosity, without being hateful; his very grossness saves him from our anger, and we feel that he plots no mischief, save as he is driven to it by a coarse, unconquerable, appetitive nature. Our moral sense is apologetic toward him, as is our

æsthetical sentiment to an interesting, though un-
couth, specimen of animal life. We feel that he is
as yet scarcely bred above his physical impulses,
and that only in the line of cunning and vanity; a
fact so palpable as to make praise and blame mis-
directed, when applied to his actions. In short, he
finds entrance and countenance in a furtive way
through a momentary remissness of an overtired
moral sense, without essentially vitiating its general judgments, or abating its force. He is no
Italian villain, whom we must know, and knowing
hate.

Taine speaks of Shakespeare as a " Nature
poetical, immoral, inspired," also as " void of will
and reason." These adjectives we think can not be
so grouped, and each retain its full force. To be
immoral is to lack in part, in one direction at least,
poetical inspiration; for the noblest creations of
character would be thereby shut out from the vision
of the soul. What, then, is Shakespeare's relation
to morality? He is not certainly a religionist; he
is not a moralist. He neither fashions precepts,
nor makes it his business directly or indirectly to
enforce them. Is he therefore immoral? Then is
nature immoral, human history and the record of
daily life; for it is these that Shakespeare reproduces. If he does not so construct his plot, so
manipulate his characters, as to give peculiar and
brilliant light to moral issues, no more does he pervert
and cover them up. He allows the moral forces,
among other real natural forces, to flow on with
events, to exercise their own share of control over

them, and to come out, from time to time, in terrific thunder shocks of retribution. He merely fails, as a showman, to arrest the spectacle, invite attention and rehearse the unmistakable lesson. At bottom, Shakespeare, instead of being an immoral, is a moral writer; because he handles powerfully and truthfully natural, real forces; those which in th world shape character, control its development, gather up its issues. In this region to be true, to be complete, is in the most important of all ways to be moral; and to be untrue and incomplete, though a thousand tags of morality be tacked to the story, or woven into it as its deceitful labels, is to be immoral. It is with the interior combination of opinions, sentiments, choices, that the artist has to do, —and the true moralist as well—with the natural issue of events, and the ripe fruits of character; and these all proceed under the laws, and disclose the facts of the world, as God ordains them. The drama, the novel, the history, the biography, so presenting them, is moral; has in it the precise morality which governs and illuminates the world. History is not printed in raised letters for the morally blind to read; it is not a Sabbath-school book for children, devising for each sin an instant disaster; yet it is, with all its crimes, its atrocities, its ninety-nine unrighteous acts, and its one hundredth virtuous one, so far moral as to be God's great and inexhaustible revelation of morality; that wherein he discloses character, uncovers good and evil, and leads ultimately to the light the excellent. the admirable, all that men do in their secret soul's honor. The religionist and the sensualist may make the same mistake, that of calculating the orbit of action from too small an arc. See deeply, see broadly, follow conduct with the patience of Providence, and there is no room for two opinions. The higher the art, therefore, the more certainly it reaches nature in its balance of motives, and in the issues of action, the more certainly is it moral. This morality belongs to Shakespeare. When crime, as in Macbeth ; or guilt, as in the King of Denmark ; or villainy, as in Iago ; or avarice, as in Shylock, come before us, they do so in their own character, and we have no other thing to say of them, than when, in the tragedy of history under the ordering of a higher hand, they move across the real stage of life. Shakespeare, also, by his high artistic power, was lifted into a purer region than that which belonged to his cotemporaries; felt less the need of low inuendo, and vulgar ribaldry ; could win and command attention by the vigor of his primary movement, and thus ordinarily holds on his way without soil from the defilement about him. That which is low, he touches lightly, and never makes his feast of it. He is full of resources, and these render him select and confident in his ground. As nature is knit to morality, and in fellowship with its purity, so is and must be its every great master. It is the petty limitations, the sad restrictions men have put on morality, its shallowness and barrenness, a clearness gained by the loss of all depth and power, that have led them to think of Shakespeare as immoral, and of the world as immoral ; and that too, perchance, while allowing God, in their conception of him, to absorb by foreordination all the sins of men into his own constitution. What we most need are eyes to see what God is about, and in this every great artist helps us.

The works of God are broader than our broadest works, fuller of sympathies, richer in beauties, mor fruitful in affections. It is the part of inspiration to see some new portion of this wealth, and of teachableness to be taught it.

Shakespeare is moral, then, by the full torrent and truthfulness of his overmastering genius, and immoral by the ooze and drainage of adjacent times. Shakespeare is surprisingly impersonal. He has written much, yet we know very little of him—William Shakespeare. He is back of his characters creatively, not sympathetically. He yields them one and all, without haste, without delay, to the laws of the world into which he has brought them. This one fact gives him a serene moral elevation. It is also surprising that Shakespeare should have been so apparently indifferent to posthumous fame. In the years that intervened between his retirement and his death, he seems to have done nothing for the editing or publishing of his plays; but to have left them to their chances, an abandoned literary progeny. There is in this a wonderful alienation from ordinary human feeling.

THE third great name of the Elizabethan age is
that of Milton. As Spenser's stands at its commencement, opening its portals backward on the
past, where the glow of the fading day of chivalry
still rests on the horizon ; so does Milton step forth
at its close, as one who has caught the prophetic
force of its spirit, and sees the light of new ideas,
of dawning ages, deeply penetrating the spaces before him and about him. Spenser is animated by a
gentle, erudite and meditative spirit, a piety and
poetry that soften and veil the harsh, unholy facts
of life ; that rearrange and represent them with a
mellow light that quite conceals the conflicts of
good and evil, and brings to the world as it is, and
yet more to it as it has been, a cheerful and benign
aspect. He is the poet of conventional forms, and
a conventional religion. Shakespeare moves amid
the sturdy, strong passions that play into and under
social events, whether they be right or wrong.
He is the poet of natural, constitutional forces,

and thus of natural religion and morality. He
deals with the fearful shocks of the moral world;
because the intellectual atmosphere of the human
soul is penetrated and convulsed by them. There
can be no terrific storms without these thunder-
claps of justice, this sharp lightning of conscience;
and Shakespeare is the poet of natural religion, because he cannot otherwise present nature. Milton
is the poet of definite and progressive dogma, a revealed religion that lives to conquer, that casts off
the past, and bestirs itself in perpetual resistance
and struggle to win a new future. The religious
sentiment had divided itself. A portion lingered;
another portion pushed onward, accepted the civil
and reformatory conflicts of the hour, and gave
itself unreservedly to a social and religious ideal.
This spirit the soul of Milton gathered with full
force into itself. His life was spent beyond the
calm of the strictly Elizabethan age. He ripened
under the conflict of its dissevered elements, adopted its progressive forces, and opened the way before them. In a reactionary hour, that brought
quiet and neglect to his old age, he gave, in poetry,
a rehearsal, in their grandest phase, to the same
ideas that had ruled his actions.

Milton was the poet of revealed religion under
its Puritanic type. The style and thought of Milton are native to this earnest and extended insight
of his mind. From the beginning he manifested
the same scope and majesty. He always spread a
broad wing, and floated serenely; moving at ease
from peak to peak. His literary life dropped into

6*

three periods, youth, manhood, and old age; and each, under one general impulse, fell to different and fitting tasks. The Hymn on the Nativity rightly opened his literary labors. There were gathered with this into his early life secondary poems, brief morning flights of the imagination, which serve to disclose the nature of the powers he held in reserve for the real labors of the day. These first hours of song were displaced by a long, sultry midday, in which Milton, forgetful of poetry, gave himself to the vigorous championship of ideas—ideas the most significant the world then held, the most formidable in action, the most pregnant in theoretical and practical results, ideas that plucked at thrones and laid the foundations of commonwealths. Without regret, driven by the earnestness of his own nature, Milton turned to the conflict of argument, and called up his imagination only that it might arm and furnish forth the truth; and send it as a thundering train of artillery to speedy conquest. The storm having passed by, a sombre, reactionary evening having set in, the heavens still cloaked with clouds, the ﹐blind warrior, finding nothing more to be done, in this hush of the senses turned again to poetry, and in the ripeness of a ripe mind took up his great labor.

An epic poem on King Arthur had been among the early dreams of Milton. From this the stern midday duties of his life had diverted him, not only diverted him, but fitted him for quite another theme. Long tossed in the most protracted, progressive and critical conflict of the century, he

naturally found himself, at its close, nerved for
the narration of a more real and pungent strife
than that of the thrice told tales of chivalry. His
eye was directed to the earliest, highest, most germinant struggle of spirits, rebellious to the moral
law ; one that opened the wide chasm that divides hell from heaven, and sowed broadcast on
earth the seeds of sedition. Here the full tension of his thoughts, his deep-toned sentiments,
found sufficient and sympathetic play. There is
still preserved in the library of Trinity College,
Cambridge, a dramatic sketch by Milton, on the
same theme as Paradise Lost, the fall of angels
and of men. This was not completed, or at least
published. It seems probable that the subject
may have opened unexpected vistas, and been
recommitted in his mind for this later and larger
presentation.

The style of Milton, not less than his depth
of conviction and stirring experience, fitted him
for the labor he undertook. So thoroughly possessed was he by classical scholarship, so crowded
was his imagination with antique imagery, that
nothing but the most overruling and dominant
impulse could give to him originality, could se
afloat and convoy these borrowed treasures of traffic. Under an independent and superior thought,
they gave scope and grandeur to the movement,
and richly furnished it out with scenic effect.

The subject of Paradise Lost is such as to
render impossible a treatment satisfactory to all
minds. Many would deny it any treatment, as in

some of its branches an unapproachable theme, one to be left in the high, unsearchable places of thought. This, in absolute, philosophical criticism, would seem to be the true view. There is of necessity a jar and collision, when the infinite and transcendant are made to enter finite limits, and that too under the unfamiliar forms of another's imagination. Yet when we remember that this is done in the person of Christ; when we recall the comparatively rude way in which, without reproach, it had been accomplished in painting, a much more sensual art than poetry, we believe that this first criticism should be waived, and the poet held only to the strongest, purest, most simple pitch of the imagination, as he makes for us a visible way through the invisible things of God.

This grandeur is conceded to Milton in approaching these dread unattainable precincts, this Shekinah of our religious thoughts. Do we not find, however, both in his presentation of the Deity and of Adam, some of the blemishes of a temper too positive and dogmatic? Art is not only not didactic, it will not allow the didactic spirit to disguise itself under its work. The Deity of the highest ethical art must not utter and enforce theology; nor should Adam, in the ruddy fulness, the sensual cast of our earliest physical life, impress upon Eve the principles of a school of philosophy. The criticism made upon Milton that seems to us best to hold against him is, that he was not always able perfectly to divorce himself from his dialectics, and, as the pure creative artist, to hold his conceptions, those of God and of Adam, aloof from every bias; the one in the grandeur of his impartial, self-poised nature, the other in the simplicity and typical freedom of his unperverted and unwrought character. A positive temperament, advocacy, controversial aims, are unfavorable to art, as they warp and limit the material, and distort it to a special purpose. There is no fullness, no repose in them, and hence these fail to be found in their creations. The intensity of the Puritan spirit, so far as it lifted Milton high up in religious sentiment, was favorable, most favorable, to his poetical inspiration; so far as it bound him under pains and penalties to a limited and precise formula, it narrowed his imagination, and gave close-at-hand and harsh limits to its creations.

Milton is also criticised for imparting to Satan heroic elements; we think unjustly. Satan is not to Milton personified sin, he is a real, historic character; and neither philosophy, nor religion, and still less poetry, requires that such an one, on the instant, through his whole constitution, should be turned to weakness and corruption by the touch of evil. There are no such utter overthrows, such violent and complete transitions, in the spiritual world. Sin is an insidious mischief, that does a slow, unwholesome, subtile work. It should find access to an archangel under the disguise of a noble, independent, courageous impulse, and, once seated in the heart, turn it steadily to adamantine pride and hardness, with such phosphorescent flashes of dying virtue as the decayed, irritable mood of a great soul may suffer. Religious art too often mistakes sin, fails of its true paternity, and true descent, by not tracing the slow, sure way in which it unknits the virtuous nature, loosens the passions, and, abolishing one divine law after another, turns all things into misrule, anarchy and night; the bitter and exasperate brood of appetite and lust. If we discern this fearful and steady descent of sin, it is far more dreadful than one mad plunge, which annihilates distance, and puts instantly the damned one beyond the range of vision and sympathy. Even physical spaces must be traversed, and so defined for the mind.

> " Nine days they fell ; confounded chaos roar'd,
> And felt tenfold confusion in their fall
> Through his wild anarchy."

This epic of Milton has helped to close the door on the epic of mere war and violence, and to affect a transfer of the truly heroic into more purely moral realms. Henceforward we wait on the battles of spirits, and the struggle of invisible and spiritual powers.

We have placed Milton in the Elizabethan age, not because he belongs there in a mere time division, but because of his affinity with the great inventive spirits that composed it. As a root sends up, at a distance from the parent stock, a rival tree, so did this first creative force, binding back Milton in close sympathy to Spenser, after its own proper era had passed by, yield one more of its most vigorous products, planted in the middle of

...ne following period. Eras lie interlaced, new forces rising in the heart of an old age, old forces lost to the eye in the heart of a new age.

We now turn to a transition period, the last half of the seventeenth century, lying between one of criticism and one of creation It is a period of violent contrasts. Society was broken up by extreme tendencies, and literature was divided and shaped by the spirit of the party to which, in its several forms, it was attached. The liberty of thought begotten by the reformation in England had been genuine and general. The nation, though aroused and strengthened by it, had, in the reign of Elizabeth, been held together. Under her successors religious and political liberty became closely united, and rapid, earnest minds began to draw off into distinct parties. The most progressive tendency, primarily religious, secondarily political, was that of the Puritans. Against them the royalists, the supporters of the established church and government, were arrayed. As in all revolutionary times, moderate and intermediate opinions became powerless, and an open conflict, ripening into civil war, swept away minor differences, consolidating the two extreme parties that held the field. Reform is rarely universal. It involves, therefore, separation, the parting of elements, which have been comparatively homogeneous, mutually restraining each other from extreme tendencies. No sooner, however, do the portions of society begin to divide, to stand in direct repulsion, than, electric equilibrium being overthrown, we have two defined and intense poles

of counteraction. Opposite tendencies, which before checked, now irritate and enhance, each other;
and cause the attitude of both parties to become
more extreme than it would be, if each were left to
its own free bent. The sweeping away of intervening persons and parties, the steady concentration
of hostile camps, the looking upon every act and
measure first of all in its belligerent character, the
blinding and distorting effect of mutual hatred, all
serve to give a violent wrench and warp to the minds
of either division, and force upon them an extreme,
and often irrational, attitude, begotten of collision,
and quite opposed to sober, constructive, proportionate thought.

It is this which makes reformatory periods so
critical. A dividing line appears, and men are
driven to the one side or the other, often sadly
against the minor tendencies of their constitution.
Those who are reluctant to cast up accounts, to
strike a balance, or to settle, by leading considerations, their method of action, find themselves tossed
about by a conflict they cannot still, and at length
compelled to shelter themselves under opinions
they would never willingly have accepted. The
reign of Elizabeth had been one of coalescence, and
thus of mutual restraint; those of James and of
Charles were marked, first by separation, then by
intense strife.

The Puritan character was not the product of
peace, but of war; it had grown up beaten on and
bowed by severe winds. It showed in every limb
and twig the twist of the strong currents in which it

had stood, and with which it had battled. We may laugh at the rigor of its precepts, its social austerity, its stubborn creed, but these had been made a necessity to it by the nature of the conflict on which it had entered. If religious laxity and social license are to be withstood, they will immediately drive the reformatory party into vigorous, pitiless, unsympathetic attack. Only thus can they separate themselves, and become belligerent. Total abstinence is the offspring of general intoxication. Thus the two parties in England forced each other to the last results of their respective tendencies. The warfare was not one merely of principles, but of principles wrought into social life, compacted and extravagantly developed in tastes, manners and literature.

The Puritan, scrupulous, unbending, severely in earnest, was railed at as a fanatic, bigot and hypocrite. The royalist, irreligious and reckless, clinging to the easy and comfortable shelter of old forms in government and faith, easily fell into levity and lewdness, and seemed to his adversary little better than a papist or an infidel. On the one hand rebuke, on the other ridicule, increased their mutual aversion. The courtier felt that he defied the Puritan in defying decency; and the Puritan rejected the follies of the world the more warmly for being the follies of the royalist. When we can hate our own and God's enemies at the same time, we are wont to hate with a will.

To carry this movement to its extreme limit, nothing was needed but a transfer of power backwards and forwards from party to party, that each in turn might suffer the tyranny of the other. This took place in the overthrow which the troops of Cromwell brought to the throne. The contempt of the royalist for the Puritan was then lost in hatred. When, therefore, at the restoration, embittered not instructed by misfortune, he once more gained control, took possession of society, opened the theatres, and assumed the guidance of literature, it is not strange that there was such an outbreak of immorality and misrule as England had not before witnessed. The evil was so excessive as to cure itself. A reaction set in, resulting in the revolution of eighty-eight. The harshness of the antagonism was once more softened down, and the elements were again so far blended as to make society possible and bearable. Thus way was made for a new era in society and literature.

In this rocking, revolutionary age, by which the nation was carried forward from Elizabeth to William and Anne, from Shakespeare to Pope and Addison, we have only conflicting and transition tendencies, conflict itself involving a transfer and readjustment of forces, the overthrow of an old equilibrium and the construction of a new one.

The first of these conflicts is that of the religious, political and social parties now glanced at, each a passionate and partial development, though the one was generally just and right in its tendency, and the other as generally wayward and wrong. Art, seeking balance, proportion, beauty in its products, suffered on either side, yet not equally. In the sound, earnest, progressive spirit

of the Puritans, there were hidden germs of
growth; in the worn out, effete, corrupt spirit of the
cavalier, there could finally be found nothing but
death, though the glow and flush of a free, reckless
life still lingered. The Hudibras of Butler presents, perhaps, the best literary embodiment of this
party. Full of wit, indicating large resources of
knowledge, it is sensual, disconnected and radically
false to the characters it satirizes. We are surprised at the wasted ability and blind bitterness it
evinces. That satire of this extreme and disjointed
character should be the best literary effort of the
royalists, while the Puritans were nourishing the
genius of Milton, and from their lowest ranks, by
the strength of the spirit that ruled them, bringing
forth the rare talents of Bunyan, shows with whom
alone a genuine and productive purpose was found.
Dislike may beget malignant satire, culture may
call forth wit, levity may make sprightly a licentious stage, and the gayety of polite society may
concentrate these products into a period of ephemeral brilliancy, but nothing noble and sincere will
thus be created, passing on for the admiration of
subsequent generations. In lyrical poetry two conflicting sentiments, the devotional and the amatory,
held the field. As in Herbert and Lovelace, strong
contrasts were everywhere present.

The literature of a theological and practical
character fell largely to the Puritans. This,
through its didactic ends and transient uses, necessarily held an insignificant place in letters. The
drama, early attacked by the Puritans, passed into

the hands of the royalists. Suppressed during the Commonwealth and Protectorate, it was revived at the Restoration, under the most immediate influence of the court party. The consequence was that the drama, while marked with some high intellectual qualities, more especially those of wit and insight, now became more corrupt than ever before, had in it less constructive power, and disconnected itself from this time onward almost wholly from literature.

Passing this period, only here and there do we find one eminent in literary art, as Goldsmith and Sheridan, whose reputation is at all associated with the theatre. The later writers of the drama, as Shelley, Byron, Browning, look for an audience and a criticism entirely disconnected from the stage; their plays are of a purely literary character; while those whose productions have been primarily composed for the theatre are, most of them, scarcely known in the literary world. Thus play-writing has either sunk to a practical, money-making art; or, reserving itself for literature, has forgotten the external, immediate ends that in the outset gave rise to it. This separation followed close upon the drama of the Restoration, most of whose products, rank with profligacy, have fallen into that decay which now so speedily overtakes this class of composition.

The abasement of this period was found, not merely in outspoken licentiousness and vile inuendo, but in the entire construction of the play. Sexual intrigue was made a chief line of adventure,

a crusade against female virtue the passion of every
spirited courtier, his traditional field of arms;
while husbands, fathers, brothers were the Saracens
and Turks who unlawfully held the holy land. No
deeper corruption of human thought and activity
is to be conceived of, and the occasional virtue
of some rare character, made to turn on sexua
purity, served only to show, in the extravagant sentiment that was gathered about it, that men sinned
wittingly, and caught single glimpses, though very
false and partial ones, of the heaven from which
they had been cast out. When the most ordinary
possession of a pure mind is exalted into a rhapsody
of virtue, we see at once how fearfully men have
fallen off from the familiar laws of morality. The
corruption of the many, men and women, no more
betrays the fatal secret of the low, appetitive life
all were leading, than the sentimental enshrine-
ment of here and there a heroine, whose mantle of
honor is after all little more than the ordinary purity of her sex. This debasement in the substance
of thought and sentiment easily united itself to a
like decay in form. Thus the dignity of blank
verse often gave way to the more external, sensual
effect of rhyme; or the comedy, stooping altogether
to the portrayal of indecency and vice, lost fellowship with fine art, became prose, and satisfied the
coarse minds it fed with the mere garbage of vulgarity, flung out in the quickest, easiest fashion.

The degeneracy of the practical drama thus
commenced has remained with us, in a greater or
less degree, for various reasons. A theatre is a

money-making institution, and must, therefore, strive to interest as many as possible. Its appeals must be to the masses seeking amusement. Hence it is confined to large cities. In these cities its efforts must be directed to those in search of pleasure, and therefore to those quite partially, rather than to those highly cultivated ; to those desiring coarse stimulus, rather than to those in love with refined sentiment. Such is the spirit of a theatrical audience, not merely from their native quality, but from the time devoted to this amusement, and the part it plays of hilarity and excitement in their daily lives. The theatre is thus compelled to bow to a money necessity, a relatively menial service, and so to miss, in whole or in part, its own æsthetical end.

This falling off from purity has all along been felt, was felt during the restoration, had been previously felt. In the period under consideration it called for censure, provoked hostility on the part of earnest minds, and thus early created a moral sentiment, which, to the present hour, pressing hard upon the theatre, has accelerated its downward tendencies If the most intelligent and moral refuse to be pleased, and withhold their patronage, much more must the classes less critical in these respects be gratified. The patrons must control the play. Thus the theatre, as a rule, in recent times, has been forced below the level of high art, first, by the interested monetary motives that govern it ; and, second, by an adverse moral sentiment, passing it over still more unreservedly to sensuous pastime and pleasure, to comedy and farce. This degeneracy of the theatre has been partial and variable, rather than complete, relative rather than absolute. There have been places and spasms of improvement, and the general moral elevation of society has told powerfully here as elsewhere.

This downward literary tendency the theatre has also accepted and confirmed by its management. Its expenditures on scenic effects have been of the most lavish character. Herein the modern stands in striking contrast with the early stage.

The rush-strewn boards that Shakespeare trod almost under the open sky, lounged on by a bantering nobility, pressed close by a rude, noisy crowd, had little in common with the luxury, the gaslight, the brilliant, sensuous appeals of the modern theatre; and we may easily believe, that the hold on reality in action was in the same stern spirit, as were these coarse, homely relations to facts.

Every possibility has been exhausted to amuse and delight men through their senses, thus transferring the chief effect from the intellectual to the physical world. A newspaper critic gives the following description of one of these modern plays: " It includes a burning house, a modern barroom, real gin cock-tails, a river-side pier, a steamboat in motion, the grand saloon or state-cabin of the steamboat, the deck of the same, the wheelhouse, the funnels, and the steamboat in flames; and all these objects are presented with singular fidelity to their originals." Here is a show in itself quite sufficient to captivate the popular mind.

Sentiment and character would be a gratuitous addition. It prepares us to hear a like critic say of a similar play, "It is not a work of literature, but a work of business. The piece is a rough conglomeration of the nothings of the passing hour—objects and incidents drawn, but not always drawn with accuracy, from the streets, the public conveyances, the haunts of profligacy. These nothings are offered for their own sake, and not made tributary to any intellectual purpose whatever." It may be doubted whether readings do not now furnish a more pure intellectual rendering of dramatic composition than does the stage.

Another cause which depresses the theatre, without affecting the drama as a written product, is the unfitness of high ethical sentiment, magnanimity, faith, love to constitute a public spectacle for a mixed, careless, critical audience of cold, superficial amateurs, such as are wont to frequent our theatres. Fine scenery, violent declamation, showy beauty, and rich attire invite a battery of opera-glasses; not so the deep, secret emotions with which the heart wrestles, nor its holiest affections, nor its purest adorations; these all draw back till they can disclose themselves, like the opening flower, in a light that quickens and renews them. How the idle claps, following hard on a scene of pathos, tumble down the airy fabric of our sympathies, like a card house, and choke us again with the dust of a noisy, conventional life.

The literary drama and the theatre parted company, because the limited and sensuous aims of the one were not consistent with the high bent of the other; and the separation dates from this deep decline of the English stage.

A second conflict which reveals the agencies at work in this transition period was that between French and English art. The French literature was now ready to exert a strong influence on the English mind. Easily uniting itself to the classical taste, with which it is so closely affiliated, it constituted the chief foreign power which affected this period. The English court was in close sympathy with France. There it had spent the years of its banishment, and returned, emulous of the tastes and refinements of its allies. The brilliant reign of Louis XIV. was in progress, the great epoch of French letters. Dryden, the earliest critic of England, favored in many respects the new refinements, as they were thought, of art. French words, chiefly of a polite, social cast, found their way into our language. Rhymed verse was introduced into the drama, and it, in keeping with this change, strove to assume in dialogue the sprightly refinement, wit and declamatory force of the French stage. These tendencies were in conflict with the freedom and vigor of the previous age, with its thorough English spirit. Thus Dryden, with eyes couched by the new criticism, was led to say, "Let any man who understands English read diligently the works of Shakespeare and Fletcher,

7

and I dare undertake, that he will find in every page either some solecism of speech, or some notorious flaw in sense."

This new art, and this freedom and refinement of manners, which the English at this time thought to win under the lead of the French, resulted in a feebleness, coarseness and debauchery, which those whom they imitated have been quite ready to laugh at. Says Taine of these years, "There were two classes, natural beings on the one hand, and artificial ones on the other; the first, with the coarseness and shamelessness of their primitive inclinations, the second, with the frivolities and vices of worldly habits; the first, uncultivated, their simplicity revealing nothing but their innate baseness; the second, cultivated, their refinement instilling into them nothing but new corruption."*

English character is so little allied to French character, that it is at once made unsound and superficial by imitation. The moral force is central in the Englishman. It is and must be momentarily operative for good or evil in his action. The French·man more easily leaves it one side, or out of sight, and can reach a free surface life, in a measure forgetful of it. Hence sin, social sin, always bears a deeper, more gross and sanguinary tinge with the English than with the French. They are compelled to recognize their own indecency, and it thus becomes a double irritation. They strike every instant against the moral law, and feel the wounding recoil. Their eyes are open in each transgres-

* Taine's English Literature, vol. 1. p. 512.

sion to their new infamy, and they are proportionately intoxicated and maddened by it. The French, as skaters upon the ice, glide gracefully along on a surface sentiment, an æsthetical tendency, and rarely pierce the film to the waters beneath, which support it, seldom penetrate the depths of their own moral being; the English sail on an open sea, they are restrained by a heavier, less manageable element, they bear more with them, and tack and turn, not in mere sportiveness, but in the pursuit of some proportionate good, while collision is irretrievable shipwreck. They cannot reach the gayety and indifference of the Frenchman, and for them to affect it, is to betray themselves at once into folly and corruption. No man is so cold and shameless as an Englishman, a Lord Chesterfield, built upon a French model. He is to the native born Frenchman what a skating rink is to the mountain lake: first there is a thin layer of ice, and then a thick layer of mud, with no interior flow, no depth, no beauty between them. A Frenchman and an Italian when they drive, crack the whip over the heads and about the ears of their horses, as if urging them on with a fusilade of musketry. The animals soon learn that this is only the froth and hilarity of motion, and maintain a quiet trot. An English horse would be maddened beyond control by such stimulus, and dash off in a break-neck race. His nerves are too many, and too much alive, to endure this extravagance of stimulus. Like his master, he must have a sober rule, or run away altogether.

The third conflict of the period was allied to

this one of nationalities, it was that between creation and criticism. We have termed the era a transition one. It lay between the two most distinct,
pronounced and vigorous stages in English literary
life. Bold, independent movement, powerful invention, belonged to the previous age. Its teachers of
art were few, of the cast of Jonson, who, with an au-
thoritative temper, enclosed art very much within
his own personal bias, was neither very attentive to
it himself beyond his predilections, nor very successful in enforcing it upon others. The most mas-
tered art only by that mastery of their own resources which belongs to power. In the period we
are now considering, invention, having gathered the
first harvest, was gleaning autumnal fields. It felt
also the force of that new, colder, more critical
phase of thought, which was approaching. Literature had expended its projectile power, and was being swept in by a rhetoric, esoteric tendency which
had sprung up in the cultivated mind, ready to control every free, aberrant thought. Times of transition are often inferior alike to those which precede
them and those which follow them. They offer no
perfect, no single and sufficient impulse, but are
distracted and distorted by conflicting forces. Dryden is full of criticism, yet presents no sustained and
consistent practice under it. He has moments of
original power, but these are lost in the waste intervals of imperfect art. Neither tendency being exclusively trusted to, but both in turn betrayed, each
fails to justify the writer. There is art enough to
offer a ready standard to censure, there is native

force enough to make us uneasy and regretful under the restrictions of a stumbling, hesitating art.

The transition persons, in whom the new movement first appeared, are usually given as Waller and Denham; and this, in large part, from the estimate in which Dryden, Pope and their cotemporaries held these poets. "Well placing of words for the sweetness of pronunciation was not known till Mr. Waller introduced it," says Dryden. And again, "The excellence and dignity of rhyme were never fully understood till Waller taught it in lyric; and Denham in epic poesy." Pope terms the latter of these, the "Majestic Denham." That poets so secondary as these two, whose excellence is at best so formal, should have initiated a new tendency, goes to show how cold and lifeless was the school of poetry ready to come forward. In this conflict between criticism and invention, the royalist and French influence favored the former. Though these themselves were transient forces in English society, united with an inherent tendency toward critical art, of which we shall speak more fully in connection with the next period, they were able to give form for a full century to English literature.

The undisputed chief of this transition time was Dryden, a man every way typical of it. He may be set down as the first autocrat in the realm of English letters; as the founder of that dynasty in whose line of descent are found Pope and Johnson. The very fact of such an authority is significant. Literary rule in the club and coffee-house falls to the critical, rather than to the inventive mind. Creation is coy, lifts a man more or less away from his fellows, may diminish, rather than increase, his control over them; and brings with it stimulus, indirect guidance, rather than instant, definite government. Criticism, on the other hand, is at once intelligible, is dictatorial, and arraigns before itself all parties. Shakespeare was not in his generation, at the Mermaid, such a ruler as Dryden in his; indeed the reins in that earlier period fell rather to Jonson, the critic of the Shakesperian circle. The seat of Dryden's authority was Will's coffee-house, and he owed his influence to the fact, that he united the critical function to his creative power; that he enforced art by that theory and precept which make the critic the expounder of his own times, rather than by that genius which pushes its possessor in advance of his age, conquering for him a kingdom in the future. Dryden held easy and sovereign sway as one who most skilfully inquired into, courted and controlled the literary predilections of the period.

His character led him to conciliation and concession. He was governed by no supreme, elevated impulse, he was a devotee to no theory, but with considerable insight and power of adaptation, adjusted his action to the predominant impressions, the passing circumstances. He undertook literary labor as work, and wrought at it as one apprenticed to the business, rather than as one who felt chiefly the control of inspiration, who built above and beyond the style about him, by impulses transcending it. He bound himself to furnish a certain number of plays each year, and, like a shrewd contractor, tried to fill the order in a manner agreeable to the taste of those who gave it. In one play, breaking through this tacit contract with his times, he signalizes the fact by the title, " All for Love." He himself says: " I confess my chief endeavors are to delight the age in which I live. If the humor of this be for low comedy, small accidents, and raillery, I will force my genius to obey it."

If his genius, as he flatteringly terms it, had been greater, he could never have bowed it to this servile work. It would, in sheer wilfulness, in simple self-assertion, have refused the servitude. As it was, it couched like the strong ass Issachar, between two burdens. Seeing that rest was good, and the land pleasant, it bowed the shoulder to bear. So much was his vision, his intellectual vision, above his practical bias, that in the end he confesses, " I have been myself too much of a libertine in most of my poems, which I should be well contented, if I had time, either to purge, or to see them fairly burned."

So far did he allow the badness of the passing years to push him from the purposes of art, that Walter Scott says of him, " His indelicacy was like the forced impudence of a bashful man." We are led to wish in him either more or less power ; more, that he may better command adverse influences ; or less, that he may sink under them unregretted. The weakness of Dryden was a moral one, a want of firmness, coherence and vigor in those ethical impulses which direct and keep true the intellectual powers. There was no one central fire in his nature, which, with a lifting current, gathered up and elevated his thoughts, stirred the flame, or bore its sparks in one brilliant shower toward heaven.

This weakness of the faith elements is seen in his religious belief. He drifted from Puritanism through the Church of England over into Catholicism, resting at length under a charge of mercenary tergiversation. There are two classes, who, by a bias of nature, are inclined toward the Catholic Church. The erudite, on whom antiquity has profoundly impressed itself, whose piety is of a meditative, poetic cast ; and who, like fragile and beautiful blue-bells, care not so much for the depth of the soil they thrive in, as to feel the rock, unbroken, earth-centred, just beneath them ; and those with whom religion is a matter of necessity rather than choice, a thing of fears and superstitions, and who covet the shelter of a church which will take all risks upon itself, and guarantee its disciples on easy terms. Dryden seems to us to belong to the second class. A superstitious feeling is shown in his casting the nativity of his son ; and his restlessness under religious influences, yet sensitiveness to them, in his dislike of the clergy.

> " Kings and preests are in a manner bound,
> For reverence sake, to be close hypocrites."

How did this ethical weakness in Dryden affect him in art? He is admitted to have possessed fine powers. Passages of striking beauty are found in his works; but they are thinly scattered, and do not cluster anywhere in such number or order as to constitute one great work. His plays are so polluted, that we no more covet their wit than the garments that smoulder with buried kings. He wrote them avowedly under the mean, mercantile inspiration of the sentiment, "He who lives to please, must please to live." Falling by these words of shrewd concession from the heights of the moral world, there happened to lie under him, for his reception, nothing but the sensuality of a court society, just passing out of life by spontaneous decay. Here, at this altar of lust, he ministered, and his plays have perished with it. In his ruling sentiment, just given, he struck the key-note of dissolution in the English drama, of its sad dissolving melody. Ceasing to be filled with its own life, and anxious only for immediate gains, it has sunk from an art to an avocation; and its composers, from artists to playwrights. Only great actors enable it for a brief period to return to the tragedies of Shakespeare.

His poems are largely satirical, didactic, polemic. The excellencies that lie on this low grade, he attained; conciseness of thought, aptness of expression, pomp and majesty of language, an occasional beautiful image, critical prefaces rivalling in interest the poems that follow them, lively versions, vigorous translations, and an increasing mastery of the formal conditions of verse. Against these attainments lie the facts, that his works as a whole are heavy, tedious; that they never quite justify his talent; that he seems to feel a better impulse than that which he obeys; to work at little things with

7*

passing visions of greater ones; and in the end is content, that his poems, for the most part, should be burned, a sentiment in which he and the world may well be at one again. Says Voltaire of him "An author who would have had a glory without a blemish, if he had only written the tenth part of his works." *

To us his weakness is that of the circle in which he moved. He lacked virile, moral force, which is to the poet what it is to the man, the spring, the coil of his intellectual mechanism, driving his ideas, giving them firm rotation, and causing them to cleave to the function and motion that are in them, as the earth revolves under its own gravitative impulse. The moral nature is looked on as merely formal, didactic, preceptive; it is rather the very essence, the organizing power of spiritual life; and unless one is by it thrown at some point into sympathy with pregnant principles, geared into the permanent world of ideas, belted to human progress, his work must be cold and poor and transient, waiting on oblivion.

* Voltaire, p. 82.

LECTURE VII.

The balance of Two Periods, the Creative and the Critical.—The
School of Pope—its Value—Relation to Poetry and Prose.—
Causes which produced it, (*a*) Natural Sequence of Criticism on
Creation, (*b*) External Influences, (*c*) Science and Philosophy of
the Time.

Social Spirit of the Period.—Improved by Literature.—The Papers
of Steele and Addison.—Service of.—Qualities of Literary Leadership.—Chief Men—Swift and Pope, Steele and Addison.

Two periods in English Literature stand in natural equipoise, both great under their own specific
forms, the creative period of the time of Queen
Elizabeth, and the critical period of the time of
Queen Anne. We have spoken of the transition under Dryden by which English Letters passed over
from Spenser, Shakespeare and Milton, to Pope, Swift
and Addison. This period of pre-eminent art is held
in very different honor by different critics, and has
been assigned a rank varying from the highest almost to the lowest. The early portion of the eighteenth century was long regarded as the Augustan
age of England. Its spirit ruled the entire century,
and only slowly lost ground at its close. It was the
reduction of its influence, the reaction against it,
that gave occasion to a second creative period at
the commencement of the present century, This
artistic tendency, made ready for in a half-century,
dominant during two-thirds of a century, and declining in the remaining third, exhibits two phases.

(155)

the first under Pope and Addison, the second under Johnson. The key-note of its spirit and method was most clearly given early in the eighteenth century by Pope, who was its best embodiment.

In the æsthetical product there are two constituents, the substance and the form. Though these are much less separable than the way in which they are sometimes spoken of would seem to imply, they may, by the manner in which they are contemplated by the mind in its productive attitudes, give quite diverse results. The intellectual substance of a conception may remain much the same, and yet its emotional force be materially modified by minor variations of expression; as the same clouds accept a hundred shades of beauty according to the light that falls upon them. The emotional element is much more subtile and evanescent than the intellectual one, and comes and goes on conditions so delicate, that we are more cognizant of the results than of the means by which they are wrought.

The form and spirit are so mutually dependent, that they only exist in and by each other. There can be no modification of the one member without a corresponding change in the other. But the mind, in its analytic, creative act, can bend its attention to the spiritual substance of its conception, made up as this is of thought and feeling; or it may direct its constructive vision to the form which the product is to assume. In the one attitude, the mind is more thoroughly creative, in the other, more carefully critical; in the one, it works more from within, and thinks of the form only as the conception grows into it, and necessitates it; in the other, it works more from without, allows the expression to react constantly on the idea, and give law to its expansion. In the first instance, we secure a living product, whose seed is in itself; in the second, an artistic or architectural or critical product whose plan has run before it, and shaped it.

We speak in this bald way of the two methods, that of Shakespeare and that of Pope, though they rarely or never stand apart as complete and exclusive attitudes of mind. Creation is not so absolute as this would imply, nor is criticism so formal. They are rather as the foci of an ellipse, which together define the curve; but in one or other of which its gravitating, illuminating centre, its sun, is located, holding the planet to its orbit, defining its periods, its degrees of light and darkness, heat and cold.

In the school of Pope, it was the critical function that was uppermost. This did not arise by accident, or by the force of circumstances merely; he early proposed to himself this precise kind of effort. Mr. Walsh, "The knowing Walsh," as Pope styles him, addressed him this counsel at the opening of his career, which met with acceptance: "We had several great poets," said he, "but we never had one great poet that was correct; and he advised me to make that my study and aim." A poet whose superiority over other great poets is to be found in his correctness, this is the project of Pope and his friend. The scheme evidently promises more formal than substantial merit. Technical precision may be reached, but what will become of greatness? There is danger that those birds of the free, upper air will hardly consort with the new-comer, notwithstanding the careful preening of his every feather. The dash and whirl of the thunder-cloud beget some ruffled plumage. The idea of great poets, who are not in the main correct poets, either springs from confusion of thought, or belittles correctness into a studious observance of the secondary rules of composition. To this labor, then, of cold, outside scrutiny, Pope and his cotemporaries set themselves. The favorite measure of the time, a rhymed, decasyllabic, two-lined stanza, was especially predisposed to a monotonous neatness of movement, an antithetic structure of the thought, an adroit, quick turn of the expression, which should make themselves sensible each instant, like waves that strike the shore under firm winds, in one unbroken cadence. Probably this poise and thrumming of the thought, by which it fell into the cold pulsations of an unvarying rhythm, have never surpassed the point of neatness attained by Pope, and accomplished all that art of this mechanical grade could reach.

The real value of this kind of excellence it is not easy to determine with precision, different minds estimate it so differently. The cotemporaries of Pope, and a large portion of those who immediately followed him, gave him rank among the first English poets. Critics of the present century have fallen off, many of them greatly, from this high praise; though some still speak of him in terms of the warmest eulogy. Thackeray says,

"Besides that brilliant genius and immense fame, for both of which we should respect him, men of letters should admire him as being the greatest literary *artist* that England has seen."* Is there not either a disparagement of art in this passage, or an exaggerated valuation of the excellencies of Pope? Either Shakespeare and Milton are not artists, o they are, according to this judgment, inferior in art to Pope. If they are not artists, what on the whole is art worth? or if they are artists, is it in the trivialities of a trade whose drift is execution, or in the sublime forces of creation that Pope surpasses them? If in the first, what does the implied praise amount to? if in the second, how does the world misunderstand itself. With a like feeling Thackeray speaks of the close of the Dunciad: "In these astonishing lines Pope reaches, I think, to the very greatest height which his sublime art has attained, and shows himself the equal of all poets of all time. It is the brightest ardor, the loftiest assertion of truth, the most generous wisdom, illustrated by the noblest poetic figure, and spoken in words the aptest, grandest and most harmonious."† When we read this passage, and then turn to the lines of Pope referred to, the praise seems to us excessive.

> "She comes! she comes! the sable throne behold
> Of night primeval, and of Chaos old!
> Before her, Fancy's gilded clouds decay,
> And all its varying rainbows die away.
> Wit shoots in vain its momentary fires,
> The meteor drops, and in a flash expires.

---

* English Humorists. † Ibid.

> As one by one, at dread Medea's strain,
> The sick'ning stars fade off th' etherial plain;
> As Argus' eyes, by Hermes' wand oppressed,
> Closed one by one to everlasting rest;
> Thus, at her fell approach and secret might,
> Art after Art goes out, and all is night.
> See skulking Truth to her old cavern fled,
> Mountains of casuistry heap'd o'er her head!
> Philosophy, that leaned on Heaven before,
> Shrinks to her second cause, and is no more.
> Religion, blushing, veils her sacred fires,
> And unawares, Morality expires.
> Nor public flame, nor private, dares to shine;
> Nor human spark is left, nor glimpse divine.
> Lo! thy dread empire, Chaos, is restored.
> Light dies before thy uncreating word;
> Thy hand, great Anarch, lets the curtain fall,
> And universal darkness buries all."

The thought in this passage barely sustains the expression. It is not the breaking out of sentiments that lift and impel upward the language.

It may help us in a just estimate of this period, as compared with the creative periods that went before it and followed it, to observe the direction which its critical temper gave it. Three leading poems of Pope are the Essay on Man, a didactic poem; The Dunciad, a satire; and The Rape of the Lock, a mock-heroic poem. Thus none of them lie in the most central fields of a creative imagination, but only skirt them. It is merely the slopes and lowlands of Parnassus that are here cultivated, made to blossom with the nutritious lentils of philosophy, or sown to the dragon teeth of satire, or purpled over with the poppy, yielding its mock visions, its weird and sportive fancies. The high, the holy, the real; the epic, the dramatic, the lyric; achievement, conflict, the song that searches the heart with its tender, echoing sentiments, are all forgotten in favor of a cold philosophy, culling precepts, and neatly putting chance principles in aimless prudential fashion; in favor of the bitter words of genuine hatred, and the mock words of ironical respect.

We shall also remember to advantage, in judging these artists, the relatively high estimate they themselves made of poets of quite secondary powers, of the calibre of Waller and Denham, in contrast with Spenser and Shakespeare.

Not only was the poetry of the time largely didactic, it was outranked, if not absolutely, yet relatively, by the literary prose of the period. The relative position of prose in English literature has never been higher than at this date. This excellence may fairly be regarded as the distinguishing literary feature of the age. Addison and Swift and Steele gave prose new force and beauty, devoted it to ends as æsthetical at least as those which engaged poetry, and made it a rival in public attention. The satire of Swift was more varied and vigorous than that of Pope, and lost little or nothing by its prose form. The essays of Addison were filled with sentiments more gentle and delicate, and hardly less imaginative and complete, than the best which belonged to the poems of the critical school. It is plain, then, that this period forsook the higher regions of art, set poetry and prose to much the same tasks, gathered and folded in one enclosure its flocks and herds whether from the rocks above or the meadows below, and entered on a safe, serviceable, dilettant husbandry of its resources, far more advantageous to the reflective and critical than to the inventive faculties; to prose, in its patient, plodding functions, than to poetry, in its bold insight, free aspirations, and tender, sympathetic responses.

Poetry had already reached the central principles of art, principles which lie a primitive frame-work of strength in all products of a truly great and original cast. It had thus comparatively little to expect from art, and lay open to the danger of a petty, superficial and exasperating criticism, that, forgetful of form as the expression of interior force, should refine upon it as a distant element, and, proud of minor corrections, set up inflexible methods and dead canons for the making of living things. Prose, on the other hand, an object hitherto of much less careful and refined attention, less sensitive in its structure, more homely and useful in its purpose, was quite ready to be profited by a new infusion of art, to be shaped as an instrument more aptly to its ends, and to accept at once a more artistic form and office. It was rescued from the harsh and exclusive service of dialectics and dogmatism, retained by the fancy and social sentiments, and set to a task of mingled pleasure and instruction. Thus the profiting of the period accrued to prose rather than to poetry; this for the first time be-

came a fine art, and in the essay, took rank as
an æsthetical product.

The causes which produced this artistic period
were various.   In the first place, a natural, almost inevitable, literary movement involved it.
Great originality and inventive power cannot last
long.   There is not strength enough to sustain
them, to hold unweariedly the gigantic stride
they involve.   Fortune is too sparing in her gifts
of genius to the race for this.   But at the advanced position reached by invention, when the
general mind is yet lively and restless, an ocean
swept by a storm that cannot at once sink into
repose, criticism and art take up their tasks with
peculiar advantage.   Unable to rival in new
fields of effort the works before them, poets and
writers are nevertheless too much lifted and
quickened by past successes to fall into mere
servile imitation.   They become pupils, inquire
into the method and details of previous products,
and conceive the idea of perfecting them.   They
have before them abundant material, from which
to derive the rules of art, to which to apply them;
they nurse a critical taste, and reach a pleasant
sense of personal power, not to say superiority
in laying down the precepts of more careful and
considerate work.   Thus it almost inevitably hap-
pens, that each great philosopher has his disciples, who correct and expand his system; each
painter of inventive power is followed by a school
of not unworthy men, who go forward to apply
the new idea, develop its possibilities, and lay

down its rules. An age of invention, in expending itself, naturally gives rise to one of art.

Such was the sequence of the age of Pope upon that of Shakespeare, growing out of it under the transition period of Dryden. It could scarcely happen otherwise than that the later poets, losing the powerful, free impulse of the earlier ones, should strive to replace it by greater painstaking, should set themselves the feasible labor of refining upon their method.

The same influences, moreover, which had wrought for art in the transition period, still remained operative. The commanding age in French literature, that of Louis XIV., was still in force; and though political events less favored than in previous years the transfer of the French spirit, the French literature itself was more controlling than ever. Pope's Essay on Criticism unites itself to the precepts of Boileau and of Horace, and shows whence the current of his ideas descended to him. The classical influence was yet more independently powerful at this time than the French. The renaissance spirit was uppermost in France and in England, and as has been usual with it in art, begot imitation and servitude rather than power. Arnold says of Pope, " The classical poets soon became his chief study and delight, and he valued the moderns in proportion as they had drunk more or less deeply of the classical spirit. The genius of the Gothic or Romantic ages inspired him at this time with no admiration whatever. He can find no bright spot in the thick intellectual darkness from the downfall

of the Western Empire to the age of Leo X." [*]
How impossible is it even for that which is best to
confer unmingled good! How much barren, unfruitful admiration has Greek art, poetry, sculpture
and architecture, begotten; drawing the thoughts
of men backward, and binding them to that already
done, rather than inspiring them for new achievement! The German must build his national Wal-
halla as a Greek temple, and adorn the palaces of
his princes with Grecian stories, and that too when
descended from an ancestry who could help to
strike out and carry forward the bolder and more
inspired styles of Gothic architecture. The classical spirit, revived in remote races and times, devotes
those who implicitly receive it to comparative ster-
ility. They can scarcely restore the past, certainly
not enlarge it; and in the effort to do this, they
waste the present and lose the future. The Greek
is what he is to us because he was intensely true to
himself, nursed and honored his own life. On these
conditions only shall we command the generations
that are to follow. They will hold lightly the
shadowy outlines of an older life that we may be
found painfully yet faintly renewing.

Taine says, "The arts require idle, delicate
minds, not stoics, especially not Puritans, easily
shocked by dissonance, inclined to sensuous pleasure, employing their long periods of leisure, their
free reveries, in harmoniously arranging, and with
no other object but enjoyment, forms, colors and

* Arnold's English Literature, 245.

sounds." * This is the Frenchman's view of art,
and the one that partially prevailed in England
at this period, prevailed so far as such sentiments could find transfer to the more earnest,
practical, English mind. What it achieved we
see, the results hardly commend the theory.
When the artist has no other object than enjoyment in view, we believe that he will find
great difficulty in realizing even this. High pleasure, like real excellence, is born of a more sturdy,
and powerfully directed spirit. Witness the severe
temperament and indomitable ideas that ruled
Michael Angelo. It is the execution of cherished
purposes, obedience to ideas, that confers pleasure,
not pleasure that enthrones ideas. High enjoyment
is ever incident to high action.

Another influence, aiding this tendency to art,
were the science and the philosophy of this and the
previous period. When natural science is pre-eminent over philosophy, when philosophy leans to
materialism, to an interpretation of the laws of
mind by those of matter, to a reference of knowledge exclusively to the perceptive and analytic faculties, we are sure to have a cool and critical, rather
than a warm and creative, social atmosphere; one
of skepticism and overthrow, rather than of belief
and spiritual construction. Science plays a most
inevitable and essential part in progress; but it
does not, especially in its earlier stages, when it is
coming in contact with many inadequate beliefs, and
overthrowing them, give inspiration to the higher,

* English Literature, vol. i. p. 332.

intuitive, trusting, ethical impulses of the soul.   It
tends to a wavering, uncertain and superficial sentiment on all questions that pertain to man and his
destiny, a sentiment like that which pervades the
Essay on Man, one of whose fundamental conclusions Pope is said to have exactly reversed under
a transient wind of criticism.   The philosophy of
Locke, the science of Newton, the skepticism of Bolingbroke, were affiliated forces, largely good in
themselves, with an immeasurable overbalance of
good in their results; yet begetting an adventurous,
uncertain, unbelieving temper, disinclined to pledge
itself unreservedly to any spiritual faith, to any
principle or precept of religious belief; and hence
ready for a cool rendering of the heart, an outlook
of immediate pleasure and comfort on society and
art.   There cannot be devotion, heroism, sacrifice
in the primarily skeptical spirit; and hence there
cannot be profound sympathy with that art in which
the human soul is tossed by deep, unquiet emotions,
refusing to be lulled into the rest of the passing
hour, but seeming to feel far off forces at work below the horizon, the promises of invisible good, the
presages of invisible evil.   The things astir in the
unseen world affect such a mind, and will not leave
it solely attentive to the lazy, measured rhythm of
a summer's day.   It floats on a sea alive with the
long swell of distant tempests.   Science had begun
its work of demolition; philosophy affrighted, was
forsaking its own principles, and seeking grounds
of alliance with the new tendencies; religion with
too little power to modify its belief, to take new po-

sitions, to reform and restate and redefend its principles, was losing hold on the minds of many, and,
like a wall that is shaken, began to show unexpected
traces of weakness and insecurity. It was ceasing
to rule by authority, and had not yet learned to
rule by reason. There was thus a loss in enthusiasm. Men were seized with worldly prudence,
were not ready for the long ventures of the spiritual
world, its patient waiting, and impalpable promises;
they cast about them for a more immediate good, a
more hasty and formal pleasure. This is the tendency which art, that has become artistic, exacting
and sensitive, is ready to accept, finding its office
in contributing a gloss of superficial excellence, an
elegance open to the senses, which, if it holds no
weighty claims against the future, redeems the
present to good cheer and elegant culture. The
lake ripples and sparkles in the sunshine, and we
stop not to ask what skeletons of death are hidden
under its waters. These were the days of unbelief
and feeble belief that were later to call forth the
reasonings of Butler, and the zeal of the Wesleys.

The political and social spirit which belonged
to the reigns of William and Anne, was more vigorous and healthy than that of the previous period.
The close, sultry, feverish air that attended on the
Stuarts, surrounding them, like the pent-up breath
of a night revel, to which the morning freshness of
a new day has not yet found entrance, had begun
to clear away. In the struggle of liberty, the cir-
cuit of aggression, resistance, reaction and compromise had been completed. The commonwealtb

had been followed by the restoration; this in turn
intolerable had been succeeded by the revolution,
and William came to the throne the representative
of progressive and revolutionary, yet constitutional
and monarchical, liberty. Thus was closed in mutual concession and the permanent gains of good
government the most violent series of events that
has fallen to the peaceful progress of England.
The political parties of this reign ceased to be fac-
tions, and struggled with each other for the guidance of a government which neither proposed to
modify or resist. The Tories by affiliation and descent had taken the place of the royalist. Their
central idea was authority; for them the chief virtue of a subject was submission. This party was
principally composed of intelligent and designing
leaders, of ignorant and prejudiced followers. No
party, as our own national experience, abundantly
shows us, responds with so firm and patient a front
to the rallying cry, as one in which the cunning of
the few is mated with the credulity of the many.
It is this inevitable union of intrigue and ignorance
that sustains selfish and unscrupulous power. Well
might such a party urge passive submission; the
high in state and church profited by it, the low
knew no other loyalty or religion. The leaders
gladly held what they had; the followers easily re-
signed what they never hoped to have. Words are
better rallying forces than ideas for the masses of
men; they involve for their partisans no discussions, and hence no divisions; they exact from
chiefs no concessions, and hence look to no sacri-

8

fices. All that was hereditary, stubborn, uncon-
cessive and selfish in English society settled by its
own weight and downward bent into the Tory
party. All, on the other hand, that was liberal,
active and progressive, yet sufficiently moderate to
hope for power, belonged to the Whigs, the political descendants of the Round-heads. Parties bid-
ding for power, eager-eyed for the possibilities of
success, are always more or less corrupt, warped
from their true tendencies. Individual ambition
will strive to lay hold of and use the party organization for its own private ends. Submission will be
enforced by urging the necessities of the party, and
thus its unity and zeal will throw it only the more
completely into the hands of the unscrupulous. The
right to think is the right to bolt. Aside, however,
from personal distractions, the central sympathy, the
prevailing purpose of the Whigs, was constitutional
liberty. They included the liberal, independent,
thoughtful minds of the nation, the midway men,
who have much to gain and much to lose, who love
their own thoughts, and covet the power to form
and execute their own plans. These two parties,
Tory and Whig, representing the old extremes,
had drawn so near together as to lay aside the
sword, and enter on a perpetual parley of words
and measures, a competition for the control of a
sovereignty both were prepared to respect.

A corresponding improvement was taking place
in public manners and morals. The literature of
the period more than concurred with this; it
advanced it in a positive way. The papers which

originated with Steele, and included the best efforts
of Addison, were a social evangel. The corrupt dra-
matists of the previous reign, who owed so much of
their taint to the court whose patronage they
sought, had passed away. William, with little literary sympathy, did not merely bring with him a
sounder, more wholesome life, one of more earnest
and serviceable purposes, he was inclined to leave
letters to a more independent and thus to a more
healthy development. The neglect of courts is
often better than their favor. The liberty and dis-
interestedness of art are both essential to its highest excellence. The moment it becomes a retainer,
and is compelled to make itself agreeable, it loses
the inspiration of freedom, the guidance of its own
creative insight. Patronage is to art a qualified
good.

These papers, which now came forward to take
the place in literary influence of the drama, and
which present the prose of English literature in its
very best dress, sprang from a broad, generous, and
skilfully conceived purpose. They aimed at what
they did much to accomplish, a social regeneration.
They depended on the general patronage, taken in
its most fluctuating form, and thus rested on their
own merit. They were able to soften public sentiment, to correct taste, improve manners, and bear
with them a genial ethical spirit, only as they could
instruct and delight their readers, and increase their
numbers. They were admirably fitted to this purpose. Short, returning at brief intervals, with no
close connection and with great variety of contents,

they could hardly fail to awaken attention, and keep alive curiosity. They were exactly fitted to the times. They were a fresh and palatable invention, and came to the club and the coffee-house with pleasing topics, offering a creditable variety of fare.

Nothing could exceed the ingenuity with which these papers were devised, and the skill with which they were written. We may also add, that this effort was animated by a correspondingly high purpose. Says Addison, in the sixth number of the Spectator, "It is a mighty shame and dishonor to employ excellent faculties and abundance of wit to humor and please men in their vices and follies." Again in the tenth number he says :—" I shall endeavor to enliven morality with wit, and to temper wit with morality, that my readers may, if possible, both ways find their account in the speculation of the day. And to the end that their virtue and discretion may not be short, transient, intermitting starts of thought, I have resolved to refresh their memories from day to day, till I have recovered them out of that desperate state of vice and folly, into which the age has fallen. The mind that lies fallow but a single day sprouts up in follies that are only to be killed by a constant and assiduous culture. It was said by Socrates, that he brought philosophy down from Heaven to inhabit among men ; and I shall be ambitious to have it said of me, that I have brought philosophy out of closets and libraries, schools and colleges, to dwell in clubs and assemblies, at tea-tables and in coffee-houses."

This purpose, thus distinctly announced, was carried forward with great fertility of resources, variety of methods, and vivacity and ease of style. Pure, idiomatic, simple English afforded fresh, flexible expression; while satire, allegory, impersonation, the changing characters of a club, letters, and many a nameless conceit besides, served to diversify and support the critical function. The inventions of Addison were exhaustless, and a benignant temper and graceful fancy adorned them all. These papers were very successful in their own time, and have since remained classics in our literature. They owe their success, first, to the nobility of their purpose, and afterward to their humor, variety, good sense, moderation, and elegance. Each of these qualities they possess in a high degree. The mirth of these pieces is mild, pervasive humor, imparting a pleasant glow of thought, and wooing the reader along a sunny, cheerful path. Satire is constantly directed against every form of social offence, but it is that genial satire which awakens attention to a fault rather than censures it, and enables us to look with the discrimination of a stranger at our own actions.

Of the second quality, Addison himself says, "There is nothing which I study so much, in the course of these my daily dissertations, as variety." Yet the arc which he and his friend Steele traversed was not the entire circle of human passion. It usually excluded profound emotion, whether of awe, pathos, terror, anger or indignation. Strong feeling, rising like a hurricane to sweep away

opposition, was consonant neither with their temper nor purpose. They looked for reform, but a
reform that should be initiated in pleasure, and
flow on of its own sweet will in the channels of
enjoyment opening before it. Hence they swept
round from satire to reflection, and reflection back
to satire, through a luminous curve of whimsi-
cality, caricature, story, portrait, description, allegory, criticism and speculation.

The cardinal quality of these papers is their
good sense; this never forsakes them. Their
philosophy presents it in a penetrative, their
humor in a pungent, form. Their criticisms on
society are as just as they are amiable. Their
analysis is correct and practical, their moral re-
flections, impressive and natural. This good sense
was most effective in securing uniform success.
It gave a restraint and proportion to what was
said that made it difficult to be resisted, and impossible to be controverted. Whatever the object
of satire, the pedantry of learning, the conceit of
rank, the foppishness of dress, the frivolity of eti-
quette, the prejudice of partisanship, the same
sober, sound opinion underlay and sustained the
attack.

Moderation was even more worthy of commendation then than now. The art of achieving a true
success is found very much in tempering zeal to a
just moderation. Steel that is too hard is fractured
at every blow; draw the temper too much and it
becomes iron. The Damascus blade, with its
tough and steady edge clings to that nice line that

divides excess and deficiency. From this middle region, Steele seems to have been inclined to range upward, and Addison downward. He complains of Addison, that "he blew a lute when he should sound a trumpet;" yet the lute notes of the one went farther than the trumpet tones of the other.

The crowning quality of these papers, as work of literature, is their elegance. This made of prose a fine art, and ranked its best productions, with those of poetry, among the permanent products of taste. This excellence was fully achieved, for the first time in our literature, by Addison; and since his day elegant culture has found constant expression in prose. The art of Addison is far less cold and critical than that of Pope. It preserves its freedom, and moves with a simplicity and ease, that are open indeed to error, but are also able to make that error seem slight and unimportant. There is in his style no opposition between nature and art; the substance and form remain inseparable, the thought lifting itself into light and being at once, rising in a single creative act out of the chaos of material.

The force of the moral element is freely disclosed in these works of Addison. Many graces and much good-will come to his aid, as he marks out a pure and reformatory path, and accepts the bias and freedom and boldness of his best impulses in pursuing it. Prose touched the meridian of art at the same instant that it culminated in a catholic, wholesome and sincere spirit. There was indeed much in the temperate, mild form of the ethical impulse to favor this sensitive and considerate art. More force would have been less appreciative, less careful; would have rushed in a heedless, headstrong way to its goal. It also favored prose as against poetry, and a poetry of art, as against one of creation. Inspiration is the life of poetry, emotion its very substance; and these are easily lost under those quiet, æsthetic tendencies which ripen prose. Poetry is likely to predominate in a vigorous age, and to master those strong spirits, whose tension of soul is sufficient for its service.

The supremacy which fell to a single person in the previous period was in this divided. During the reign of Charles, a reckless and corrupt temper controlled literature. This spirit Dryden accepted, and consolidated his authority under it. In the reign of Anne, different opinions found recognition in popular productions, and the influence of the leaders of literature was affected by their political sentiments. Pope and Swift were Tories, Addison and Steele Whigs, and this fact was one ground of divided authority. The temper of the two typical literary leaders, Pope and Addison, was a farther occasion of separation. Pope, sensitive, exacting and irritable, was early displeased with Addison, misinterpreted the counsel he gave him, and found in him too mild, or, as it seemed to Pope, too cold, a temper for his own moods of bitterness. Addison could not unite with Pope in his harsh, personal asperities. The irritation of Pope passed into aversion, and the two maintained as unfriendly a relation as the gentleness of Addison would admit.

The natural powers of neither of these leaders fitted them for the undivided control which fell to Dryden. Pope was too feeble in body, and too irritable in disposition, to venture on the late hours, exposure and hard-won supremacy of the club and coffee-house. Addison was too diffident and taciturn, too select and retiring in his tastes, to seek or to enjoy the public and familiar intercourse of a literary coterie, or at least to make it a means of self-assertion and uncontroverted authority. Hence there arose a quiet partition of power in the domain of letters. Addison, in the line of regal descent, held sway at Button's, opposite Will's. He gathered to himself Budgell, Tickell, Phillips, Steele. Pope, unable to endure the physical strain which the rollicksome clubs of the coffee-house put upon their members, and with a secret disrelish of dependence, retired to Twickenham, and there, in his own villa, maintained a more moderate and splendid court. Swift was strongly attached to him. Garth, Arbuthnot, Bolingbroke, Gay, Prior belonged to his circle of friends.

These four men, Swift and Pope, Steele and Addison, gave by their individual characteristics the controlling personal elements to the age, and constituted two groups of rival power, but unlike temper. Indeed the secondary vigor and artistic force of the time are seen in the absence of any overshadowing personal power. The composite tendency had the upper hand of separate life.

8*

Swift possessed a sharp, most incisive mind, which he was wont to use as the cruel weapon of morbid, exacting, unhesitating passions. He was powerful to do mischief and had the practical predilection for it of a street brawler. He was himself incapable of happiness, and could not but worry and wound those whom he approached, and those the most who were the most attached to him. His insanity and idiocy were the physical and spiritual fruits of a morbid temper, and were, as germinant seeds, long and deeply hidden in his constitution. The contempt, almost hatred, of men, shown in his satires, evinces a mind at war with itself, ceasing to delight in its own activities, chafing at its pursuits, and clashing in a mad way with its own good and the good of others. The most undeniable talent and wayward temper united to make him formidable, one who was sure to inflict injury, though the portion which fell to his enemies was hardly greater than that which he brought to himself and his friends. He won love to outrage and waste it; he gained power to plant fierce, bruising blows in the teeth and eyes of men, leaving to accident and prejudice to decide who should be his adversaries. Yet, viewed from within, his character at times assumed quite another appearance, and was lighted up by generous and sincere emotion. We are led to feel that he himself was overborne by those biting passions which made him, in so much of his outward activity, the fierce assailant, the bitter and cruel satirist.

Pope was a man of great and obedient talent—

some would say of genius. He brought ample resources to the tasks he set himself, but there was less inspiration in them, either of belief or of feeling, than in those of any other great poet. The invocation with which his Essay on Man draws to an end, well expresses his temper and his triumphs

> "Come then, my friend, my genius, come along;
>   Oh master of the poet and the song!
>   And while the muse now stoops, or now ascends,
>   To man's low passions, or their glorious ends,
>   Teach me, like thee, in various nature wise,
>   To fall with dignity, with temper rise;
>   Formed by thy converse, happily to steer,
>   From grave to gay, from lively to severe;
>   Correct with spirit, eloquent with ease,
>   Intent to reason, or polite to please."

Here is the diplomatist of letters, who coolly studies his times, the temper of men's minds, and adroitly guides his steps among them. He drives his Pegasus in embossed harness, in tricksy fashion. Pope added to an irritable self-consciousness something of the biting passion of Swift. They were confederate and rival masters of satire.

The second fraternity, that of Steele and Addison, was most gentle and humane. Steele exemplified the strong, heedless, generous impulses of his Irish nationality. He would have been consistently good, had he not so relished the pleasures which lie on the border-ground of evil. These he gathered, tearfully cast away, and recklessly gathered again; his sins each time giving a new purchase and provocation to his virtues. While we owe much to him, and feel a sympathy with him, paled in the light of his powers by the over-shadow-ing presence of Addison, we yet accept as our chief debt his indirect service in calling Addison to the support and development of the first serials, the Tatler and the Spectator.

Addison's tact, skill and resources were those of genius. A spontaneous fecundity and power of adaptation had fallen to him, and Steele stepped in at the critical moment to determine the form of the result. Addison led a prosperous and pleasant life, and, with a kind and generous nature, scattered freely its blessings. His chief fault was social; he sometimes smothered the fires of intellect in the va-porings of intoxication, an inverted torch quenched in its own oil. Addison occupies in English litera-ture a place only second to that of its great mas-ters. We admire the balance, goodness and fruit-fulness of his faculties, yet can hold intercourse with him without the separation and awe of sur-passing greatness. A polished shaft in the temple of letters, we are more struck with the beauty of workmanship than with the weight supported. Our tribute to him is one of good-will even more than of admiration, though admiration is never wanting. It is not often that so large a social obligation adds itself to a literary one; we put as the supreme point in the man the purity of his spirit, the gener-osity of his temper, and rejoice that his excellent work stands fast by the altar of worship. There are two deeply shaded walks, the one at Oxford, the other at Dublin, associated with the name of Addison. They well express the gentle, meditative.

benignant temper of the man, drawing inspiration
from the quietness of nature, and giving it in the
quietness of his own soul.   The points of loving
contact between man and the external world help
to define the quality of that secret life which the
mind cherishes.   They disclose its most free and
tender affinities, and that on which it is fed day
by day.

LECTURE VIII.

WE are now to speak of the second phase of the artistic period, falling to the middle of the eighteenth century. Again we see that periods, as indicating the prevalence of particular influences, have no definite bounds. There is very little in intellectual forces, either in their origin or their end, which is instantaneous or abrupt. They overlie each other, interpenetrate each other, and gradually grow out of each other, under the slow victory of new tendencies, under the slow expenditure of old ones. Associated conditions secure a ganglionic centre, and increase and diminish in power as we approach or recede from it, while the forces that are to rule a subsequent age are already springing up among them. The art which in English literature had culminated in Pope and Addison did not pass away quickly. It was a vigorous and deep-rooted tendency, and did not easily yield possession of the national soil. It assumed a second form before it began to give ground to the forces that supplanted it. There was far too much strength,

too much freshness and individuality of thought, too
little extravagance and affectation of method, too
much common sense and English sympathy, in the
writers of the reign of Queen Anne to allow them
to be easily pushed aside. For one full generation
after them, the literary momentum of their works
was unabated; and only slowly, as the last century
was drawing to a close, and the present century was
opening, did vigorous reactionary tendencies disclose themselves.

Yet the second phase of this period, that which
is marked by the autocracy of Johnson, differed in
some decided features from the first, under the
divided rule of Pope and Addison. In the early
portion, poetry and prose stood in fair equipoise.
The influence of Pope was not secondary to that of
Addison. If he is not to be ranked with the great
creative minds of our literature, yet this was not
the feeling of his cotemporaries concerning him.
There were no honors which they of his own time,
or the times immediately subsequent, were disposed
to withhold from him. That he has fallen to a
lower position is due to the verdict of later judges.
The artist who rules by art, who, in the incipient
conflict that is always springing up between creation
and art, sides with the latter, almost always leads
his generation. Art, passing from its unconscious
and creative to its conscious and preceptive stage,
in its clear, critical, formal procedure, flatters our
vanity of knowledge, and meets with easy and quiet
admiration. It is only when it strikes upward or
outward in growth farther than we can follow it,

that it is compelled to wait for a first, second, or third generation to reach its level, and enter into its spirit. Art that is merely garnering the past is popular; it is only when it attempts to break new ground for the future, that it encounters the barriers of prejudice.

In the later portion of this period, no one in poetry stood up in the place of Pope. No one possessed equal weight with him, or could for a moment challenge his rank. Poetry that many would now prefer to that of Pope belonged to the time of Johnson, yet there was no poet who was so productive, who held the same available power, or could command any considerable part of the influence which fell so easily to the corypheus of art. Quantity has some weight even in poetry, and the prodigal abundance of a fruitful mind gives to it a position it cannot claim by any single production, though that production be its very best. The second moiety of the artistic period differed then from the first, in the pre-eminence of one mind, and differed from it and from every previous period in our literature, in the pre-eminence of prose over poetry. As the poems of Johnson are related to his other works, so was the poetry of his time to its prose productions. There is an unmistakable predominence of this secondary branch of literature, which indicates the period to be one peculiarly degenerate in art. Poetry had become sparse, sporadic, and was waiting for a new development; prose was prolific, dominant, critical, taking vigorous possession of new fields.

The reason for this, or rather one reason for it,
it is not difficult to render. Criticism always makes
for the relative enlargement of prose in several
ways. Art, in its critical, speculative bearing, is a
triumph of the intellect over the emotions, and is
thus an extension of the sphere of thought. The
didactic spirit is uppermost, and finds in prose its
ready and fitting instrument. The dominant tendency is one which stands in direct, intrinsic affinity
with this simple, and, for mere truth, primary, form
of composition, and cannot fail, therefore, often to
prefer it. The impulse which at another time would
expend itself in a poem, will now be taken up by a
critique; and a dissertation on method will be substituted for performance. Further, art being everywhere active as a formative, external force, will lay
hold of prose, reshape it, give it new excellencies, and
be proportionately enamored of it. There was little
for the critical feeling merely to prefer in the poems
of Pope above the papers of Addison. In some
respects, the latter held the advantage as against
the former. Their beauties were fresh, spontaneous
and natural. Poetry was passing its zenith, prose
was mounting to it. This was for the first time
coming into the power that belonged to it, while
that was only gathering a second and inferior harvest. The intrinsic force of the two, their spon-
taniety, was naturally proportioned to this fact. This
fact, then, so peculiar to the period, of the ascen-
dency of prose, we hold to be a direct issue of the
cold and critical temper which ruled in literature,
calling the thoughts into unwonted activity, and

proportionately restricting the spontaneous expression of the emotions. Those wrought best in poetry who, like Goldsmith, were inevitably emotional, and could not be driven from the fastnesses of a tender, passionate nature, by the fashion of the time, or the ridicule of men.

Another difference is found between the earlier portions of the century and its later years in the style of Johnson as contrasted with that of Addison. Johnson, in accepted tendencies, in the grounds of his critical judgments, was in the line of direct descent from Addison; though, by the formation of his own mind, he was very diverse from him. Following in the same form of composition, he supplemented the Tatler and Spectator with the Idler and Rambler, and these papers closed this chapter of prose art in our literature. In their moral tone, social purpose, and critical spirit, the unequal portions contributed by Addison and Johnson to the splendid completion of Steele's fortunate conception, were identical; in aptness of execution and ease in style they were very different. These two men, working with one spirit and under similar circumstances, admirably illustrate the importance of the factor of original endowment. The manner of Addison was impossible to Johnson; his rugged and ponderous nature utterly forbade it. Johnson puts himself in inevitable and unfavorable contrast with Addison by a style inflexible, weighty, not to say heavy, and full of a controlling mental habit. He thus brought a powerful, personal element to the portion of the period he so strongly influenced. The tendencies of his own nature must be added to those of his time, as second to them only in weight. His style has been thought to owe its impression to the choice of less familiar words, especially those of Latin origin, and thus to fall easily into pomposity. This is scarcely a sufficient statement of the case. His style acquires its chief characteristics from the penetrating, analytic mind of the author. This imparted a reflective, discriminating form to his language, and led to a choice of words critical and explicit. His composition is full of antithesis; he carefully balances the thought, limits it on this side and on that, and exhibits it in various relations. An exact poise of ideas and correspondence of considerations accompany him in his composition, whether it be grave or humorous; while passages made cumbersome by words merely, are infrequent. He himself has ridiculed this pretentious verbiage in Rasselas. "To live according to nature," said the philosopher, "is to act always with due regard to the fitness arising from the relations and qualities of causes and effects; to concur with the great, unchangeable scheme of universal felicity; to co-operate with the general disposition and tendency of the present system of things. The prince soon found that this was one of the sages whom he should understand less as he heard him more."

Johnson himself was not often misled by the pomp of words, or occupied by mere sound. A

thoughtful and dignified manner, inborn to the
style in his very conception of the topic, prepared
the way with him for a full and formal phraseology. The idea was no more colloquial than the
manner in which he put it. It was not a choice
of words, but a ponderous quality and gait of
mind, that made Johnsonese so distinguishable a
style. The classical taste which Johnson shared
with his time, served indeed to color the large
vocabulary to which his discriminating, analytic
thought gave occasion, and helped to impart an
appearance of pomposity.

The following examp'e from the Idler, of
March 15, 1756, shows the well defined, formal
path by which he threaded his way through the
most familiar topic. "I lived in a state of celibacy beyond the usual time. In the hurry, first
of pleasure and afterward of business, I felt no
want of a domestic companion; but becoming
weary of labor, I soon grew weary of idleness,
and thought it reasonable to follow the custom of
life, and to seek some solace of my cares in
female tenderness, and some amusement of my
leisure in female cheerfulness.

" The choice which is long delayed is commonly
made at last with great caution. My resolution
was to keep my passions neutral, and to marry only
in compliance with my reason. I drew upon a page
of my pocket-book a scheme of all female virtues
and vices, with the vices which border on every virtue, and the virtues which are allied to every vice.
I considered that wit was sarcastic, and magnanim-

ity imperious; that avarice was economical, and ignorance obsequious, and having estimated the good and evil of every quality, employed my own diligence and that of my friends to find the lady in whom nature and reason had reached that happy *mediocrity* which is equally remote from exuberance and deficiency."

The humor of this composition lies very much in the deliberate, cautious manner in which a great, unwieldy mind moves among trifles ; selects the few points that promise a plausible support in its progress, and tempers itself to a good-natured tenderness toward the safety and pleasure of others. So an elephant might walk among sportive children.

Here is a stiffly outlined portrait of Square Bluster: "He is wealthy without followers ; he is magnificent without witnesses ; he has birth without alliance, and influence without dignity. His neighbors scorn him as a brute ; his dependants dread him as an oppressor ; and he has the gloomy comfort of reflecting that if he is hated he is likewise feared."

Johnson, though grounded in the same principles of criticism, stood in marked contrast to the simple, genial Addison, and united with him to illustrate the very different phases which one school of art may present.

Addison and Johnson were alike primarily prose writers. In this department lay their chief work and their crowning excellencies. Both, however, ventured into the field of poetry, with something of the boldness that falls to criticism, yet with unequal success. The Cato of Addison received the highest praise from Voltaire, and is one of the best plays of the Franco-English school. Few have done the Irene of Johnson any reverence.

Having sketched the relations of the two portions of the artistic period, we wish to deepen two impressions concerning its later years; first, the rapid development of prose; second, the coldly critical dictatorship of Johnson. We have seen these two things to lie in the normal development of the forces at work. Prose henceforward in English literature is varied, artistic, voluminous, spreading far and wide into many realms of thought, like a swollen torrent that has escaped its mountain fastnesses, and covers the plain, leaving rich alluvial deposits on every arable field. Theological composition, which more than any other kind of prose constituted the continuous, central current of this stream, was scarcely abated in its practical, stereotyped form, while in its defensive, speculative aspects, it showed new vigor. The age was critical, not formally so in art merely, but centrally so in thought also, and this too increasingly. New departments of knowledge were rapidly opening in the natural sciences, new methods of investigation were gaining ground. The minds of men were putting in many directions bolder questions, which called for other than conventional answers. This movement was met in a vigorous and truly national method by such writers as Berkeley, Paley and Butler. New defenses were thrown up to suit the new attack. A force was developed within the church which showed the hold of Christian truth on the mind to be vital and sufficient. While Methodism was giving new proof of this practical control, its theoretical force was as signally shown by its apologists. The works of some of these authors are remarkable for their insight, as Butler's Analogy; others for beauties of style and clearnes of statement, as Paley's Natural Theology, and Horæ Paulinæ; and others for a combination of these characteristics, as Berkeley's Alciphron.

Metaphysics was relatively more fruitful even than theology. The Positive Philosophy has rightly grouped these two phases of thought, for they are closely dependent. In this field, the writings of Hume at this time mark an era; most modern unbelief traces its line of descent through him. Often sophistically met, rarely indeed answered, and requiring for their complete refutation a profounder philosophy than has yet been attained by us, at least with any generality, his views have slowly penetrated the purely scientific mind, till they are now entrenched in it as an invincible prejudice against the supernatural, against every distinctively spiritual view. A philosophy so immediate and fatal in its theological inferences could not but call forth much activity in this department, and the Scotch school of metaphysicians, Reid, Stewart, Hamilton, began to follow in a reactionary line; while an equally able series of writers developed the tendencies included in the works of Locke and Hume.

Thus it fell to metaphysics to commence a skep-

ticism suicidal to its own line of investigation. Its
overthrow was a *felo de se*, not the work of physics.
It is due to Hume, pre-eminently a metaphysician,
and to an argument to its very core metaphysical,
more than to any other one agency, that mental science has fallen into such general disrepute, and been
so far lost in physical inquiries. The end is not yet.
We here only mark the fact, that the earlier sieges
were laid, and the first manifest breaches opened,
at this pregnant, critical period, in the invasion of
the laws of mind by those of matter. No discussion more central was ever sprung upon the thoughts
of men than the one involved in miracles; and the
loud acclaim with which, from time to time, the victory of the scientists is rung out, only shows how
far off the real issue of the battle is. The most obvious English date of the origin of this universal
and irrepressible controversy, which colors every
department of knowledge, and is daily gathering its
pros and cons from every field of thought, is found
in the prose of this time.

From the cold speculative outlook of this era,
there came denials which set at jar and controversy
the two elements of creation, the natural and the
supernatural, and strove to reduce under the rigid
formalism of immutable law its entire handiwork.
No discussion could be more purely critical, yet
more profoundly significant, than this. It rested
with it to decide in religion, philosophy and art
whether we were to have the mere colored rind of
wax fruitage with which to staunch our hunger, or
the inscrutable, unformulated life of free and inex-

haustible forces—a being offered not as a finality, a finished product, but as a first term in the vocabulary of wisdom and of love.

The speculative, germinant character of the epoch is also seen in political, social science. The English constitution and law found presentation and historical discussion in The Commentaries of Blackstone; and Political Economy, in the works of Adam Smith, Malthus, Ricardo, rose to the proportions of a distinct science. That wakefulness of thought is here first shown which has since busied itself with so many social questions, past, present and future.

Indeed no one thing more discloses the character of a period than its estimate of historical inquiries, and historical methods of investigation; than a tendency to look for the explanation of present states and facts in their relation to previous ones. Herein is a due appreciation of the force and continuity of causes, indicating a thorough scientific and reformatory tendency. In this period there arose a very conspicuous group of historians, grading upward in the order given, Hume, Robertson, Gibbon, the last being from our present point of view, the most interesting. History has two complete products, which it slowly approaches. The first is a narrative of events, correctly and exactly sketched, proportioned one to another by intrinsic value, by the aggregate of human-weal involved in them, and rendered with the light and coloring of real life upon them. The historic picture thus shows

9

knowledge, insight, and feeling. It is no bald outline, nor do its leading figures lack the symmetry and support of a thoroughly wrought background of those conditions and companions of life which lend to them pre-eminence and value. Nor are the historic events merely given in light and shade, they are deeply tinged by the sympathies, passions, affections which made them, in their own day, living experiences of the generation then passing. The second product is philosophical, a philosophy of histoiʷ The narrative now clings to the connection of causes. It treats slightly chronological dependencies. It cares not to be full in the statement of facts; it would gladly assume a knowledge of these, and only brings them forward as they serve to mark the line of action, of significant forces transmitted through them, and modified by them. It searches for the channels, the deep under-currents, on which have floated down the pomp of historic events. Its facts are buoys and light-houses along this line of progress. The eddies and shallows and silent pools which are mere topography, failing to define the strength and direction of currents, the interlacing lines of force, it passes in rapid survey. It seeks only to outline events, and give their osseous frame-work, on which, as fulcrums and levers, the muscular and nervous energy of the time has been expended.

These two products are reached by a long road. Legendary and historical traditions; chronicles of easy credulity; annals with barren dates, mere

pegs divested of the tapestry which should hang
upon them; histories that busy themselves only
with kings and warriors, with the trappings, the
glitter and clatter of life; historic criticism that
pulls to pieces this poetry of the past in search of
the scattered, germinant facts out of which imagi
nation has grown its luxuriant, tangled and fanciful
narratives; the philanthropic estimate of human
life, that seeks for it in quantity and quality wherever found; the philosophic impulse, that wishes to
master causes, and through them effects, all these
lie between the beginning and the end of history,
between the period in which the human mind takes
pleasure in dream-land, cloud-land only, and that
in which it strives to repeat the glowing dyes of
fancy in the sombre fields of its daily experience,
setting more store by the simple flowers at its feet
than by the crimson banks of color that come and
go as transient shore-lines of flitting vapor.

Gibbon claims especial attention, because his
work made so sudden and decided an advance in
history. It is possessed by the critical spirit, deals
constantly with causes, and presents a style quite
in keeping with the formal rhetorical tendency of
his time. The very objection which has been taken
to him, that he over-estimates the natural agencies
connected with the propagation of Christianity, and
under-estimates, or altogether overlooks, the supernatural ones, indicates an excellence in his method,
while it discloses the unsympathetic and somewhat
barren nature with which he performed his too
purely intellectual work. Neither he, nor the spirit

of the times which he expressed, was aglow with
conviction, nor alive to the hopes and fears of life,
its emotional issues near at hand and far off. Gibbon presents in a cold, it is true, yet in a clear,
striking and valuable form some of the best results
of the new critical tendency in the then fresh department of history.

Another branch of literature, that of oratory,
reached remarkable excellence in this last half of the
century. Chatham, Fox, Burke, Sheridan, Erskine,
Pitt, Grattan form a group not since equalled.
The greatest of these, Burke, well presents in his
personal history the influences which attended on
and secured this growth of eloquence. Bold political criticism, new political principles, and wakeful independent sympathies, furnished the conditions and
grounds of his oratory. A period that is fresh and
vigorous in thought, exacting in style, and aroused
by urgent, practical, yet national interests, gives
the best possible conditions of eloquence. The
years under consideration were of this character.
Its critical spirit was at once formal and substantial, rhetorical and philosophical, brilliant in statement and bold in speculation. Weighty political
interests, no longer amenable to laws of conquest
or of violence, gave occasion for the enunciation of
new principles in the government of colonies that
had suddenly grown into national strength in the
progress of English commerce. Allied to this oratory, were the Letters of Junius, which carried political criticism to the height of boldness, force and
severity.

As was to be expected, rhetoric and criticism as arts began to receive some of their best contribu tions. The works of Campbell, Kames, Blair, have been for a century manuals in this department Blair, though light in calibre, copious and some what superficial, has by his simplicity, clearnes and correctness held his ground against many mod ern writers. He well presents in precept those formal excellencies of style of which he found such ample illustration in Temple, Addison, Atterbury.

We urge this unusual productiveness of the period in prose at only one more point, the novel. From a merely literary, artistic view, the novels of this era, when we consider their number, variety and merit, constitute its most interesting, as they do its freshest feature. The novel is the last stage of prose in its progress toward poetry, and the first field that offers congenial cultivation as an author declines from verse. The novel of this period was reached in both ways. Sterne, Smollett, De Foe climbed up to this art-level from humbler labor; Fielding turned back to it from dramatic poetry. That the barometrical column should have rested in literature at this point, unable to rise permanently above it, shows how rare and light the intellectual atmosphere had become by continuous criticism, and that it was waiting to be toned again to its usu- al tonic force and productive power by a revolution, a storm of sentiment, seeking the conditions of new and higher order in freedom, and in living, spiritual convictions.

De Foe possessed the measure of genius which

attaches to thorough realization. He sought and attained the minute truthfulness, the verisimilitude of the pre-Raphaelite art. But as this perfect mastery of details was animated and directed by no unusual insight into forces, nor knowledge of principles, he only reached, as in Robinson Crusoe, the level of an excellent story, an object-book, the delight of boys. Richardson adopted the most cumbersome form of story-telling, that of letters. This method, in its tedious indirection, is to the novel what dialogue is to philosophical discussion, a piece of mechanism fitted to check the thought, iron it thin, and deliver it in the largest number of sheets. Richardson's patient assiduity was at one with his chosen method. By minute invention and almost insensible accretion, he worked up his plots, entangling his characters in a net not the less severe in its constraint, nor tragical in the issues involved because of the thousand gossamer threads of which the insect ingenuity of the author had spun it. Aiming directly as he did, at moral influence, it yet may well be doubted whether the sensual passions which he chose to delineate will admit to advantage of this slow, anatomical exposure.

Fielding is every way different. His narrative is easy, his characters genuine and spirited. Morality is not with him a law, and his scenes and heroes are often vicious and vulgar. Yet a certain nobility, generosity or sincerity of nature goes far to redeem those whom the author likes; while opposite vices stamp with legible censure his real reprobates. Truth to English nature and sympathy with manly

quality perf.rm in Fielding, to a degree, the work
of morality.

Smollett is much less worthy of commendation.
He tells a story, not with the zest of insight and a
loving appreciation of character, but as men rehearse in bar-rooms tales made up of grotesque and
gross incidents, and coarse physical jests. He
generally gathers his material from a low region,
and has little disposition to shake it clean in the
getting. The English novel has hardly touched a
lower point than in Smollett. The prying, sensual
inuendo of Sterne, alive to mischief, is yet redeemed
by greater humor. Such was the industry of prose
composition in this period, opening all the veins of
thought that have since been so assiduously wrought.

The second fact to which we were to revert was
the rule of Johnson. There is nothing quite like it
in our literature. The great minds of our English
race had come and gone, but none of them had held
such absolute authority. Nor was this due to any
inferiority of power in the literary cotemporaries of
Johnson. No cluster of names in any one period
brings before us greater or more varied talent, than
those of Reynolds, Burke, Fox, Goldsmith, Garrick,
Gibbon, Sheridan, Adam Smith, and Warton. We
may be sure that it was no easy, indolent supremacy
which such men as these yielded to Johnson.

A singular instance of the deference paid him
appears in the round-robin addressed him by Burke,
Gibbon, Sheridan, and others requesting a slight
modification of the epitaph he had written on Goldsmith. If there was some intentional humor in this

method of appeal to the literary leader, making the
thunderbolt of his wrath harmless by the circle of
points that drew off and dissipated its impatient
fire, there was also in it a sincere regard, and an
unwillingness, on the part of these men, each great
in his own way, singly to injure his feelings, or
provoke his resentment.   Johnson, in his later
years, held a quiet, undisputed supremacy.   This
was due, as we have intimated, in its first ground,
to the fact that the period, as one of criticism, prepared the way for immediate and personal control
on the part of any one pre-eminent in this art; and,
in its second ground, to the character of Johnson.

Sound   intellectual   qualities,   common   sense,
continuous and protracted composition, led him to
criticism, and, in spite of his dictatorial tendencies,
kept his conclusions within safe and acceptable
limits; vigorous thought sustained what he wrote
and said.   While this is true, he was greatly defi-
cient in that profound, philosophic spirit, in that
unbiassed opinion, that calm, ready candor and delicate sympathy which deepen, while they moderate,
the mind's action.   His was the attitude of the con-
troversialist, who sees clearly on his own side, feels
to the full all the prejudices that sustain him, and
is conveniently blind to the positions of an adversary.   He was acute and analytic rather than profound and comprehensive.   His powers were thoroughly disciplined in spirited, personal intercourse,
and the free methods of conversation.   He used
arguments as weapons, now of defence, now of
offence, with very little quiet, thorough investiga-

tion of the whole subject. Like a professional soldier, he took up arms and laid them down again
without primary reference to the justice of the cause.
His own opinions, such as had fallen to him with
an honest, but strongly biassed nature, were the
ground which he set himself to defend in sturdy,
English fashion. He could enjoy victory, and suffer
keenly under defeat. Goldsmith said of him, "There
is no getting along with Johnson, if his pistol misses
fire, he knocks you down with the butt of it." Yet
even then he knew how to give either the force of
wit or the color of truth to the blow. Burke
affirmed of him, that "Whatever side he advocated,
he gave good reasons." Clear-minded men are of
all persons most sophistical when they choose to
be; most easily convince themselves and others
of the justness of what they propose.

To this keen rather than clear insight; to this
wilful rather than firm bent of mind, Johnson added
in conversation quick, dexterous, unsparing wit.
This rendered him a formidable adversary. It gave
a precision to his blows that made them instantly
effective. He rebukes in this wise the timidity of
Bolingbroke, who would not allow the publication
of his works till after his death: "Sir, he was a
scoundrel and a coward, a scoundrel for charging a
blunderbuss against religion and morality; a coward because he had not resolution to fire it off himself, but left a half-crown to a beggarly Scotchman
to draw the trigger after his death." Miss Hannah
More expressed to him surprise that a poet, who
had written Paradise Lost, should compose such

9*

poor sonnets. He silences the critic without the labor of vindicating the maligned poems, without perhaps himself appreciating them. "Milton, madam, was a genius that could cut a Colossus from a rock, but could not carve heads upon cherry-stones."

If we add to these qualities the reputation which attached to him from his diversified, protracted and successful literary labors, and the evidence he always gave of an honest, upright and even tender nature, we see sufficient personal grounds for his influence. This massiveness and soundness of mind and heart were not to be hidden by a little irritability of temper, nor grossness of appetite, nor coarseness of taste. That he could command devoted and disinterested affection is seen in Boswell. The unmeasured contempt that Macaulay has expressed for the friend and biographer of Johnson is not altogether deserved. There is a sincerity of admiration, and a forgetfulness of personal claims in Boswell, which call for some lenity. If he had possessed more pride, and a more irritable egotism, he would doubtless have escaped the scorn which has been so freely bestowed upon him, but he would also have lost the pleasure of much profitable intercourse, and we a most enjoyable narrative. Let us be content with our own nettlesome independence, and not deride the assiduity of one who could profit by the virtues of a rare, good man even in submission to his petty faults. As long as we concede so much to the duplicity and intrigue of ambition, to complaisance that is prompted by interest, we may grant something to the vanity and adulation of an unequal friendship.

The control which Johnson exercised especially concerns us as expressing the critical character and appreciation of the period. There is much to be commended in Johnson as a critic; his common sense and breadth of intellectual activity stood him in good stead. Yet there is in him a lack of emotional insight, and a tendency to seek everywhere formal excellence rather than inherent power. This is seen in his unqualified acceptance of Pope and Dryden, and his evident relish of their art. In his Lives of the Poets, he gives the famous verses of Denham addressed to the Thames,

> "O could I flow like thee, and make thy stream
> My great example, as it is my theme !
> Though deep, yet clear; though gentle, yet not dull ;
> Strong without rage, without o'erflowing full."

and adds, that "Since Dryden has commended them, almost every writer for a century has imitated them." After a slight criticism he proceeds to say, "The passage, however celebrated, has not been praised above its merit." The thought and imagery of these verses doubtless constitute them a neat piece of poetic work, but not one fitted to be the text of a century, and the model of a school. So used they could hardly fail to tether the fancy. They compare but poorly, we think, with the kindred lines of Wordsworth :

> "O, glide fair stream! f rever so
> Thy quiet soul on all bestowing,
> Till all our minds forever flow
> As thy deep waters now are flowing."

In the same spirit he echoes Pope's **praise of** Dryden :

> " W..er was sm oth ; but Dryden taught to join
> The varying verse, the full resounding line,
> The long majestick march, and energy divine."

This in spirit and form is as brim-full of sound as the march of boys to drum and fife. With feelings akin to those which led to this commendation of Pope's, Johnson accepts under protest the blank-verse of Milton, "verse only to the eye." as an ingenious critic had pronounced it. He prefers the heroic, rhymed measure to which so much of our English poetry has timed its dreary, methodical march, as soldiers that plod wearily through a dull day.

It was this opinion, with kindred faults in his estimate of Milton, which led Cowper in his Letters to say, " As a poet Johnson has treated Milton with severity enough, and has plucked one or two of the most beautiful feathers out of his Muse's wings, and trampled them under his great foot. I am convinced that he has no ear for poetical numbers, or that it was stopped by prejudice against the harmony of Milton's. Was there ever anything so delightful as the music of Paradise Lost? It is like that of a fine organ, has the fullest and deepest tones of majesty, with all the softness and elegance of a Dorian lute—variety without end, and never equalled. Yet the doctor has little or nothing to say upon this copious theme, but talks something about the unfitness of the English language for blank-verse, and how apt it is, in the mouths of

some readers, to degenerate into declamation. Oh,
I could thresh his old jacket, till I made his pen-
sion jingle in his pocket!" * Doubtless, yet the
doctor so attacked, with unmollified temper and
fresh sagacity, would have broadened his principles
of criticism, and, in doughty championship, stamped
hard the grounds of debate without once surrender
ing them. His definition of genius, given in the
life of Cowley; and of poetry, in his Preface to
Shakespeare, both exhibit the same preponderance
of intellectual, formal action over intuitive, spontaneous power. " The true genius," he says, " is a
mind of large general power, accidentally determined to some particular direction." What is here
assigned to accident is rather the very essence of
genius. The irrepressible impulse betrays the
force that predetermines it, the genius that controls it. His is a definition of talent, not of genius ;
and the men of this artistic age were men of talent
rather than of genius.

" The end of writing," says Johnson, " is to instruct ; the end of poetry is to instruct by pleasing." Exactly, Pope would have said ; hardly,
Shakespeare would have replied. Under this definition he proceeds to criticise the great dramatist
in this wise : " He sacrifices virtue to convenience,
and is so much more careful to please than to instruct, that he seems to write without any moral
purpose. * * His precepts and axioms drop
casually from him ; he makes no just distribution
of good or evil, nor is always careful to show in the

* Reed's British Poets, vol. ii. p. 18.

virtuous a disapprobation of the wicked." If Johnson had censured Shakespeare as wanting a hearty appreciation of virtue, a sufficiently deep insight into it, and noble sympathy with it, his criticism would have had some hold ; but certainly the poet can be excused for not making over, in the way here commended, his dramas to didactic morality.

Johnson puts in a personal shape, and lends personal force, to the great feature of his period. He is in intimate action and reaction with it. The life about him serves to explain much that is in him ; yet he, by his individual vigor, gives an ultimate element to it also. It is thus always. Men are not ciphers, in search of some integer of the physical world to give them value. They themselves are a final law to much that is around them. What proportions of heat and cold, of wet and dry agents, were able to give, then and there, to English society, the positive character known as Johnson ? A solid Doric column, chipped into outline and assigned position by circumstances, he nevertheless chiefly interests us by the rugged strength of his own native texture.

Hawthorne thus speaks of him : " I was but little interested in the legends of the remote antiquity of Lichfield, being drawn here partly to see its beautiful cathedral, and still more, I believe, because it was the birthplace of Dr. Johnson, with whose sturdy English character I became acquainted at a very early period of my life, through the good offices of Mr. Boswell. In truth, he seems as familiar to my recollection, and almost as vivid in

his personal aspect to my mind's eye, as the kindly
figure of my own grandfather. ✿ ✿ Beyond all
question I might have had a wiser friend than he.
The atmosphere in which alone he breathed was
dense ; his awful dread of death showed how much
muddy imperfection was to be cleansed out of him,
before he could be capable of spiritual existence
he meddled only with the surface of life, and never
cared to penetrate farther than to plough-share
depth ; his very sense and sagacity were but a
one-eyed clear-sightedness. I laughed at him
sometimes, standing beside his knee. And yet,
considering that my native propensities were toward Fairy Land, and also how much yeast is generally mixed up with the mental sustenance of a
New Englander, it may not have been altogether
amiss, in those childish and boyish days, to keep
pace with this heavy-footed traveller, and feed on
the gross diet that he carried in his knapsack. It
is wholesome food even now. And then how English ! Many of the latent sympathies that enabled
me to enjoy the Old Country so well, and that so
readily amalgamated themselves with the American ideas that seemed the most adverse to them,
may have been derived from, or fostered and kept
alive by, the great English moralist. Never was a
descriptive epithet more nicely appropriate than
that ! Dr. Johnson's morality was as English an
article as a beefsteak." ✿

This English character of his was after all his
chief excellence. Though it could not, under a

* " Our Old Home," p. 142.

spiritual exigency, blossom into flowers, like Aaron's rod, it nevertheless could and did bring many a sturdy buffet to the back of fools. One who so embodies national traits as did Johnson those of the English tends strongly to confirm them. He presents them in their most effective and brilliant form, one in which they best win the sympathy and command the respect of the nation. Though the faults of such an one are as salient as his virtues, the glamour of the latter disguise the former, and cause them, in their milder aspects, to pass for piquant eccentricities. The force, therefore, with which a nation realizes itself in a man like Johnson makes him a new and vigorous agent in its history.

LECTURE IX.

A statement of the periods of English Literature, and of their rela tions to each other.

Second transition period.—Churchill, Akenside, Thomson, Goldsmith, Gray, Collins, Cowper, Burns.—Forces at work to produce a new era, (a) Revival of early English Poetry, Percy's Reliques, Warton's History of English Poetry, (b) German Influence, Relations of France, Germany and England, (c) Political and Social Questions, (d) Philosophy and Religion,—Skepticism.

WE have now advanced sufficiently far in English Literature to point out completely and finally the dependence on each other of its several periods, as we divide and designate them. Aside from the individual, the national and the foreign influences at work in them, we draw attention to their natural sequence, as indicating a connection which went far to determine their character, and more particularly that of later ones. The first or initiative period was arrested by the retrogressive one, and literature made a second start in the first creative period, that of Elizabeth. This, by an easy, natural transition, passed into the first critical period, the so called Augustan age of Pope and Johnson. This again, with a more obscure transition closing the eighteenth century, gave place to a second creative period, the opening years of the nineteenth century, the years of Scott, Byron, Coleridge, Wordsworth. This has been followed by our own times, an age more marked by diffusion, the volume and variety of literature, than by any one pre-eminent quality of it. Indeed its quality is largely determined by this very fact of its universal circulation; that, for the first time, literature is percolating down through all classes, and seeking to quicken them all. We shall strive later to show how this diffusion has been occasioned. We now refer only to the order of sequence between the three great eras, the determinative epochs, of our literary art, the first creative period, the first critical, and the second creative, each separated from the other by years of transition. Our own age is in turn, doubtless, one of transfer, though the diffusive powers of modern civilization have come in to impress upon it its most salient features.

The first of these three periods being given, it tended to draw after it the other two in order; as the wave heaped up before the wind furrows the sea behind it, and is then followed by a second. We cannot expect a creative era to last long. The forces at work too much transcend ordinary experience. The clustering in of influences and the sudden unfolding of national genius under them are as necessarily transient as fruit to the plant, or summer to the seasons. When, however, these forces begin to abate, they do not subside at once. Though none are able to open up in art new directions, or quite equal its masters in old ones, there are many who can catch something of the spirit abroad, and who are able, in various ways, to perfect the movement already initiated. The products of art that were secured while the inventive power, in its first intensity, was at work in the national mind, now on its partial decline, give both the occasion and the principles of criticism.   The busy workmen cease indeed to quarry the living rock, but they chisel diligently at the Titanic blocks already lifted from their bed.   In architecture no sooner has the new style struck its initial idea, found a master under it, and been pushed to a magnificent realization, than many come in to modify, mingle, manipulate ; uniting the new to the old, exhausting the new in its manifold applications.

Genius can scarcely discern all that is in it, or stop to unfold it.   Talent can hardly fail to take up with critical delight this unfinished work, flattered at once by laboring with the masters of art, and seeming to improve upon them.   Genius gives occasions, suggestions to talent; and talent patronizes genius, while really doing its servile work. Criticism follows invention, completes it, and makes its gains permanent in rules and principles.   It prepares the national taste, in its moderated, habitual action, fully to appreciate and relish great works. It enters analytically into the good achieved, and makes way ultimately for its more thorough appreciation.

But art easily forgets and oversteps these its natural limits.   As it is liable to mistake, in the very outset, the power to criticise and improve for superiority, so is it afterward inclined to delight in rules and lines of order, aside from any completeness or fulness of life expressed by them.   Criti-

cism at the beginning, true criticism, is very delightful. It is passing beneath the form to the force
which controls it, and seeing the two in their inter-
dependence. But when the fatal excess that is in
it overtakes it; when it dreams that because the
form expresses the force, the force may be reached
through the form, it passes rapidly into superficiality
and coldness, wearying at length its most devoted
disciples. Thus in the art referred to, architecture,
the expansion of a style is almost sure to lead to
degeneration, to the excesses of a profligate, ill-
governed fancy, and thus to be brought to an un-
timely end.

But when the harvest of invention has been
gathered, and the rich field exhaustively gleaned by
criticism, there must needs be a second seed-time.
None can say how long the winter of discontent
that follows the barrenness of mere criticism will
last, but it must be brought to a close by a second
creative period, a vigorous, independent reaction in
some direction. The new period is provoked by
the manifest call for it, by the disrelish and ennui
of the hour; and sooner or later national forces, if
vigorous, will respond to this claim upon them.

Thus the three periods which interlock the
other periods of English literature, and disclose the
inter-dependence of its history, succeeded each
other. Shakespeare initiated the movement, Pope
refined upon it, Wordsworth rebelled against the
excesses of criticism, and returned anew to nature.
Creation led to art, and art, having faithfully spun its
last silken thread, lay a dead chrysalis, till a new life

was ready to eat asunder its sepulchral cerements, and betake itself again to the air.

In the present lecture, we are to deal with a second transition, to trace, in individual poets of the closing half of the eighteenth century, the changes by which poetry finally passed from the school of Pope to the freedom indicated by Wordsworth. It was an unpoetical period, the critical tendency was very slowly expending itself, and giving place to new impulses ; so slowly that for sixty years there was no poet of the first rank, scarcely one undeniably of the second rank. Churchill, so popular in his own day, so nearly forgotten in ours; a rival then in fame to Dryden and Pope, now known chiefly by name, seems to have carried to its last and most superficial form the rhetorical, satirical phase of poetry. Akenside, didactic in matter, stiffly classical in manner, with a coldly poetic elevation of diction, was not fitted to help his age onward either in freedom, depth or boldness. When a poet gives himself to an analytic rehearsal and eulogy of the pleasures of the imagination, we may be pretty sure that his poems proceed neither from the bold, battling flights of phantasy, nor from the loving, cooing frenzy with which it feeds and nestles it callow young. The mood of mind in which we write about the passions is not that in which we most strongly feel them.

Thomson presents one element of progress, a glowing and fairly faithful description of natural beauties. Of this inspiration he seems to have drunk much deeper than his predecessors. If he had added to this love of nature equally earnest human sympathies, and could have given these the bent of a creative purpose, he would have possessed the endowments of a great poet. As it was, his power was too unsupported and single to yield large results. He justifies his chosen subjects to himself, and gives them an apologetic introduction to his readers, in a formal appeal to the ruling poetic taste.

> "Such themes as these the rural Maro sung
> To wide imperial Rome, in the full height
> Of elegance and taste, by Greece refined." *

He is thus reassured, since Greeks and Romans had done the like, that it is safe, poetically and conventionally safe, for an Englishman to sing of "fostering breezes," "softening dews," and "tender showers." So cold an enthusiasm and fearful a search for precedents might well be followed by a feeble dressing up of homely things in poetic verbiage, like the following:

> "Hushed in short suspense,
> The plumy people streak their wings with oil,
> To throw the lucid moisture trickling off." †

Or this:

> "Urged to the giddy brink, much is the toil,
> The clamour much, of men and boys and dogs,
> Ere the soft fearful people to the flood
> Commit their woolly sides." ‡

When we can wash sheep in a way no more straightforward than this, our muse is too dainty for husbandry.

* Spring.   † Ibid.   ‡ Summer.

Observe the coldness of the following personifications :

> " Half in a blush of clustering roses lost,
>   Dew dropping Coolness to the shade retires ;
>   There, on the verdant turf, or flowery bed,
>   By gelid founts and careless rills to muse :
>   While tyrant Heat, dispreading through the sky,
>   With rapid sway, his burning influence darts
>   On man and beast and herb and tepid stream." *

Such abstractions as coolness and heat are here personified without the slightest descriptive clue by which the imagination can give them a bodily form; or rather any form which the fancy may assign them springs up instantly to contradict and make absurd their nature and functions. Imagery that is present as comprehension is absent, and steals away on its approach, is at war with any completeness of thought. Thomson, though in vassalage to his times, is in part saved from them by the dreamy sympathy of his nature with the physical world about him. He has this one point of living contact and hence of freedom and power. So far we stand indebted to him.

There was in Goldsmith no such force or independence of intellectual character as to free him from current impressions, or lead him to new results. There was, however, in his Irish heart a tenderness and a profusion of sympathies that take from his poems all coldness, and lift them above the school to which they belong. His personal and his poetic merits both rest on the same emotional basis.

Perhaps no one poem is a higher, a more suc-

* Summer.

cessful expression of the type of poetry under discussion than Gray's Elegy. We would rank it with
the productions of the critical school, not because
of the date of its composition, but because it owes
so much of its excellence to the exactness and easy
elegance of its form. With no peculiar depth of
insight, or vigor of imagination, it confers unfailing
pleasure, by its naturalness of sentiment, its simplicity and aptness of expression. In the highest
work, adverse tendencies always meet; form and
substance concur. Hence any unusual strength in
either element is sure to bring with it fair power
in the other. While there is this unity of qualities
in the Elegy Written in a Country Churchyard, its
predominant excellence seems to us to lie in the
studied simplicity and exactness of expression, in the
easy precision with which the sentiment assumes the
imagery, and both, the metre and rhyme, gliding on
with them the clearest and most peaceful of streams.

In Collins we meet with a poet of a much bolder
spirit. His own time no more accepted him than
he it. His poems were received with almost complete neglect, and rose to rank slowly by their own
buoyancy. There belong to Collins a new intensity
of emotion, a vividness of personification, a broader
sweep of imagination, which decidedly distinguish
his composition from that of his cotemporaries, and
impart to the reader a sense of larger, freer, glad-
der motion. As a vigorous bird proportions his
curves of flight to his power of muscle, so Collins
adopts a more varied and continuous rhythm. His
successive impulses gather up and weave together

more lines, and we are borne on the strong wing of
a single image through a series of varying melodies,
that will not fall apart into brief, measured stanzas.
This is observable in the opening of his Ode to
Liberty; also in his Ode to the Passions:

> " Who shall awake the Spartan fife,
>   And call in solemn sounds to life,
>   The youths, whose locks divinely spreading,
>   Like vernal hyacinths in sullen hue,
>   At once the breath of fear and virtue shedding,
>   Applauding Freedom, loved of old to view?
>   What new Alcæus, fancy-blest,
>   Shall sing the sword, in myrtles drest,
>   At wisdom's shrine awhile its flame concealing,
>   (What place so fit to seal a deed renown'd?)
>   Till she her brightest lightnings round revealing,
>   It leap'd in glory forth, and dealt her prompted wound."

This fearless and impassioned movement of Collins
put him out of sympathy with the tame, restricted
temper about him. He had anticipated the season,
and must needs wait the approach of coming summer months.

We now pass farther on in the century, and meet
with two poets quite divorced from the old, and, in
very different ways, ready to usher in the new,
Cowper and Burns. The connection of Cowper
with the approaching and better spirit of poetry is
quite generally recognized. Says Craik: "As the
death of Johnson closes one era of our literature, so
the appearance of Cowper as a poet opens another.
* * His opinions were not more his own than
his manner of expressing them. His principles of
diction and versification were announced, in part, in
the poem in which he introduced himself to the

10

public, his Table-Talk, in which, having intimated his contempt for the 'creamy smoothness' of modern fashionable verse, where sentiment was so often

> " ' Sacrificed to sound,
> And truth cut short to make the period round,'

" he exclaims,

> " ' Give me the line that ploughs its stately course,
> Like a proud swan, conquering the stream by force :
> That, like some cottage beauty, strikes the heart,
> Quite unindebted to the tricks of art.' " *

Cowper recognized the formality and rigidity into which literature had fallen under the influence of Pope, and complains of him that he has

> " Made poetry a mere mechanic art,
> And every warbler has his tune by heart."

This independent criticism shows that he caught sight of a new era, and designedly hastened its coming. To the last degree timid and self-distrustful, his mind nevertheless moved independently and vigorously under its own laws. This inner strength and courage of the soul, are quite distinct from confidence in action, and are often met with without it. Indeed the timidity with which such a mind retires upon itself leaves it only the more free to follow its own bent. It was the seclusion of a diffident nature that hemmed Cowper about, and left him to his own independent judgment.

The fresh impulse which Cowper brought to poetry is found in the genuineness, depth, and pervasive character of his sentiments. While his

* English Literature and Language, vol. ii. p. 372.

poems have in them much that might be thought
didactic, this matter is given in so natural, reflective, and yet more, in so emotional, a manner as
quite to escape the censure that might be implied
in the word. The thought does not, predetermined,
so much seek for the image and rhythm wherewith
to enforce itself, as flow out in an incidental living
way from the scenes and objects present to the
poetic imagination. It is not thought, but its cold
statement, or perceptive enforcement, that poetry
rejects. Cowper has a large measure of that power
which brings interpretation to natural objects, and
looks upon them with a rapid interplay of suggestions, uniting the visible to the invisible, and lending to passing events a scope otherwise quite beyond them. Especially is he able, in the manner
of Wordsworth, to see and feel the twining and in-
tertwining of facts and sentiments, which often so
closely bind the buoyant spiritual mind to the physical world, and make this the resounding loom in
which are woven with wonderful rapidity, variety,
and beauty the patterns of its highest and noblest
thoughts. The quiet, earnest, subtile, pure, pervasive mind of Cowper made him a poet by the innate
force and character of its conceptions. There is
everything in his history to confirm the view, that art
finds its germ in natural endowment, and nothing
to sustain the theory, that it can be compassed by
external conditions. Attached to one of the least
interesting portions of England, he was yet pre-eminent in his love of nature, and penetrating observation of it; in close intercourse with the devotees

of Calvinism, his poetry is marked by sympathy
and tenderness of sentiment ; diffident and distrust-
ful beyond self-control, his verse moves, as he fain
would have it, with the quiet force of a swan breast-
ing the stream, seeking and, to the full, enjoying
its own.

The devoutness of Cowper was too deep, directly, formally to control his poems. It and they
grew together out of his entire intellectual and
emotional life. Religious sentiment and spiritual
insight gave the same strong traits to his productions that they imparted to his character. Without
these he would have been another man and another
poet. Though his religious views received a severe
and melancholy cast, which, concurring with natural
temperament, led him at times within the limits of
insanity, this spiritual vitality was not less the normal disposition of the man ; and was connected
with a volatile temper deeply impressible by mirth
and the quiet joys of life. Though his nature made
answer most fully to religious sentiment, it was with
no loss of the attachments which fall to a lively
temperament.

Burns imparted to poetry an impulse at once
like that given by Cowper and diverse from it.
Both were in a high degree natural, spontaneous, sincere ; but the sincerity of the one was
that of a melancholy and devout temper, and
that of the other of a joyous and passionate one
Few characters so elicit sympathy and regard,
passing into regret and sadness, as that of Burns.
With large and generous impulses and an eager

relish for pleasure, he sought it impetuously, and missed it early and almost utterly. His warm, emotional nature made him as ready to impart as to receive enjoyment, yet his fatal haste and disobedience brought the same bitterness to others as to himself. His love was as deadly as the hate of another man. The flowers he plante lost their fragrance, and the blossoms he plucked distilled blood upon his fingers. We share something of his resentment and impatience at the stern, cold, cruel features of the social life and religious faith of his country, yet we are forced to remember, that out of his own more tender sentiments, as expressed in the Cotter's Saturday-Night, there came no strength, no power to plant, to harvest, or to enjoy the good he coveted. His own failure was early and complete.

As a lyric poet Burns deserves the name of great. In the most essential qualities of this form of verse; in fire, tenderness and naturalness, none have surpassed him. The earnest devotion of Cowper united him in meditative sympathy to nature; the warm passions of Burns set him aglow with human interests, and made him the poet of tender, heroic, mirthful, wilful impulses. He keenly felt, and uttered melodiously what he felt; and by this force of a strong, impetuous nature became a fresh, creative poet, working vigorously for the new era. With lively and sympathetic feelings he entered into the homely experiences of life about him, both frolicsome and serious, gay and sombre; rendered them with his own appreciation, and colored them with his own transfiguring fancy. The human sympathies of Burns wrought like the spiritual sympathies of Cowper, and put him, at times, as in the Mountain Daisy, in living concord with nature.

The class to which Burns belonged, the dialect in which he wrote, his limited education, all lightened the weight of conventional influences, and left him chiefly to the push of his own nature as he produced his lyrics, first for himself, and later for the world. Though Burns stands at the entrance of the new period, none of the great poets that followed surpassed him in individuality of faculties, a freedom which yet left him in full mastery of a varied and most melodious verse. Here again in the life of Burns we have a large, constitutional, original element, which shaped itself into the development of his times without being governed by it. Pope had been made the subject of admiring study by Burns, yet cast no reflection of himself in the dancing, sparkling, rollicksome stream of his verse.

We now turn, having touched a few of the significant features of transition in the works of individual poets, to the general forces which helped to bring about a new intellectual activity, a fresh era of invention. We have referred to the weariness into which art, mere art, finally falls, the ennui which forces the spirit to some new form of activity. But this is a negative rather than a positive force, a divorce from the past

rather than a promise of the future. We still need
to see what awakening energies, what living
ideas, were then at large in the intellectual
world, to take the guidance of a new movement,
and impart to it impulse.

A literary influence which accompanied and
indicated this change of taste was an increase.
interest in early English poetry. The nation, weary
of the products of classical criticism, turned to the
fresh, wild fruits of its own literary youth, and
sought in its early ballads the relish it had lost in
didactic art; as old age seeks to renew its languid appetites with the fruits that delighted its
boyhood. It is always a sign of health when a
people is interested in itself, its history, its art,
and the tendencies native to its growth. A
submission to foreign law, and a sedulous imitation of works more or less alien to the soil
and temper and wants of a people, are the
marks of flagging invention, and the precursors
of still farther decay.

The publication, in 1765, of Percy's Reliques
of Ancient English Poetry was a leading and very
influential indication of the wakefulness of the
nation to its own work. "I do not think," said
Wordsworth, "that there is an able writer in verse
of the present day, who would not be proud to
acknowledge his obligations to the Reliques; I
know that it is so with my friends; for myself I
am happy to make a public avowal of mine own."
Walter Scott, who felt so pre-eminently, and who
so fully followed out, this tendency to legendary

and romantic history, to restored nationalism, says:
" From this time," the date of his reading the
Reliques of Ancient English Poetry, " the love
of natural beauty, more especially when combined with ancient ruins, or the remains of our
fathers' piety or splendour, became with me an
insatiable passion, which, if circumstances had
permitted, I would willingly have gratified by
travelling over half the globe." So ready and
inflammable was the material prepared for these
living coals, unraked from the ashes of departed
years. The Reliques were largely composed of
the lyrics of earlier and later writers. The ballads yielded the key-note, and then gave place to
the melody of more modern verse, the most free
and national in its character. Lyric poetry, less
ambitious than other forms, more close to the
individual sentiment, is wont to be the refuge of
the most genuine, simple and passionate strains;
to be most deeply infused with the national temper.

The impression made by this work of Percy's
was confirmed by Warton's History of English
Poetry. This history covers the early years of our
literature broadly and thoroughly, and indicates at
once enthusiasm and patient research. The awakened interest in the past is also indicated by the
literary forgeries of the time. These sprang up
in connection with the general interest that attended on historical research. Evidently Macpherson
and Chatterton found something in this eager temper of the public mind which prepared the way for
their deceptions.

A second literary element, which marked and helped to cause the shifting spirit of the period, was the incipient influence of German literature. Immediate entrance was given to it through Walter Scott, and still more, through Wordsworth and Coleridge. Coleridge was well fitted for the reception both of its philosophy and poetry. His methods of thought concurred with his knowledge to render German influence powerful with him. From this date onward German literature has been gaining ground in England and America, and has for many years been quite the most vigorous of European forces. England, France and Germany, together supreme in philosophy, science and art, hold toward each other independent and diverse positions. The artistic element, in its more separate and complete form, belongs to France. The active, the brilliant, the formal, in social organization, in social intercourse, in criticism, in creation, are found with the French; the sluggish, practical, powerful and useful rest with the English; while to the German belongs the theoretical, the speculative, the profound, the laborious. The three occupy in reference to each other the points of a triangle. For the English to draw near the French is to be quickened in execution, but to lose weight; to be made critical, captious and superficial: for them to draw near the Germans is to deepen and enlarge inquiry; is to be renewed in thought, and enlivened in invention.

Taine reproaches the English as lacking philosophy. The reproach is not just, and, if it were,

10*

would come but poorly from a Frenchman. The philosophical tendency is not as controlling in England as it has been in Germany; nor is it likely to flash out in as extreme, rapid, and perchance brilliant speculation as in France; yet, as we shall later show, as settled, consistent, continuous and fruitful a philosophical movement has fallen to England as to either of the other two. The philosophy of England shows a history far more independent than does that of France, and one, we believe, whose results have kept much closer to the truth than the speculations of either France or Germany.

It is now urged, and with a measure of correctness, that the scientific temper is one of relative indifference to the bearing of the results reached by inquiry; that it schools itself to accept one result as freely as another. As against controlling prejudice, this claim must be granted, not, we think, as against every cautious, constitutional tendency. The English, as contrasted with the Germans, pursue philosophy distrustfully, with a predisposed and interested spirit. Questions of religion, of society, and of government are so present to their speculations, that they are always forecasting the issues and tendencies of a theory, suffering practical exigencies to react upon it, and turning aside from troublesome conclusions. It may be questioned whether the fruits of their philosophy have for this reason been less valuable. Additional caution, repeated consideration by various minds, a stern resistance to extreme, erratic tendencies, have been the result, and have made the gains of thought, if

slower, less bold and captivating, more safe and
reliable. The German mind, from its intellectual
freedom, from this very divorce of its speculative
processes from practical questions, its separation
from the interests of the hour,—for in Germany one's
philosophy is especially disconnected from his so
cial, political and religious relations,—has lost some
of the balance and steadiness which the retardation
of immediate and material interests would have imposed upon it. Moreover, the practical relations of
a theory do afford a partial, even though it be an
inadequate, test of its correctness. The German
mind, with all its subtlety, breadth of knowledge,
and boldness of inquiry, seems not especially well
fitted to weigh evidence, and to reach reliable conclusions. A wild, dreamy speculation sweeps in
upon it from this side, and is shortly followed by
another as erratic from that side. It is impossible
for any of us to preserve an ideal attitude of indifference to evidence, and to be prepared to weigh it exactly and completely as it is offered. If the thoughts
were thus to loosen themselves, to drop the great
burden of practical issues and previous conclusions
that sober them, they would be seen to play fitfully,
like idle weathercocks, rather than to mark deep
undercurrents, like anchored buoys. The new as
new, the fresh theory because it is the last theory,
our thoughts as our own have a peculiar hold on the
mind, and should be met by the inertia of old tendencies. An index that plays with some friction
shows the stronger forces, and escapes the fluctua-
tions of lighter ones. An Englishman can hardly

be as extreme and visionary as it is possible for
a German to be, and because he has more of this
national habit of mind upon him, feels more of its
conservative tendencies.   Now this inertia of a
nation, putting to perpetual use its knowledge, does
often embarrass philosophy, but often saves it also;
makes it stupid at times, it is true, but always renders it serious, and faithful to whatever has been
entrusted to it.

The English, as contrasted with either Germans
or Frenchmen, owe much to their political organization, to their compact, slowly developing, social and
religious life, by which every question assumes a
national bearing, and is kept at all hazards within
the limits of safety.   If much is due to the boldness
of individual thought, much also is due to the slow,
half-instinctive movement of a nation, as it creeps
hesitatingly on in its organic development.   This
judgment of every theory by its power to play
safely into the daily facts of life is a wholesome restraint on erratic speculation, is allied in philosophy
and religion, in the checks it affords, to those offered in science by the special phenomena under
discussion.

At this second creative period in her literary
history, England began to come in contact with the
freer, bolder, more speculative mind of Germany, and
to be awakened by it.   The English make awkward
disciples of the French, as a slow practical person
appears poorly in the presence of one audacious,
quick-witted and accomplished.   They unite more
hopefully to the obscure, patient and intellectually

productive Germans; turning readily to an immediate purpose, and presenting on their valuable side,
the fruits of these diligent laborers. The practical
strikes hands advisedly with the theoretical, and is
sure of the larger half of the common harvest.
The ore that is brought to the mine's mouth is thus
quickly reduced, and made marketable.

In a characterization of nations, only a general
and partial truth is aimed at, or can be reached.
Individual exceptions will spring up on all sides.
England, France, Germany, have each many citizens who share the national virtues, and in large
measure escape the national faults. Certainly the
individual never appears to better advantage than
when, availing himself to the full of the nation's resources, he yet tempers them all to a broader and
more catholic spirit; the Englishman adding to his
own firm-footedness the nimble celerity of the
Frenchman, and the sustained strength of the German; or the German enlivening his thoughtful path
with the vivacity of French insight, and bending it
to the sober, serious purposes of his Saxon kins-
man; or the Frenchman, casting the brilliancy of
his national spirit over the solid substance in character of the other two. It is also to be remembered,
that national tendencies are always the most clearly
shown in social, political and religious questions,
and in philosophy and criticism as they bear upon
these. In science the conditions of progress are
more fixed and independent, and personal bias is
less influential. All nations are more nearly one
on those topics which pertain less immediately to

character.   The order of European influence has
been Italian, French, German; and the long arm
and strong hand now rest with Germany.

This creative period was also profoundly affected
by political causes.   The movement toward religious
liberty which had been so efficient a force in the
Elizabethan period had at length, under favoring
circumstances, issued in an equally decided and
extended claim for political liberty.   The religious
precedents and drift of the past had not been more
sharply questioned, nor its conclusions more broadly
denied on general principles by the Protestant Reformation, than were the opinions pertaining to society and government by the American Revolution.
This revolution, while favored by circumstances,
had not been their blind result.   It had not been
made ready by mere physical forces; with these
there had been a steady ripening of opinions, a
practical use and theoretical proclamation of the
principles of political freedom.   This revolution was
not allowed, therefore, to transpire in the dark, its
underlying truths obscured by the turmoil of conflict, or lost sight of in the interests of the hour.   It
was ripened by convictions, and accompanied by
the clearest announcement of its justifying reasons.
Its social bearings were thus much more important
than its immediate political ones.   Though it was
the starting point of a great nation, it helped to set
in motion, and gave a permanent, unmistakable
form to social truths, which overleap all national
bounds and carry discussion and commotion everywhere.

Questions of government and social organization have, from that hour to the present, been the
themes of the most earnest, enlarged, varied and
urgent consideration. The destiny of the leading
civilized nations has been rescued, in part, from the
blind flow of physical forces, from the awards of
battle, and shaped by a conscious and ever returning struggle for enlarged rights, for social gains to
be secured and fortified under new organizations.

England was compelled to take a prominent
part in the practical, passing solution of these problems. True to her history, she was divided in sentiment against herself, throwing her physical weight
chiefly upon one side, and her moral weight largely
upon the other. The American Revolution was
followed by the French Revolution, in part begotten, and certainly hastened by it. The first kindled
those latent tendencies which wildly flamed out in
the second, on a broader field, in the midst of more
valuable and critical interests, and with less of the
restraint either of reason or surrounding circumstances. Questions of rights thus received at once
an emphasis which did not allow them to be set
aside. Here again England was a leading belliger-
ant, was driven by her sluggish, jealous and conservative temper into an extreme attitude of resistance,
out of harmony, at least in the outset, with her
own best sentiment, and finally covered up and
made admissible only by the extravagance of the
French, and that blind martial mania of theirs
which slowly resolved the entire controversy into
one of conquest.

We can hardly in our country and in our time, when questions of government, and our rights under it, are in constant discussion, and are every day finding an easy and safe settlement, appreciate the shock which these inquiries brought at the beginning, before men had become accustomed to them, or society supple under them; when they carried with them the imminent danger of such bloody crises, and half-fruitless struggles, as those of the French Revolution.

In these political and social conflicts, the second brood of the Spirit of Liberty, we have a force fitted to stir the mind of England scarcely less deeply, and quite as broadly as those religious rights which called forth its earlier strength. The leading minds of the incoming period were borne rapidly forward by these incentives. Johnson resisted the progressive spirit. He personified the stubborn English temper, slow to acquire anything new, and yet slower to part with anything old; that accepts with composure the revolutions of the past, but has no sympathy with those of the present. Burke, less timid, favored for a time revolution, and lost sympathy with it only in its excesses.

Coleridge, Southey, Wordsworth, were carried away with the first enthusiasm of liberty, and slowly returned to a conservative temper as experience, reflection, constitutional tendencies, or disastrous revolution restored to each the balance of thought.

Shelley, Byron, Landor remained more extreme

in temper. Shelley especially drank to intoxication of the glowing promises of speedy, social regeneration. All the great minds of the period encountered at once these questions of liberty, and were aroused to fresh activity, strange hopes, or sudden alarms by them. It is to be observed, however, that those somewhat secondary in ability were alone shaken from permanent composure; while the larger minded and more sedate ones came slowly to receive the promises of revolution with abatement, and to cling to the old, as at least presenting the soil out of which the new must grow, and by which it must be nourished. The slow organic evolution of society held the thoughts of those sobered by experience, and taught the continuity of events, as against all violent and precipitate change. There is very little difficulty in society that is simply one of organization, and can be sufficiently met by constitutional shifts. The wise caught the lessons of the French convulsions before the revolutionary drama was half closed, while the enthusiastic were left to misunderstand events, to look wearily about for the reasons of failure when the last sad scene was over.

In philosophy and theology, the influences at the close of the eighteenth century were vigorous and progressive. Science was rapidly enlarging its acquisitions in all directions. The skepticism of Hume was calling forth a new school of Scotch metaphysicians. The critical, materialistic, utilitarian tendency of English thought

was meeting with farther enlargement by such vigorous men as James Mill and Jeremy Bentham.

Coleridge was a zealous party to these inquiries, and gave new emphasis to the truths
of our higher, our intuitive nature. By his extended influence, especially through the medium
of conversation, he was able to carry these discussions into literary circles, and quicken and
deepen interest in the profound questions of
our being. The practical religious life of the
nation, strengthened by the zeal of many able
and devout men, held the grounds of faith with
stubborn resistance to the skeptical philosophy
of the time, and with the changing methods of
defense which the advance of inquiry made necessary. Since the time of Locke there has been
no material cessation in the conflicts in the English mind between science, philosophy and religion.
The later lines of struggle, however, those which
rest back on the reason, the intuitive nature of
man, were beginning to be more clearly taken, as
this second creative period came forward; and
helped to enlarge and deepen its spiritual impulses.

The conflict was also made more intense by
a reflex wave of English philosophy returning to
it through the French. The tendencies to materialism latent in the doctrines of Locke had
been more rapidly and fearlessly unfolded in
France than in England, and had there taken
their secondary form of religious unbelief and
revolutionary social theories. The celerity and
recklessness of the French mind enabled it to

give back, as the startling infidelity of Voltaire,
and the destructive socialism of Rousseau, what
it received as a safe, quiet denial of innate ideas.
So differently do the same seeds of thought ripen
in distinct national soils! On this period were
converging the political revolutions which sprang
from Puritanism, and those quickened by the feverish theories of French materialism. If the
sober-minded were thrown forward by the one,
they were quickly flung backward by the other.
On this period were converging the tenacious,
slowly-progressive theology of the English mind,
its deep-seated, half-unconscious materialism, always prone to shirk and deny its own corol-
laries; the abstruse theories of Germany, too remote to be to many either the grounds of belief or unbelief; and the extreme, startling and
varied social and religious skepticism of the
French, alarming the most tender and deep
sympathies of the soul. It is not strange that
many minds, so played upon, became erratic,
and that retreat followed quick upon advance.
Thus the century opened, a pregnant spring-
time, in which the useful, the beautiful and the
worthless struggled together for sun-light.

Every quarter of the civilized world was
coming to be subject to intense influences from
every other. Assertions, which went forth as
harmless speculations, came back as revolutionary frenzy. Nothing was at rest, nothing un-
assailable; nor had men yet learned the value
of revolution, the power and worth of a mere

change of organization. The hopes of men were as extravagant as their thoughts were feverish, and they were ready in all directions, to make short roads to the millennium, and take by vio- ence the kingdom of heaven. On this religi- ious and political ferment the century opened, and set itself to the task of eliminating its false- hoods and embodying its truths.

The interlacing of different tendencies, the striking modifications which national and indi- vidual character brought to the same fundamen- tal principles, are seen in the social, political philosophy of Locke as expanded in England, in America, in France; and also in the posi- tion of free, protestant Holland, sheltering in the seventeenth century the Puritans of Eng- land, and in the eighteenth the skeptics of France; giving its types, now to an English Bible, now to the Social Contract of Rousseau; and becoming at length the "great printing press of France." * It fell to this century to decide between nation and nation, statement and state- ment; and to discover that truth is truth only as it is wrought into coherent, social and in- dividual life.

* Rousseau, vol. ii. p. 57.

LECTURE X.

THE second creative period, the first thirty
years of the present century, finds but one rival
era in our literature.   In this, as in that, revolutionary forces were at work, and the minds of men
were awakened by various and powerful causes.
As then, though foreign influences were active,
native, national tendencies were pre-eminent.   England, in the first instance, stood proudly on the defensive, the champion of Protestantism ; and now,
at least as she deemed it, of national constitutional
development.   No continental wars have been to
England more significant than the struggles with
Philip II. and Napoleon I.   In each instance, she
awaited a great invasion ; and in each the conflict
of arms was united with one of opinions.

This second period was equally fruitful with the
first, and more varied in its productions.   It does
not, indeed, reach quite the elevation of the Elizabethan era ; it lies under the shadow of one or two
of the great men of the earlier age ; but, this admitted, it shows a more diversified, vigorous and pervasive literary activity than even that first outburst of
life.   In it, as in every great literary period, poetry
was clearly pre-eminent, and this, notwithstanding

the fact that prose, in an unbroken and enlarged volume, came down from the previous time. Inquisitive, laborious, artistic prose multiplied in all directions, and added to its previous forms its most careful essays and best novels. Criticism, especially in the review, the magazine, the journal, began that prodigious productiveness which has at length filled every portion of our atmosphere with its floating spores, springing up as moss and lichens on every stalwart trunk; or as the literary must and mildew of the time on every decaying thing.

Notwithstanding this unchecked power of prose, working for science or art, for use or pleasure, as it was able, poetry was the distinguishing feature of the time, and this under its best forms. Narrative, dramatic, lyric poetry prevailed, and when the didactic element was present, it took so meditative, intuitive, emotional a form as to impart a new, more spiritual, more profoundly poetic temper to our literature.

We now turn, having spoken of the character of the period and the general forces at work in it, to the individuals who fixed its precise type, and made it exactly what it was—to Scott, Byron, Wordsworth, Coleridge, Shelley. There is earnest discussion as to what shall be done with the individual in a philosophy of history. Some are willing, as Spencer, so to magnify the aggregate of external conditions; the influence of climate, race, cultivation, the accumulated products of descent; the precise circumstances of the time and place on which he has fallen; the social movement into

which he is educated, as to leave him hardly more
than a waif on a mighty current, whose direction
and force he may indicate, but can do very little to
control.   Others, with much less reason, far more
superficial in observation, are struck with the prominent part that a few great men take in affairs, and
are ready to look upon them as the chief forces a
work, as giving direction to events by their single
volition.   To these Spencer makes answer :

"If, not stopping at the explanation of social
progress as due to the great man, we go back a
step, and ask, Whence comes the great man? we
find that the theory breaks down completely.   *   *
Along with the whole generation of which he
forms a minute part ; along with its institutions,
language, knowledge, manners, and its multitudinous arts and appliances, he is the resultant of
an enormous aggregate of causes that have been
co-operating for ages.   *   *   If, disregarding
those accumulated results of experience, which
current proverbs and the generalizations of psy-
chologists alike express, you suppose that a Newton might be born in a Hottentot family, that a
Milton might spring up among the Andamanese,
that a Howard or a Clarkson might have Fiji pa-
rents, then you may proceed with facility to explain social progress as caused by the actions of
great men.   But if all biological science, enforcing
all popular belief, convinces you that by no possibility will an Aristotle come from a father and
mother with facial angles of fifty degrees ; and that
out of a tribe of cannibals, whose chorus in prepa-

ration for a feast of human flesh is a kind of rhythmical roaring there is not the remotest chance of a Beethoven arising; then you must admit the genesis of the great man depends on a long series of complex influences which has produced the race in which he appears, and the social state into which that race has slowly grown. If it be a fact that the great man may modify his nation in its structure and actions, it is also a fact that there must have been those antecedent modifications constituting national progress before he could be evolved. Before he can re-make his society, his society must make him. So that all those changes of which he is the proximate initiator have their chief causes in the generations which give him birth. If there is to be anything like a real explanation of these changes, it must be sought in the aggregate of conditions out of which both he and they have arisen."*

This presentation of Spencer has force as against the limited view of his adversaries, and is to be preferred to the flippant theory of Taine, which refers so much of the history and character of Englishmen to external conditions. "They are," says he, "never comfortable in their country, they have to strive continually against cold or rain. They cannot live there carelessly, lying under a lovely sky, in a sultry and clear atmosphere, their eyes filled with the noble beauty and happy serenity of the land. They must work to live; be attentive, exact; close and repair their houses, wade boldly through the mud behind the plough, light their lamps in their shops

* Popular Science Monthly.

during the day.   Their climate imposes endless in-
convenience, and exacts endless endurance.   Hence
arise melancholy and the idea of duty.   Man naturally thinks of life as a battle, oftener of black
death which closes this deadly show, and leads so
many plumed and disorderly processions to the si-
lence and eternity of the grave.   All this visible
world is vain; there is nothing true but human virtue,—the courageous energy with which man attains
to self-command, the generous energy with which
he employs himself in the service of others.   On
this view he fixes his eyes; they pierce through
worldly gauds, neglect sensual joys to attain this.
By such internal action the ideal is displaced; a
new source of action springs up—the idea of righteousness." *

It would seem strange that the unbearable mud
and weather, in themselves not less abundant in
earlier than later times, left the Saxons so blood-
thirsty a brood, such lawless revellers, and yet
wrought righteousness in the English.   If France
lacks conscience in lacking clouds, misses reflection
in missing the dismal retinue of storms, the English
may indeed congratulate themselves on elemental
conflicts which, displacing those of men, leave the
streets of their capital unstained with blood, and
beat out the germs of hasty, cruel and futile revolution.   We should hardly have looked for so much
moral power in a drizzling rain, but if it be what
Taine thinks it, we may well compose ourselves to
its frequent return.   On the whole, we accept the

* History of English Literature, vol. i. p. 101.

11

philosophy of the Englishman, laboring though he does under the epithet "unphilosophical," as against this ready theory of the Frenchman.

The truth would seem to be, that, setting aside foreign forces often very influential, a nation's growth in kind and degree is determined by external conditions of climate, soil, position; by constitutional national character and general cultivation, accumulated and transmitted in physical and intellectual and moral descent; and by individuals. Which of these three is the more controlling it may not be easy to decide, nor do they always maintain toward each other the same ratios of force. As national character becomes vigorous, external conditions are cast into the background. It is only in the earlier, the incipient stages of growth, that these seem to have a decisive control, and then over the direction rather than over the degree of activity. They constitute the conditions of necessity, and doors of opportunity, which in the beginning compel and invite action, but which, if growth follows, are soon overmastered by the forces which it supplies. The English are now commercial by a stronger fact than the possession of harbors.

In striving to strike the balance of power between the nation and the individual, between its combined movement as controlling its personal life, and its personal life as shaping and reshaping its combined movement, we are to bear in mind, that the two agencies are so interlaced as to be inseparable in their action. The individual worker, the great man, holds both elements in himself;

he adds the personal type to the national type, and gives new efficiency to the general bias by the individual bent of soul that he brings to it. If it be true, as Spencer says, that before he, the man of genius, can remake society, society must make him, it is also true, that when he is actually at work on society, his efficiency is due more to what he brings to the common stock of qualities, than to these stock-qualities as held by him ; more to the moral altitude given him by personal endowments above the table-land of national character, than to the height of these plains themselves, whereon are mustered the nation. It is the head and shoulders of his own supremacy that give him dominion, though this dominion is to be expended in actual work on the level of the faculties which belong to his race.

These two forces, the race-force and the personal force, mutually limit each other. If genius is conditioned for its quality to the nation to which it belongs, the nation is also conditioned upon the presence of men of genius to express, intensify, and make effective in growth the national strength. If talent, for its efficiency, is dependent on the intellectual and moral state of those with whom it labors, so are these, in turn, dependent on their leaders for the full realization of their next step of progress. The nation and the individual grow together, and are, therefore, in instant living interplay. Each is what it is through the other, and neither can hold independent ground. If we wish critically to estimate their claims, we shall be able to do it best, not by watching the erratic, brilliant career of genius, to whom all forces seem secondary; nor by turning to the slow, irresistible steps of national growth, which, in the steady progress of centuries, sinks into seeming insignificance the individuals who have been partakers in it; but by more carefully observing the momentary interplay of national and private life, by which the one is slowly transmuted into the other.

In this common growth the individual is always primary. He alone thinks, he alone advances with a self-sufficing force. Take the nation at any stage of progress, early or late; it must be gotten beyond that stage by the new views, the discoveries, inven tions, prowess of persons. It will remain inert till some one man, or class of men, move, pioneer the way, and teach others to follow. So all progress has been achieved. The growing point is in every case the individual. The position he shall start from is determined for him by the nation, that is by previous individual workers, the men of genius and talent that have gone before him; but the next step of progress, for himself and the nation, he must take. The individual, therefore, is always primary, initial, the seat of living activity; while the nation is secondary, residuary, receptive, the trunk-growth, or, as in the coral, the rock-growth, left behind. The terminal buds on a tree owe their position to the organic development that has preceded them; but this growth has all been initiated by them, as must be all farther growth. All that is really additive, then, is due to the individual, while preservation.

continuity, the conditions of increase, come from the nation. The nation is the storehouse wherein are treasured the fruits of individual labor.

In reference to society, to the nation, the men of genius, so far as they have genius, are supernatural forces, that is, forces unexplained by their antecedents. As men normally endowed with the national constitution, tastes, disposition, they are natural products, sufficiently explained by the circumstances of their birth. In the conditions under which their powers are expended, the work that falls to them, and the general limits of its efficiency, they are also included in the national development. But in so far as they have genius, in so far as they transcend the national type, as they are a peculiar and personal power, they remain unexplained, are an original and independent source of influence. We have no recipe for the production of a Shakespeare, no hint as to the causes which will yield a Bacon. Shakespeare, as Shakespeare, is a primitive, supernatural power in English history ; working indeed under the conditions of that history, but not included in them or explained by them. He expounds history, our literary history, more than that history can ever expound him. If genius is altogether a natural product, one of ways and means, it is to us, as yet wholly ignorant of its productive conditions, as a supernatural force, one that comes and goes without challenge. The soil may determine what trees shall be present in a forest, those already in possession may still farther restrict its form of growth, but the vital force of each species has helped to

decide, and must continue to decide, its make-up.
Great is the constitutional force of society at any
one moment ; but into it, the force of a thousand
individuals has already been wrought; into it other
independent spirits, in part only its own progeny,
may press their way, and, living influences, living
in and with the national life, may move as it moves,
yet cause it to swerve more and more under their
steady pressure. The constitutional vigor of society, great as it may be, is yet plastic to the individual hand, and in time may receive any form from
it. To this last element in the second creative
period, that of genius, we now turn.

The outside influences which went to the composition of Walter Scott, as a poet and novelist, are
very obvious. The national character and history
were vigorously at work in him. An intimate
knowledge of the minstrelsy of the Scottish border,
and of its wild traditions ; a spirit thoroughly imbued with the mediæval, chivalrous temper, softened
and transfigured by a poetic imagination ; and
familiarity with the natural beauties of Scotland,
with an enthusiastic appreciation of them, united to
give shape and tone to his works. He was not a
product of the present, nor of the past, but of the
past history of his country as transfigured by the
present, sifted of its harsh features, and wrought
into the lively, humane dreams of poetry. These
historic forces were not merely felt and transferred
by Walter Scott, he had a peculiar affinity with
them. He transformed them in the presentation,
and gave them a power and life native to himself

What he added to them by a glowing fancy is as observable and essential as the material itself. The trend of the banks accounts for the bed of the stream, but not for the torrent that fills it. This is fed by the deep fountains of the earth and the passing clouds of heaven ; the great forces of nature are every moment busy with this labor.

Walter Scott was endowed with the powers of a very large and loving observation of outside life. With comparatively little spiritual penetration or interpretation, he easily seizes in nature and in man their sensible, significant features. The insight involved in this, and it is very considerable, belongs to him ; but he does not go much beyond it. He renders actions in their outside spirit and power, but does not care to analyze them, to study their sources, relations, issues. He gives a glowing, active picture, renders in a lively way the flow of events, and leaves us to query as we will about the impulses, the good and the evil that are in them ; to search for the problems of life they contain, and the answers they make to them. Yet there is so full a rendering of character, such a catching of the flavor of men and things, that we are at once endowed with the lively observation of our author, and may, though we are not provoked to, go deeper than he in our inquiries. The light, fleeting impressions with which he crowds the imagination are well shown in his picture of Loch Katrine in the morning light,

> " The mountain shadows on her breast
> Were neither broken nor at rest ;

> In bright uncertainty they lie,
>> Like future joys to fancy's eye."

Thus he touches the symbol and the meaning beneath it, the action and the life that prompts it, and lets the two glide on together, without division or discussion. With this temper of mind, so personal to him, so spirited, active and objective, Walter Scott deals with wholesome, energetic, out-door forces. Reaching little that is either direct or high in intellectual stimulus he puts us in contact with robust life, and extracts mental health from physical inspiration and courageous action. The morbid, mean and cowardly skulk away ; the faithful, magnanimous and bold are in the foreground.

The likings and tastes of Walter Scott were at one with the spirit of his works. Chivalrous, aristocratic proclivities, in their best form, entered largely into his character. He had little in common with modern democracy ; the amenities, sympathies, and social dependencies of the old *régime* he thoroughly appreciated. The revolutions of his own time had slight effect upon him. While others were stirred by their social promise, he, called into actual service by the threatened invasion of Bonaparte, was composing his Marmion, as he walked " his powerful steed up and down upon the Porto Bello sands within the beating of the surge, and now and then plunged in his spurs, to go off as at a charge with the spray dashing about him."* So lightly did these events, ploughing deep furrows in more philosophical minds, slide over or lose themselves in his pre-engaged

* Reed's English Poets, vol. ii. p. 81.

fancies. Walter Scott was a very genuine man, though a somewhat antiquated one. His strong bias makes him limited in the range of his works. He left poetry and turned to fiction, as he himself said, because he "felt the prudence of giving way before the more forcible and powerful genius of Byron." Had he not also exhausted the particular vein of poetry which his tastes and attainments fitted him to work? Endless production was here an impossibility. The material at his disposal became more available in the novel than in the poem. A monotony of form had begun to show itself as the result of a monotony of matter. Variety is a sterner necessity in high art than in fiction, and the want of it is more immediately apparent. The very felicity of adaptation of material, language, metre in the best of Scott's poems cut him off from continuous production. Emphatic in their kind, they could not return again and again. He grew weary, and others were weary with him. It is true, moreover, that Byron's works "wonderfully excited and intoxicated the public mind at first, and for a time made all other poetry seem spiritless and wearisome." Scott stands alone in his poetic works. Some may hastily depreciate them ; none can speak slightingly of their execution.

Personal passion was to Byron what national romance was to Scott. Strong, restless, ungovernable emotion, seldom beneficent, often startling and destructive, underlay his volcanic nature. An irritable, overbearing self-consciousness, the product of lawless, selfish impulses, of appetites and passions keenly alive to pleasure, and forever baffled in its pursuit, of a soul in proud wilfulness and real strength refusing to be taught, was the distinguishing spiritual feature in the character of Byron. He was constitutionally immoral in the sense that he constantly felt, and as constantly chafed at, moral law. The infidelity of the time wrought no repose in him. He did not accept unbelief indifferently, quietly as a philosophy; he fled to it as a poor defense against belief, as a refuge from the bitter rebukes and endless strifes of his own restless spirit. He was intensely immoral because he felt so intensely the moral law, and so struggled to break his way through it. He could not for a moment overlook or forget it. Mere stupidity, mere brutishness and mere speculation were alike impossible to him. He took the fears of unbelief, the extinguished hopes of materialism, home to a high poetic temperament, that to its very core revolted against them, and could only have been assuaged, lifted, inspired by pure and profound belief. From the strife about him for social liberty he gathered little save more wind for the flame of his own passions. With the restraints of liberty he had no sympathy, and was only once blessed by its spirit, when helped for a brief period by the Greek revolution into a more generous and objective life.

The intense, passionate nature of Byron, while it was the propelling force of his art, yet robbed him of that large, catholic success which his lively wit, fruitful imagination, and quick intuition of beauty seemed to promise. It narrowed down his percep-

tions of character, and at the same time perverted
them. His ideal man and his ideal woman stand
over against each other, complements in passion,
but alike false to the true nobility of their sex.
On the one side are pride, strength, disobedience,
indulgence ; on the other concession, devotion,
the smothered fires of a soul that cannot escape
beyond the heat of its own narrow, intense, blind
life, but must needs, with none of the rallying
forces of self-respect, smoulder and perish in it.
There is in the one no patience, no restraint, no
magnanimity, no nobility; in the other there is no
worthiness, no independence, nothing holy and
uncontaminate. The poems of Byron are comparatively lost, by the lie which, hidden in his own
soul, so often reappears in them ; by the futile
and ever renewed effort to unite beauty, first to
license and then to the sullen, resentful moods of
impotent rebellion. His wit, as in Don Juan, thus
plays phosphorescent about things dead and corrupt ; his pathos springs suddenly up with no sufficient nourishment in the worth of the characters
that call it forth ; his yearnings for that which is
better are only regrets, momentary rents in hurry-
ing, wind-sped clouds. His cry is a single, plain-
tive, despairing note, as of a bird lost in the
darkness :

> " No more, no more, oh never more on me
> The freshness of the heart can fall like dew,
> Which out of all the lovely things we see
> Extracts emotions beautiful and new."

Don Juan, the work on which Byron squandered

his ripest intellectual strength, lacks most of all the beauty of character, the coherence of healthy, wholesome life. It more than any other of his poems is breaking out everywhere with his own corrupt, defiant spirit, hastening on to death. The flowers grow, but they are passion flowers, and we catch the rank odors of the saturated soil that bears them. The mischief which his own nature wrought in him is seen in this increased distortion of his works, in the intense resentment it called forth in him against any restraint or criticism, and in his personal antipathies to those of a nobler spirit.

The immorality of Byron's works consists superficially in their licentiousness ; far more deeply and pervasively in his confounding lawlessness with strength, accepting proud despair as the portion of the soul, and presenting pleasure as the bait by which free, noble spirits are caught and hopelessly entangled in the net-work of malign world-forces, the providences of a demiurge. He had no power to perceive the beauties of faith, or the loving guidance and strength of the God of the faithful. Byron is fitted to captivate bold, active, restless, unreflective spirits, who have not yet exhausted the fountains of their physical life, and can still give a dash of freedom and a relish of appetite to rebellion ; but the sober, disciplined, deepened, dispassionate mind finds increasingly less to love and to cherish in him.

"The Byron-fever is in fact a disease belonging to youth, as the whooping-cough to childhood— working some occult good no doubt in the end. It has its origin, perhaps, in the fact that the poet

makes no demand either on the intellect or the conscience, but confines himself to friendly intercourse
with those passions whose birth long precedes that
of choice in their objects—whence a wealth of emotion is squandered. It is long before we discover
that far richer feeling is the result of a regard bent
on the profound and the pure." *

Byron himself is the best antidote to his works.
That life and those poems put side by side, and
read together, are a chapter in ethics which few can
mistake. As the rocket is driven aloft by the reaction, the spurn of its own spiteful forces, and, reaching the upper air, explodes in yellow, purple and lurid
light, so Byron forced his way upward with scorn
and repulsion, flamed out in wild, explosive, brilliant excesses, and disappeared in darkness made
only the more palpable.

> " Man's a strange animal, and makes strange use
>   Of his own nature."

As Scott was the poet of the chivalrous temper
of the past, so was Byron the poet of the wild, passionate, lawless one of the present—a bold, appetitive spirit, spurning resentfully at restraint. Each
added genius to a constitutional tendency of society,
and secured a large following.

Coleridge and Wordsworth were closely united
by friendship, by an agreement tempered by a
diversity of tastes, and by a union of sentiments.
They both accepted with the generosity and impet-
uosity of youth the new hopes of liberty; and both,
as years ripened the understanding, came to see

* Alec Forbes, by MacDonald.

more clearly its conditions and limitations. Southey
shared with them this oscillation between the enthusiasm of sentiment and the caution of judgment,
the latter gaining with him early and easily the
mastery.

Coleridge possessed the most undeniable and
wide-ranging genius of any one of his time. Its
practical force, its sustained insight were greatly
restricted by a vacillation, a weakness of will, which
loosened his powers, and lost for them their true
pivot of revolution, their smoothness and harmony
of action. His naturally enervate temper was enhanced in early life by the lack of vigorous disci-
pline, and later by an indulgence in opium. He
thus fell into pitiful imbecility, taxing for support
the charity of friends, and craving from the charity
of Heaven a forgiveness that issued in no new
strength. Thus natural gifts so varied and so great
that they only called for patient and wise use to
put him among the few great masters of men were
humbled and in a measure lost.

Philosophy, a philosophy that sprang from and
expressed the insight of the soul, was the seat of
his strength; but philosophy was so united in him
to a creative fancy, that as many remember the
poet as the sage. These two even-handed gifts
made him the very best of critics; and appreciative,
suggestive criticism became a third endowment.
The influence of these three gifts was enhanced
by their harmony, and by his unusual conversational
powers; or better, perhaps, by his ability to impress
himself upon others in harangues which took the

place of conversation. If what Carlyle says of him be partially true, "I have heard Coleridge talk, with eager, musical energy, two stricken hours, his face radiant and moist, and communicate no meaning whatsoever to any individual of his hearers, certain of whom, I for one, still kept eagerly listening in hope, "* the force and inspiration of the man wh could hold, and, on these hard conditions, sufficiently reward, superior men, ever reluctant to be mere listeners, are only the more apparent. He says farther, "Coleridge's talk and speculation was the emblem of himself; in it as in him a ray of heavenly inspiration struggled, in a tragically ineffectual degree, with the weakness of the flesh and blood."†

The centre of his philosophy was a stern resistance to materialism, a reintroduction of spiritual intuitions, a reassertion of the reason. This gave new faith to his love of freedom, new devotion to his religious belief, deeper insight to his criticism, a loftier inspiration to his poetry.

An enervate will, and that too in connection with an indulgence that was undisguised sin before the keen, rebuking eye of his own soul, was especially fatal to the upward, poised, independent flight that belonged to his spiritual temperament. All are struck alike by the fragmentary character of his work. His great poems are comparatively brief; some of them odes that could receive form under a single, undivided impulse, the subtly woven words

* Introduction to Coleridge's Poems. Little & Brown.
† Ibid.

springing at once from the emotion, as "the flame from its feeding oil." This "sublime man," as Carlyle calls him, possessed of "a prophetic or magician character," to whose actual endowments men were ready to add a halo of mystery, wielded an influence quite beyond the direct results of his works. He gave truths, easily lost to the English mind, a fresh lighting up, and startled with them, when he did not disperse, the shadows of materialism. It is minds like his that furnish turning points of thought. By them we pass a headland, or double a continent, and find new waters and new tracts before us. If we are tempted profoundly to regret the dislocated products of such a mind, the vast fields of broken ice-floe that it sends drifting by, we are yet proportionately impressed by the brilliant lights; the strange, weird forms; and deep, exhaustless and inscrutable forces, that are here. Coleridge, as Coleridge, appeals to the thoughts and imagination hardly less than if he had carefully planned and perfectly finished his works. The quick view that we catch from some bold Alpine summit finds the foil of its wealth, its fascination to memory, in the very indistinctness and haste that make us wish to return to it. Carlyle acknowledges with too little appreciation the great fragmentary thoughts that fell from the lips of Coleridge. They sometimes found the richest soil, and brought forth their one hundred-fold. Wordsworth, DeQuincey, Hazlitt presented minds with whom a suggestion was a harvest.

Wordsworth is in important respects the foremost poet of the period under consideration. He

gave with deliberate purpose through a long life
his undivided and growing powers to his own favorite pursuit. He coveted success, not so much as
an ambition as a thirst of the soul for high spiritual
insight and an effective, sufficient rendering of the
things seen.

> "Blessings be with them—and eternal praise,
> Who gave us nobler lives, and nobler cares—
> The poets, who on earth have made us heirs
> Of truth and pure delight by heavenly lays!
> Oh! might my name be numbered among theirs,
> Then gladly would I end my mortal days."

Wordsworth is among the most voluminous of
English poets,—the omnipresence of the poetic sentiment was an article of his creed and practice—
and none of them have more decided or original
characteristics. He was the centre of the Lake
School, a name that sprang from local connections,
and turned, in its application, more on personal
friendship and sympathy, a general concurrence of
feeling, than on a single theory of art shared by its
members. Southey was most nearly united to
Wordsworth in critical views, but between their
poems there is no close agreement. The ability of
Wordsworth, his steadfastness and faithfulness, won
him pre-eminence in the new movement; and with
these, other causes concurred. He announced a
theory of poetry, and gave it in his works extreme
illustration. He suffered the harshest criticism,
and slowly conquered bitter, dominant prejudice by
expansion in his own line of effort under his own
conceptions. This forcing growth against the ac-

cepted canons of art, laid down by the acknowledged
critics of the day, like Jeffrey, and under the contempt of popular poets, like Byron, drew attention
and sympathy to the independent power that
achieved it. Wordsworth has hence been assigned
a position that hardly belongs to him. He has
been looked on as founding a school of poetry, giving birth to a new era, rather than as one who best
embodied and most completely presented a spirit
that had in various forms, for years, been gaining
ground in English literature. Though not the first,
he is the highest, and most central, summit in the
mountain range skirting the new realm of poetry;
and stands disclosed, quiet, serene, eternal in the
clear transforming light of an earnest, reflective imagination.

It is not altogether strange that Wordsworth
should have met with severe criticism. His theory
of art was not well put; some of its illustrations, as
The Idiot Boy, were extreme; while criticism, bur-
dened with a large inheritance of conventional opinions and conventional praise descending from Pope,
his cotemporaries and subsequent admirers, was
still inclined to the cold, formal and preceptive in
art. The pith and truth of the theory of Wordsworth, as shown by his poems, are found in the fact,
that all forms of life have in them poetical elements,
and require only a sensitive, intuitive presentation
for their disclosure. Herein lies the genius of
Wordsworth, that with intense, pervasive feeling;
quick, penetrative sympathy, he is able to move
among all objects, touching the lowest in human

life, and those in nature most remote from ordinary
insight, and bear everywhere with him an inspiration and a rendering that disclose their hold upon
the human soul, their share in the problems of the
universe. This is what he has actually done, and
this we may well believe is what he intended to do.
His own statement, however, of his principles of
art is not convincing, and seems to have been
shaped in part by contradiction, by resistance to
the coldly elevated and critical spirit that had gone
before him, and whose influence was still predominant. He described "his object as being to ascer-
tain how far the purposes of poetry might be ful-
filled by fitting to metrical arrangement a selection
of the real language of men, in a state of vivid sensation." Herein he failed to do full honor to the
appreciation, the interpretation, that always abide
with the poet, and which so distinguish him from
other men. "He goes out of his way to be attacked."* How easily Wordsworth's omnivorous
poetic fancy invites ridicule, the criticism of Taine
suffices to show.

Wordsworth affords an admirable illustration of
a new tendency in art, mounting rapidly into full
power, and henceforth made dominant, by virtue
of its contact with one soul in which it lights and
feeds the flames of genius. An influence before
but dimly perceived became speedily enthroned,
and gave a date for a new intellectual dynasty.

The social and political forces were at first as
keenly felt by Wordsworth as the poetical ones,

* Landor's Conversations.

though his own strong spirit tempered them to moderation as he slowly and painfully struggled back to the footing of experience and faith. His placid, thoughtful and retiring disposition could hold no terms with fruitless and bloody revolution. He loved too well the peaceful promise of nature and society. He thus prays in behalf of his own nation :

> " Oh that with soul-aspirings more intense,
> And heart-humiliations more profound,
> This people, long so happy, so renowned
> For liberty, would seek from God defense
> Against far heavier ill—*the pestilence*
> Of Revolution, impiously unbound ! "

How diverse this from the feeling which had led him earlier to exclaim of the French Revolution :

> " O pleasant exercise of hope and joy !
> For mighty were the auxiliars which then stood
> Upon our side, we who were strong in love !
> Bliss was it in that dawn to be alive,
> But to be young was very heaven ! "

It is not easy for us fully to understand the darkening down of the entire spiritual heavens incident to the bitter disappointments of blind, futile progress, which has served to express the passions of men, rather than to establish their convictions. It is not easy to get again the foothold of faith after the shock and paralysis attendant on the overthrow of too sanguine hopes. Wordsworth was a reflective, meditative poet. It was not the form and garniture of the world that he loved to present, but its emotional force, its suggestions to the spiritual nature. It was not action in human life, but its under-current of sentiment, that he delineated. He is especially undramatic, for it is not the surface-play of events that occupies him, but the secret nurture of the soul, its half blind responses to the circumstances that try it. Wordsworth above all other poets calls for a spiritual sympathy of his readers with himself. On this condition only we pass with him those invisible lines which divide mere facts from the Elysian fields of the poetic fancy. Says Taine, "When I shall have emptied my head of all worldly thoughts, and looked up to the clouds for ten years to refine my soul, I shall love this poetry. Meanwhile, the web of imperceptible threads by which Wordsworth endeavors to bind together all sentiments and embrace all nature, breaks in my fingers; it is too fragile; it is a woof of woven spider web, spun by a metaphysical imagination, and tearing as soon as a solid hand tries to touch it." *

Ought not Taine to have asked, How came this man to spring out of English mud and English utilities? Genius, even in an English soul, breaks, in a troublesome way, the cobweb threads of a too ingenious philosophy. Tenuous as are the connections of Wordsworth's poetry, they are too strong for the reasoning of Taine.

To the great personal forces represented in Scott, Byron, Coleridge, Wordsworth, there are to be added others of diverse and somewhat inferior power, Crabbe, Southey, Moore, Keats, and above all, Shelley. In vigor and boldness of poetic fac-

* History of Eng. Literature, vol ii. p. 262.

ulties, Shelley is scarcely surpassed by any. **No** region was too remote, too ethereal for his sustained and sweeping flight, no path was so slight or sinuous as to be altogether lost under his searching eye. In him the imaginative impulses were in excess; he felt commonplace too weakly, and returned to it, and its ally, common-sense, too rarely. He was instantly lost to the slow, plodding steps of judgment. Above all the poets of his time, he was fired with revolutionary hopes, and struggled resentfully on toward the better times which the successive stages of change served only to postpone. He found himself at war with religion, with society, and government, a war prompted by the compass and humanity of his sentiments, and a resistance to restraints whose ground he failed to comprehend. Shelley needed only more sober and solid thought, a mind ballasted by more common and cheap qualities, to have moved among the highest. The poetic elements super-abounded, and allowed him to be driven before a whirlwind of sentiment, which found in him magnificent, though too often wild, utterance. What his biographer says of Landor,—who also deserves more attention than he receives — was equally true of Shelley; though the one was impelled more by will, and the other by affection: "What was wanting in his books and in his life was submission to some kind of law." *

The beauty of his poetry never quite covers with its verdure the volcanic forces at work under

* Life of Landor, p. 676.

it. A sense neither of safety and sufficiency nor
of quiet hope settles down on his landscape.
We are dealing with agencies that work with
terrific energy, nor always with a sober fore-
sight of results. One cannot but love Shelley,
and delight in him. The generosity and elevation of his sentiments cleanse him from the soil
that attaches to the selfish passions of Byron.
We can but wish that a safe substratum of
thought had upheld and nourished all this splendor of imagination, this enthusiasm of soul. He
thus states his own purpose in his preface to
The Revolt of Islam :

"It is an experiment on the temper of the
public mind, as to how far a thirst for a hap-
pier condition of moral and political society sur-
vives, among the enlightened and refined, the
tempests which have shaken the age in which
we live. I have sought to enlist the harmony
of metrical language, the ethereal combinations
of the fancy, the rapid and subtle transitions of
human passion, all those elements which essentially compose a poem, in the cause of liberal
and comprehensive morality ; and in the view of
kindling within the bosom of my readers a virtuous enthusiasm for those doctrines of liberty
and justice, that faith and hope in something
good, which neither violence nor prejudice can
ever totally extinguish among mankind."

Who can fail to sympathize with this daunt-
less effort of a noble mind, though it misses the
conditions of success, or breaks restively through

them when they lie before it? Shelley was as foreign to the English temper on one side, as Wordsworth on another, and both must find interpretation and honor in the depths of natures akin to their own. Such men bring to us the trying test of appreciation, by which we define our place among men, and settle what in heaven and earth lies open to us.

LECTURE XI.

THE last three centuries, the seventeenth, eighteenth and nineteenth, have each opened with decided literary tendencies. The first dawned in the clear, growing light of the Elizabethan era, when the early forces of our literature were in full play ; the second came forward with less fascination, with more tame and tempered light, as our Augustan age of art ; and the third restored us again to the impassioned powers and dewy freshness of our national growth, broke once more in a day of creative energy, clothed anew with beauty and with strength. The middle of this century, which opened so auspiciously, it is too early to characterize in its relation to those periods that have gone before and those that are to follow. Not till the issues of an age are seen, can we certainly say for what it is making ready, in what direction it is modifying the life it has received. Certainly, these midway years of the present century, are not distinctively creative in art, as compared with those that preceded them. They seem rather to indicate a gentle subsidence of those inventive powers which so exultingly lifted the national mind in Scott, Byron, Wordsworth.

The present may prove the slope and expansion of these high summits into beautiful and arable plains, to be joined again on their farther side to rival mountain ranges ; or it may be, so wakeful is the critical feeling with us, but the opening of one of those prairie stretches of great fertility and slight diversity, consoling the appetites rather than inflaming the imagination of men.

The present is a prose rather than a poetic era, and this by the bulk, central body and quality of its productiveness. There is, perhaps, more poetry written to-day than ever before, and much of it is very good ; but there are very few poets who command the attention of the English nations,—those distinct or united nationalities, that have laid down liberal boundaries of present and future power in every quarter of the globe. It is difficult, indeed, to send a tidal wave along these conjoint, mobile lines of language and literature, spreading through every branch of the great English people, and few are doing it. Questions of science, new theories, new fictions, chase each other more rapidly around the English globe, than new poems.

While, however, it is a prose period, one of very diversified and very busy inquiry, of sharp and destructive criticism, of bold theory, and of practical reform everywhere, and especially among English-men, cisatlantic and transatlantic, it can better be considered, waiting for its final literary relations to disclose themselves, as one of diffusion. In this particular, it is broadly and nobly distinguished from every age that has gone before it. This very startling fact of diffusion, this spread of richly-laden waters over every cultivated field, this leaving a deposit of thought, not merely along conventional lines in rich river bottoms, but over the scant and remote acres of the poor, may have little interest for mere literati, but is of profound concernment to the philanthropist. Above all ages, our own deserves honor for this enlargement of thought, this scattering everywhere of some scant measure at least of the treasures of literary art. From this practical side, we shall chiefly consider this practical period, this period, that halts a little in the merely intellectual march of the race, that it may send its voice abroad and backward, gathering on every side enlarged numbers into the fellowship of its strength, and waiting to compact its ranks, before it renews its advance.

The scientific is, on the whole, the predominant phase of thought with us. Philosophy suffers disparagement ; historical, religious and social dogmas are kept in perpetual agitation and irritation by the bearings on them of the scientific spirit, its theories and its facts. This science reaches the people in inventions and discoveries, in innumerable lines of industrial improvement. It is not content, however, with this ; popularized in a great variety of ways, it seeks and everywhere finds an enlarged and enlarging audience. This cannot be called an age of oratory, for the same reason that it is not a poetic one ; but certainly, no period

ever beheld so many who have sought the general
ear for purposes of instruction. If the resounding
oration has been displaced by the more modest
lecture, this truly has been attended with results
as benign and as far-reaching as have ever fallen
to oratory. It has become the office of speaking
more frequently to present and expound the truth
than to enforce it, and into this branch of instruction men spring up everywhere by tens, by
hundreds, by thousands.

The love of facts, near and remote, that belongs
to science, shows itself also in history. Historical
research, criticism and composition, have been
greatly enlarged in the present period. The philosophy of history, the leading forces that have
wrought in it, have been diligently sought into by
such men as Hallam, Buckle, Lecky, Stanley, Tylor,
while history in the common acceptance of the
term has been voluminously written with more than
wonted insight into the connection of events, and
more than wonted wisdom in their selection. Kings
and conquerors have ceased to occupy the entire
historic stage, and the condition, customs and opinions of the masses of men, claim their share of
attention. The list of historical writers has never
been larger, or indicated better perception or more
power, either here or in England, than during the
forty years which have just passed away. Macaulay, Grote, Arnold, Merivale, Rawlinson, Milman,
Mahon, Froude, Kinglake, Freeman, Bancroft,
Prescott, Motley, constitute but leading figures in
the laborious group.

The two departments of literature, however,
which have had the widest popular influence, and
are most characteristic of the period as one of diffusion, are the novel and the periodical.   Gathering
the last in its manifold forms under one term expressing the most typical member of the group, we
may say, the novel and the newspaper are the mos
peculiar and influential of the literary forces at work
at the present time.   The novel is the most purely
artistic prose production, and is most closely allied
to history, also with us particularly ambitious of
literary excellence.   The novel adds poetic to prose
qualities.   The creative faculties are uppermost in
it, since it calls out and orders events in the strict
development of a subjective purpose, in the expression and execution of a conception.   The poem is
not more plastic, does not more wait on the mould-
ing touch of the thought which creates it, than does
the novel.

As primarily and immediately does the novel
deal with the emotions.   All emotions, under every
variety of condition, fall to it, and one supreme emotion, one supreme sympathy, waits habitually upon
it, that of love.   All that can be made of human life
in its conjoint and individual unfolding, in its serial
forces, is open to the novelist ; and none, therefore,
can search more deeply the human spirit, put
together more constructively its passions and impulses, or trace more consecutively and freely its
types of character, the varieties and issues of its
action.   No field can be more free, more interest-

ing, closer to the human heart, and to human life than that traversed by the novel.

While it has free access to these highest elements of poetry, while it is charged with no cumbersome, didactic duty, but can hold itself open to the allurements of pleasure, it is still possessed of much more liberty than the poem. Criticism, theory, insight, observation of every sort can be woven into the narrative, making its progress instructive and brilliant. It is not held to the close conditions of the drama. It can talk of, as well as through, its characters. The novelist, as a third party, can interpret, criticise, open up on unexpected sides his personages, cast on them, and bring out of them every variety of side-light. At all events, this is the style of the English novel, and we hold it to be the true liberty of this prose poetry. The novelist is not bound to evolve, in and under his characters and their actions, his entire thought, leaving the reader, as before a painting, to penetrate and unfold the conception as he is able. The novelist stands on more intimate terms than this with his audience. He is present in his own person, in his own studio, and may throw out such lively hints, or give such clues of thought as he thinks best, provided always that he keeps all eyes directed to the characters delineated, and unites in an easy, living way, every sentiment to their development. This personality of the writer and progress with us from one to another picture in his art-gallery, constitute a large part of the attraction of the novel. It moves in an easier, more familiar and less commanding way than the poem, and has a thousand chances offered to say what is uppermost. Not merely in preface and initial chapters, but in any moment of leisure, it takes up its readers on familiar terms of cheerful gossip, and binds them to itself with new links of sympathy.

Works of fiction may be divided into romances and novels. The two differ from each other in the element of truth. The typical novel has this complete. It adheres to the line of characters it has chosen to delineate, with thorough and exact representation, striving to make them clearly drawn counterparts of those real persons whom they represent. The romance lacks truth, and that in the worst of all ways, by insensible departures, by excessive coloring, by glaring and false lights. The romance chooses its characters from remote, unfamiliar quarters, gives them a fanciful elevation in power and prowess, surrounds them by novel circumstances, verges on the supernatural or passes its limits, and makes much of fictitious sentiments, such as those which characterized chivalry. The poor, sensational novel has points of close union with the earlier romance, represented by Walpole in The Castle of Otranto.

It is against the romance element, ever likely to appear in historical novels, as it appears in history itself, when it runs like a child after the glittering march and sonorous sounds of war, that most of the moral objections to works of fiction hold. Unreality, giddy show, easy victory, the sensuous gliding on of a dream, are, indeed, most enervating to the moral nature, and evaporate the sweet, genuine sentiments of the heart in a dry, hot, peevish and indolent atmosphere. The novel, so far as it adheres to truth, and treats of life broadly, descending to the lowest in grade, deeply and with spiritual forecast, seeing to the bottom, is not only not open to these objections, but rather calls for the reverse commendation.

The novel is divisible into two general kinds, the pictorial and the ethical. Pictorial novels may be subdivided into four kinds: those which deline-ate, under historic characters, the traits of a nation; those which give renewed life to a period present or remote; those which present a particular rank in society; or a particular calling in life: or historical, descriptive, social and professional novels. Ethical novels may be divided in two classes: those which enforce some especial reform; and those which offer a general study of character: or reformatory and creative novels. No novel is purely of one kind. They are classified by predominant features. The most strictly historic novel will still present a study of characters, and may offer a good epitome of the manners of a particular period or of a certain rank. Yet most works of fiction are constructed under such definite aims as to assign them readily, by predominant tendency, to one or other of these classes. We see from what quarter the light enters the picture, the rays come in aslant from left or right.

Of historic novels, many of the works of Walter Scott, as Kenilworth, afford an example Of novels presenting a particular period, or descriptive novels, the Hypatia of Kingsley offers an illustration. Of the social novel, bringing forward a given grade of social life, Mansfield Park and Emma, by Miss Austen, may be adduced as instances. Of professional novels, having also a national and historical cast, we find examples in the nautical tales of England, as those of Marryat. Pictorial novels have all an historic character, though the word, historical, is more strictly applied to those works of fiction in which historic characters appear, thus giving the closest attachment of the narrative to history. This use of one or more historic names, may, after all, be a secondary feature, and the real historic element be found in the care and exactness with which imaginary facts reflect in their form real ones. This they may do very imperfectly under the most familiar historic names, and very perfectly without such names. That novel is truly historic which puts us in living contact with a given phase of national life. The pictorial novel is always primarily presentative in its character whichever of the forms it takes.

The ethical novel belongs to a higher class than the pictorial novel. It presupposes this, and adds something to it. It seeks historic truth, but more than historic truth. It renders life, and at the same time renders in it some of its deeper lessons. It translates it into an earnest spiritual language. It is not content with facts, near or remote, with living and veritable persons. Like advanced history, it hankers after the philosophy of these facts, and gives

12*

them a definite drift in solution of some of its own
theories, or ideals, or impressions of society. When
this is done in a limited way, in the enforcement of
a particular phase of progress, we have the reformatory novel, of which the Caleb Williams of Godwin, a writer very deeply imbued with the liberal
and progressive spirit, is an early example; and
Uncle Tom's Cabin by Mrs. Stowe, a recent one.
The narrative, however life-like and real, is made
to offer a constant mirror to certain conditions of
society for the sake of the censure and the sentiments thus elicited. A reformatory and satirical
purpose thus runs through the works of Dickens,
sufficient, in some instances, to classify the novel, as
in Bleak-House and Nicholas Nickleby.

The second ethical novel, the highest novel,
that of character, makes a study of human life, not
so definitely in the interest of any one reform, but
penetratively and profoundly, in view of its many
issues. This novel is most strictly ethical, as is all
composition which deals searchingly with the human
heart. It cannot fail to have a decided moral flavor.
Dombey and Son by Dickens, Vanity Fair by
Thackeray, Romola and Middlemarch by Mrs. Lewes, are illustrations. This ethical tendency, this pre-
dominance of character, human character, the seat
of moral life in its thousand phases, each as certainly ethical as it is rational, is the leading index
of power in the novelist.

All the kinds of fiction of which we have spoken
are good or bad, as they disclose discreetly and intuitively, under the drift of the writer's feeling, char-

acter. This is the crowning quality, and the novel
is poor without it. In whatever class, therefore,
the particular work of fiction may stand, it approaches this last class according to its excellence ;
and if no one feature is so predominant in it as this,
then it falls to this highest division. Thus, Romola
by Mrs. Lewes, though an historic novel in one aspect, and a descriptive one in another, is rather an
ethical novel, so pre-eminently is it a study of character, of human nature in its deep and permanent
bearings. To return to a former comparison, the
landscape, always the same, owes its transient ex-
pressions to the light and mist and clouds, the floating unbraided beams of morning, the intense, accumulated splendor of broken storm-clouds, or the
brilliant long-lined cirri of evening, fading, trem-
bling into night. If one of these effects is singled
out and strongly treated, it classifies the picture
more than the fields, woods, mountains, which lie
under this play of the heavens upon them. Yet,
there is always the scene itself to be studied, and
so presented, that while we have no hesitancy in
discerning the wonderful lights and shades at work
in it, these are all woven into the landscape itself,
and find their utterance through it.

A relatively cheap excellence in the novel, are
the surprises, doublings and rapid evolutions of the
plot. To be hurried on by events, and exhilarated
by the mere swiftness of the current as it glides into
the rapids, is a child's pleasure, and one that with-
draws the eye sensibly from those many beauties,
near and remote, which make the voyage profitable,

and cause it to linger in the memory as if we had floated down a stream on whose enchanted shores were grouped, with strange disclosure and divination, things past and things to come. A novel of adventure is a boy-book, and when we hasten on under the excitement of a story, a temper of weak and boyish curiosity overtakes us. The ethical novel implicates its events in its characters, and gives them intensity, as we impart meaning to common words, by the impulse put in them. The great novelist finds a tendency to cling close to ordinary life for it is events like these that are daily unlocking the souls of men, and startling circumstances serve to divert attention from character, to confuse, prejudice and overbear its development. The child, playing by the pond, scarcely thinks of the wind and the water in their constant fellowship and wonderful interplay, so interested is he in the immediate fortunes of his little vessel, its freighting, its voyage, and its wreck. In like manner, to mere sport, does the feeble novelist reduce the events of life, starting his characters, like mimic boats, with rudders fixed for the farther shore, righting them with the power of a superior deity under the squalls and mishaps of the voyage, and directing the eye always to the outside action of these empty nondescripts, and the gallant way in which they reach the predetermined port.

There is no more profound, philosophical and moral study than that of the novelist, when he conceives a character, puts it in action and into interaction with other spiritual entities, like and unlike itself; sets, as it were, the varied currents of physical, social, intellectual forces, good and evil, at play upon it ; and then strives to follow out results, not make them, as they flow from the double and complex causation of the outer and inner world, of the heavy yet mobile waters of life, acted upon by the invisible winds that come stealing forth from unknown spiritual realms. It is only that genius which intuitively reads, which intuitively and reflectively unfolds, characters and events, that can watch over its creations, and make them disclose to duller minds all the forces, above and below, that determine their final haven. It is because this work is often done in so childish a way, in so false and incomplete a way, in so wicked a way, that the novel suffers such deserved censure, and constitutes a dangerous, wasteful, or vulgar literary element.

No period has equalled our own in this department. Its names stand among the first. This is the era of fiction; Dickens, Thackeray, Bulwer, Charlotte Brontë, Mrs. Lewes, are not likely soon to be equalled. The creations of Dickens, outlined with a few strong strokes, almost of caricature, united to our sympathies by the abounding humor and humanities of the author; the more carefully delineated, but less liked and less familiar personages of Thackeray, often built up under the cold criticism of the writer, rarely evoked under his affection; and the men and women whom George Eliot brings before us, full of physical and intellectual life, a life that begets appetites, passions, noble impulses, lending itself to every variety of incentive, and disclosing many secret springs of conduct ; these are not soon to be forgotten.

The novel, moreover, is interesting as the field in which woman has fought her first literary battle, and won her first victory. Here, she stands with the foremost.   The intuitions of her nature, her quick sympathies, and the lively, searching activity into which these are called by the daily conditions of her being, have made this with her a favorite method of composition.

The newspaper, like the novel, mingles freely good and evil in its literary results, with even a more decided advantage in general knowledge. The quarterly and the daily stand at the two extremes of the periodical press as regards time, and equally so as regards matter and circulation. The dailies discuss those current themes which attach to the hour, and few of which extend beyond it ; and present the ephemeral news, the mere sheen and dust of the marching host.   The quarterlies cling to the abstract, theoretical, general ; keep thought alive, and return often to those social, philosophical, religious principles which are built together as the framework of society.   The periodical assumes an evanescent or permanent value in proportion as it approaches the one extreme or the other.   The periods of gestation in the animal kingdom are scarcely more indices of varying strength than are the times of return which belong to serials. The highest literary influence falls, perhaps, to the monthly, equally removed from the slow ponderous movement of the review and the rapid execution of the journal.

The startling facts concerning the periodical press, are quantity, and, this being considered, quality and rate of increase. Though the review dates back to the opening of the century, and the daily to a period a little earlier, the rate of increase has been so accelerated, that the influence of the newspaper press may be said to belong distinctively to the last forty years, In the United States, the circulation was in 1850 twenty-fold that of 1810; in the next ten years it more than doubled, and reached in 1860 an annual aggregate of nearly a thousand million copies. The years intervening between this period and the present, have shown a corresponding growth. Every age and class and calling, and scientific and literary taste, have been addressed, each with its own appropriate publications. Our time not only stands alone, it is a constant miracle to itself in its productiveness. It swarms with the ephemera of literature, and only the happiest and most diversified mechanical art makes possible this creation and diffusion of printed matter. The steam-press is a royal instrument, and right royally gives to the four winds all that the busy mind of man can furnish or crave.

Though there is much to be deprecated in the press, though it imparts a whirl and dizzy rapidity to life otherwise unknown, a gossipy and trivial character to daily thought ; though it drags to light much that should be left in darkness, awakens a prurient curiosity, and confounds notoriety with fame, yet as an educating, quickening, propelling power, it offers the most peculiar and pleasing feat· ure of our time.

It especially favors the discussion of social, reformatory questions. These questions, rife at the opening of our century, have multiplied with its succeeding years. In minor and graver forms, they are constantly coming and going. The newspaper press offers the best facilities for the rapid evolution and solution and disposal of these problems. Attack and defence, assertion and denial, are immediate and from all sides. The entire community is sought out by these organs of the press, and held to constant deliberation on every question of general interest. It at once receives from every variety of temper, of interest and of power a corresponding form of presentation. The substance of its facts and theories is rapidly sifted out, and the results, as far as they are practical and tangible, speedily reached. The grades of intellectual insight represented in these periodicals, from the confident, hasty and bold journal, to the cautious, conservative, thoughtful review, favor this result; each according to the light that is in it, taking up, in one way or another, the discussion. The effect has been, that in England and America, where the press is rapid, free, prolific, social questions have lost most of their revolutionary power. Any theory, however radical, however great and urgent the interests involved in it, may be propounded and considered without endangering or loosening the ties of society and government. The latest reform in America, which has cost mobs and revolutions, was that of anti-slavery, and this seems to have cleared finally the atmosphere of those storm elements which could not rest till they had filled the heavens from side to side with the roar of their ineffectual thunder.

In the United States, the census of 1860 gave the following ratio, expressing the relation of periodicals to each other, according to their avowed purpose. Eighty per cent. were devoted to politics, seven per cent. to religion, seven to literature, and six to miscellaneous objects. As politics admits of a great variety of secondary ends, the proportion of attention devoted to it is not as great as it seems to be. The political journal universally unites to its partisan purposes the duties of a newspaper; and these, save in the crises of politics, are by far its greater labor. It is the medium for the rapid treatment of all passing questions of general interest, whether of a scientific, religious or social nature.

This portion of the press, therefore, more than any other, indicates the force held in constant readiness to circulate theories, chronicle pertinent facts, report and enlarge discussion, and in every way keep the public mind simmering and seething till the moral power of a topic is exhausted. Such are the physical and intellectual appliances which a free press offers to social progress, and, as a result, ten years are frequently more fruitful in England and the United States of growth, than whole centuries of an earlier *régime*. These two countries owe their general exemption from bloody revolution, and that in connection with rapid development, to nothing more than to a free, pervasive press, drawing the innocuous thunderbolt from every political cloud.

The most delicate questions of political policy, social police, commercial regulation, of education, of religion, and the adjustments of law to exceptional territorial conditions, as in Ireland, are constantly before the people of England, and peacefully reaching with each year, a safer, more just and philanthropic solution. So powerfully have this diffusion of intelligence through the press, this confronting, quickly and thoroughly, every measure with the results which social experience and philosophy are ready to assign it, this steady exposure of chronic, constitutional evil, wrought for progress, that, at no time, have the reformatory forces been compelled to heap up in sheer violence, and deal physical blows against the barriers of truth.

A second result of the newspaper press, is the vigor of public sentiment, issuing more and more in its soundness, sobriety and candor. Sprightly, racy, incisive, the daily and weekly press must be; this is with it a necessity of existence. Its best articles live on the hurried attention of a moment, are sandwiched in between courses at the breakfast-table, between items of business in an active morning, fall to the moments of transfer from place to place in lines of labor, or are caught by the weary eye at the close of a day's toil. To hold the time thus stolen, to improve this opportunity, which never returns, to impart a new, a sensible force to a mind already spinning on its axis like a whipped top, the editorial must be quick, decisive, energetic. This demand, so urgent, will not seem to tend at once to soundness and soberness of judgment, but we believe that these qualities are reached, and in a very high degree, by this active observation, this continuous and protracted meeting of the varying problems of many years.

A practical sobriety of judgment is a marked characteristic of the English and American mind, and we believe this is to be attributed, in large part, to the rapid business way in which it is called on to meet and answer the many questions of the hour. The most eccentric judgment, the most remote theories are found with those pre-eminently speculative. The mind dwelling by itself, suffering little contradiction, and giving optical clearness and enlargement to its own speculations, is the one that wanders farthest from soundness, breadth and sobriety of opinion. Extreme as are many of the statements current in the press, increasing insight and reliability of judgment fall to the veteran journalist. Like the business man of many years and many complexities, he hits easily and quickly on the practically safe course, on the average chances. The sins of extravagance and chimera come back so often and so surely to vex the guilty for their correction and the correction of the public ; journalism so strengthens the general memory, and so often confronts to-day with yesterday, the events of this year with the theories of last, that sobriety of opinion and practical prudence, become, more and more, the criteria of power. English journals are as remarkable for the sober, sure-footed principles they bring to every passing phase of life, as for the testy, vigorous way in which they are applied. Wisdom, which takes the form of a wide-reaching sagacity, is an offspring of journalism in an intelligent, thoughtful community. The severe and constant criticism to which journals are wont to subject each other tends to the same result, brings home every mistake, and furnishes the strongest motives for its correction.

This vigor and temperance of thought issue also in candor. Notwithstanding all the political abuse prevalent, no period has approached our own in candor. The numberless occasions for minor and larger differences, the rapid changes which public sentiment undergoes, and the many instances in which unexpected conclusions are reached, concur to secure caution of statement and candor of advocacy, whatever the truth defended. We doubt not, moreover, that truth is more sincerely coveted, and more quietly enforced now than hitherto, when the search for it is so free and uncontrolled, and the results to be reached by it in practical life, in society and in science, are so momentous. Vigor and candor and universality of inquiry, do all that can be done to call forth in English society the penetration and patience, the wise demand and wise concession, which leave the social elements to constant and peaceful readjustment ; nor do the malice, misrepresentation and falsehood of the hour, permanently affect the result.

Public sentiment, with whatever independence and soundness may belong to it, finds also, in times of social and political corruption, its most vigorous application to the prevalent evil through the press. Our own recent history has served to bring this redemptive power clearly forth. Exposures, censures, measures of redress, incentives to fresh effort have, in our struggle with municipal corruption and a wide-spread mal-administration in every branch of government, come chiefly from bold, earnest and independent journals. These have rallied and combined the people in each reformatory movement, and held the common mind steadily to the duty and labor of correction. Journalism, in some of its branches, seems likely to rank among the most incorruptible of public agents.

This pervasive power and freedom of the press make popular education effective, and at once soften and confirm the influence of the pulpit. Without this constant use and enlargement of knowledge, its mere rudiments are of little avail, and the machinery which most diligently awakens the popular mind on the greatest variety of themes, and in reference to the most practical interests, is that of the press. The people are kept in movement, are put to the use of their knowledge by the newspaper above all other agencies. Without this, the rudiments of education would be of small account.

The pulpit is liable to become circumscribed, rigid and conventional in its methods, except as the common mind is stimulated by other intellectual considerations, and brings a somewhat independent and critical temper to the Sabbath's discussions. The more stern and pressing the necessity laid on the pulpit for grounding and regrounding its strength in broad, rational and suggestive truth, the better for its permanent hold on the people. Its prescriptive power and privileges are its greatest enemies, those which put its common-sense, its vigilance and its piety to sleep. The pulpit is helped by the press as an independent rival power ; one that has its own standards and brings them to bear unsparingly.

The power of the press emanates chiefly from the great cities. These are the seats of its most influential organs ; not only does the metropolitan journal itself have the largest circulation, and that among the most intelligent, it exerts a strong influence on the weaker journals, scattered through the country. The press, therefore, is an assertion of the intellectual life and strength of cities, and a flowing of it forth over all parts of the land. The rusticity and deadness formerly found in country and village have largely disappeared, and the remote citizen is put in daily and living contact with the great seats of national activity. There is thus a pronounced circulation which carries the life-blood briskly through the body politic, equalizes the advantages of position, knits the nation together in knowledge, and imparts a common urbanity to its members.

It may be said against this and much more that may be urged for the periodical press, that it is in large part instrumental, that it is a great whispering gallery, carrying light things and scandalous things and wicked things a long way to many ears that might otherwise happily have missed of them; that the press is often but the tell-tale mechanism of disgraceful national gossip, that has nothing whatever to recommend it. Granting freely the truth of this and other accusations, still we must remember, that village-gossip is better than family-gossip, town-gossip is better than village-gossip, state-gossip than town-gossip, and national-gossip than either. Gossip loses something of its bane-fulness, obscurity and petty personality and private hate at every remove, and the country scandal of a low tavern is as much more concentrate, vicious and unclean than that of a news-room or county paper, as its range is more restricted. Simply to get men out of doors, away from the trite, stupid vulgarity of their cronies is a great gain. A national interest and the air of national intelligence make way for national truth, and these for universal truth.

It may also be urged against the press, that it gives ready circulation to vice. The accusation is most true. Such, however, is not the natural fellowship even of news, much less of popular dis-cussion. Pestilence may fly on the wings of morn-ing, but these more often distil the dewy fragrance of abounding life. Publicity is allied to light, and favors virtue. Vice, as a rule, has more to gain from concealment than exposure. It settles as a miasma in dark and secluded places, rather than on wind-swept slopes under open heavens.

The literary accusation is thought to lie strongly against newspaper influence, that it debauches language, introducing questionable words and street-phrases, passing them from one grade of literary recognition to another, till, forgetful of their low extraction, they are able in quiet effrontery to usurp good society. Here, too, there is truth in the statement; but the fact expressed by it has also its compensations, and by no means unimportant ones. Mere formal criticism, a cold conventional pedantry, the literary barrenness that overtakes letters from time to time, encounter resistance in the somewhat coarse yet vigorous popular appetite; and language is kept more flexible, lithe and nervous, than it otherwise would be. The purely literary tendency cannot safely be left to itself. It is too overwrought and finical. If it is wedded to creative power, well; but when this is wanting, its place may be supplied in part by the popular impulse, by the homely, changeable, but always lively service to which language is put in the newspaper world. As a matter of fact, recent years have been characterized by a large number of critical works on the English language. Some of our periodicals assiduously cultivate style, and many works of the present time could be pointed out, which show a high popular estimate of pure, simple composition. It remains to be shown that the language has really been injured by the freedom and license of the popular press. Departure at one point from the staidness of ordinary

labor no more incapacitates us to return with
relish to it at another, than does the raciness
of conversation unfit us for the formalities of
sober speech.

One pronounced tendency, which has been with
us through the entire century, is literary criticism,
bold, fearless criticism in all departments. This
is the fruit of the large and varied audience
which the press gives to every leading work.
The world's estimate of it, the discrepancies of
opinion which it calls forth, are as instant and
inevitable as the sympathetic approval or censure,
or the divided feeling that runs through the
gathered multitude, listening around a political
stand. Aside from systematic and direct criticism,
aside from that involved in discussion, there are
many popular writers who, with open, inquiring
eye, arraign topic after topic before them for
judgment. Our popular novelists are often of
this character, Dickens, George Eliot, George
MacDonald; and in more general literature, Carlyle,
Ruskin, Emerson. Such men are personified criticism, who search all they see.

The present diffusion of literature, so hopeful
a sign to philanthrophy, does, indeed, intensify the
struggle for literary life. In the tossing of the
multitudinous waves, much floats for a little that
is of slight value, and works that can ill be
spared are occasionally engulphed, overwhelmed
by things more trivial but more buoyant. Composite tendencies, the half-unconscious conjoint
movement of many minds, interlocked in their

13

life, take the place of individual leadership, and thus the conditions of progress are removed, more and more, from the hands of single men. Some pictorial interest, some individual development, may seem to be lost in this upheaval, this uprising of the masses, this general diffusion and stir of intellectual life; but an organic, social growth, that indicates a conquering force at work freely on many minds, is much the more stable, and, at bottom, much the more stimulating and spiritually interesting, development.

Moreover, the man of genius finds this compensation, that his works and words, though losing some of their primary, magical force, nevertheless enter into the final product with a more intellectual, free, conscious control than ever before. They drop like living things among living things, and though their direct, obvious sway is lost, the powers really evoked by them are more subtile, more pervasive, more permanent than hitherto. He who possesses the intelligent popular mind, holds the highest, deepest dominion that belongs to man. The night suits well with auroral flash, but the day, in its accumulated glories, floating the sun-beams on a sea of light, as, many and divergent, they lie along in tranquil strength, is a better image of social joy and life.

LECTURE XII.

THE present lecture will be devoted to English Philosophy, the undercurrent of belief that has upheld our intellectual life. England has been remarkable, on the one side, for a commercial, practical temper; on the other, for an earnest, independent, religious spirit. Assiduous traffic and remote, irresponsible colonization have co-existed in each later generation with earnest piety and zealous philanthropy. The philosophy of England has had one decided and growing tendency, compared with which every other development in mental science has been sporadic and transient This prevailing drift of speculation has been on the side of material, rather than spiritual interests; though the piety of the nation has steadily held it back in the national mind from the logical conclusions contained in it. Religion has waged a double war with greedy practical tendencies and stubborn speculative ones. The continuous growth of English philosophy has been materialistic, though the imputation has almost always been repudiated, and the last finishing deductions been forbidden.

(291)

Let us understand our terms. Idealism ultimately resolves all facts, phenomena, into mental states. This has found very little acceptance with the English. Realism divides, with the strongest lines, mental from physical facts, and believes that the mind has sufficient proof of both. This must needs be the underlying philosophy of religion and daily life, though it has rarely, aside from the Scottish school, found clear statement in England. Materialism, in its complete form, identifies mental with physical facts.

Few, in any country, have had the hardihood to state and defend it in this, its last position. From typical realism to typically complete materialism, there is a long and gentle slope, down which English philosophy will be found, from century to century, slowly sliding. When refusing with Spencer to accept either materialism or idealism, it is yet fully open to the charge of a materialistic tendency, because it is ever over laying the mind with the laws of matter; subduing its true spiritual domain, and subjecting it, as conquered territory, to the principles and forces of physical science. If this philosophy has not poured down headlong like a river into the morass and lowland, it has like a flexible, dissolving glacier, though seeming to hang on the hill-side, slowly crept hither. The glacier, with its gelid stream, turbid with the débris of rock it has ground to powder in their mountain fastnesses, forcing its slow way to the fields and flowers below, and disappearing as fast as it reaches their warmth and life, yet from its frozen, mobile centre thrusting forward new masses of ice, is a symbol of the unceasing push of materialism, grinding along its hard, tortuous way, among the beliefs and hopes of men.

This descent of thought with its reactions and exceptions, we wish to mark. We can only do this clearly, in so brief a space, by confining attention to some central point in philosophy, some especially significant feature, whose position shall serve to determine the changes going on about it. Such a feature we find in the origin of knowledge, the faculties involved in knowing. Realism must hold to two sets of powers, one, which receives the impressions of the physical world, and, as inseparable therefrom, of the mind also—since a sensation has a double aspect, pertaining both to mind and matter, involving both; and another, which lays hold of, analyzes and rationally divides these phenomena, and attributes each, under its own laws, to its appropriate sources. Thus the facts of a certain transaction, as, for instance, the firing of a building, are perceptively received. The mind then inquires, under ideas present to it by its own intuitive force, where it occurred, when it occurred, why it occurred, and the thought-process therein completes itself. Any falling off from this duality of the mind, its passivity and activity, its power to receive and to use independently, rationally, what it receives, is sure to result in idealism or materialism. If the active power prevails, and the mind is set constructively at its own mental facts, if the power of logical evolution is made to contain and overrule all others, till the material of thought is included in the forces of thought, we reach idealism. If passivity prevails, if the mind is made simply receptive under the play of sensations, then we steadily approach materialism. This has been the bias for centuries of the English school. It has busied itself in denying and belittling the active, original faculties of mind, and studiously developing those which turn on its sensational, receptive power. We shall make this idea—the source of our knowledge — the guiding light of our discussion. If we know whence our knowledge comes, we thereby define what it is, how far it reaches, and the nature of the issues it involves. If it come by the senses only, all talk of a spiritual world is delusive and visionary.

Sir Francis Bacon was the pivot on which English thought turned decidedly and finally to the physical world. The movement, as he proposed it, was necessary and most profitable, but, none the less, it was partial. He directed attention from deduction to induction, from the forms of thought to an inquiry into the very subjects and objects of thought. This effort favored most decidedly natural science. It sought a physical basis for knowledge, and opened the senses as its chief avenue. Seeing and hearing became the conditions for thinking, and the external world suddenly sprang forward in study as a rival to the mind. This tendency was altogether healthy, healthy for philosophy itself, for this, too, needed to be reinvigorated by a new hold on facts. It is set down by us as the initiative of materialism only because it, in turn, became excessive and one sided. All deductions to be fruitful must rest on exact statement, or exact observation ; and when the premises have become feeble, fluctuating, verbal, remote from the facts they seem to represent, then the conclusions are futile and visionary. The galvanic current is due to acids in instant action on metals, a fresh surface of the one must be exposed constantly to the dissolving agency of the other. So must thought and fact stand in constant, living reaction, if the evolved force is to be abundant and effective. The world in the time of Bacon had few well-established facts, its premises were mainly word-facts, and its reasoning, hence, idle word constructions, the chopping of logic, logomachy. Yet the bent, excellent in itself, which thought received from Bacon, was physical, and easily became opposed to true mental science, in which other elements play so important a part.

Hobbes is the next name in our sketch, and in him materialism is more declared. Indeed, he so far overstepped his time, and was so little able to support his extreme views, that his influence on philosophy lingered a good deal in rear of his own opinions. The points at which he gave a decided materialistic impulse to thought, were liberty and right. He denied the applicability of the notion of liberty to the will itself, and affirmed every man free, who is physically free to follow his own choices. The choice, itself, like other activities, is determined by the influences at play upon it. This, the often-repeated view of English philosophy, doubly favors materialism. It denies, in its most central acts, the original force, spontaneity of mind; traces into and through it those external, physical influences which act upon it; and beholds these simply in a new form in its out-going and on-going action. Thus the material current is no more stayed in its flow by man than by beast, by beast than by plant, by plant than by rock. Each modifies it, includes it, and is included by it in a more subtile way as we pass upward, that is all. This view also favors materialism, because the very idea of liberty, an intuitive perception, is denied. Necessity and chance, its opposite, are all that are recognized, and human freedom, it is affirmed, must be one or the other of these.

Hobbes, in morals, adopted, in its grossest form, the doctrine of utility. This doctrine, always, as we believe, false in theory, becomes practically coarse and unendurable, or proximately elevated and serviceable, according to the author's estimate of human nature, of its predominating impulses, and the circle of its enjoyments. Hobbes held human nature very low, and right became consequently with him, little more than the law or ravin of rude appetites, the eager assertion of selfishness. Here, again, we have materialism, not merely in the coarseness which these doctrines assumed, but in the denial of that original, ultimate law in our constitution, the law of right, which the human reason, by its own penetration and with its own power, sets up.

Though the deepening current of English philosophy, its transmitted and almost national force, has lain in one direction, there have always been dissenting voices, some of them of clear and startling emphasis. It is our purpose to speak, however, of the schools of philosophy, of its continuous lines of development, and to pass, with slight mention, those side efforts which, oftentimes more valuable than the prevailing line of thought, were yet unable to secure any general following. It is impossible to settle exactly the degree of prevalence of any one form of philosophy at any one time ; we can only infer that those speculative streams, which flow steadily on with enlargements in each successive generation, do, for the most part, draw the national mind. Yet, even this inference is not always correct.

Next succeeding Hobbes is Cudworth, a fine representative of the dissenting tendency. His philosophy is Platonic in its cast. A few others labored with him, and they represented the older, better phases of thought unsubdued to the new temper and at war with it.

The next great name in the line of materialistic succession is that of Locke. So full are his works, and so influential have they been both in England and on the Continent, that modern English philosophy dates from him. A philosopher does not owe his position exclusively to the novelty, or

13*

to the logical force of the views presented, but largely to their acceptance as issuing from him, their subsequent reference to him, and their historic connection through him. Locke gave such an enunciation of his view of the origin of knowledge, that it entered in a central, germinant principle of many subsequent forms of thought. It was just at this point, that Locke was peculiarly influential. His view became almost axiomatic with his disciples. The materialistic philosophy followed his lead, rarely stopping to rechallenge his premises. We give his opinion in his own words: "Let us, then, suppose the mind to be, as we say, white paper, void of all characters, without any ideas; how comes it to be furnished? Whence comes it by that vast storehouse, which the busy and boundless fancy of man has painted on it, with an almost endless variety? Whence has it all the materials of reason and knowledge? To this I answer in one word, from experience; in that all our knowledge is founded, and from that it ultimately derives 'tself. Our observation, employed either about external, sensible objects, or about the internal operations of our mind, perceived and reflected on by ourselves, is that which supplies our understandings with all the materials of thinking. These two are the fountains of knowledge whence all the ideas, we have, or can naturally have, do spring."⁕

He then proceeds more definitely to state the sources of knowledge to be two,—sensation, reflec-

* Human Understanding, B. II. chap. i. sec. 2.

tion; meaning by reflection, the mind's observation
of its own acts and states, now usually termed consciousness.

As Hobbes had called forth from Cudworth a
strong declaration of the inborn conceptions of the
mind, so he in turn gave occasion to a staunch
denial by Locke of innate ideas, and this clear assertion of experience as the sole ground of knowledge. The struggle thus opened is not one merely
of words; whether "innate ideas" expresses well
or ill our original intuitive knowledge, but whether
we have any such knowledge; whether mental
states are not in their entirety the primary or secondary products of sensation. This Locke affirmed
them to be, and would not grant in thought the
presence of any element not traceable to the senses.
Thus time and space, the most obviously super-
sensible of ideas, he yet refers to this origin.

The point was clearly put, and vigorously defended, that the mind contributes nothing to the
material of thought, but that this is always either
directly sensible objects, or the states of mind
which sensible objects have occasioned in it. The
mind may occupy itself with objects, or with the
sensations, feelings, these objects occasion; it can
go no further. It were truer to the spirit of the
philosophy to say: These occupy the mind, expend
themselves on its passive powers, and there repro-
duce the order and the connections that are in
themselves. The image is orderly and beautiful,
because the objects are so which cast it upon the
screen,—the blank sensorium of the soul. White

paper expresses the maximum power in the mind itself. The fruits of this philosophy we shall find so clearly unfolded at its next step of development, that we shall delay their consideration till that is given. It belonged to Hume, following in the line of succession, to develop this view with a startling consistency and recklessness of consequences. Never did a philosophy, that touched daily belief everywhere, stand so at war with it, as that of Hume. Never did a philosopher inquire in so quiet and indifferent a way, what are the conclusions locked up in his premises, and proceed to open them, not stopping to remember, or seeming to care that he was dealing with the box of Pandora. Though the eye passes at once from Locke to Hume in the development of materialism, a considerable period lies between them, and demands some notice, especially for the reactionary efforts in philosophy called out by the works of Locke. The first of these, following immediately upon Locke, was the effort of Shaftesbury to reassert the power of the mind, and emphasize anew, especially in ethics, its contribution to our judgments. There is this change impressed on the phraseology of the realists by their controversy with the disciples of Locke. They cease to speak of "innate ideas," a conception which came from Plato, and defend the intuitive powers of the mind. Samuel Clarke is next to be mentioned in the line of defense. He renewed the à priori argument for the being of God. Such force did he attribute to the mind's conceptions that he thought them to carry with them a suf-

ficient proof of an external reality, a view quite at
war with the doctrine that referred all belief to experience. He also took up the defense of liberty,
and attempted to rescue the ethical nature from the
degradation cast upon it as the enforcement of conventional motives of interest. He saw in it a
power by which the mind discerns the "fitness of
things," and enforces it as a law.

The most extreme reaction to the Lockian philosophy, is presented by Berkeley. His point of
attack was the connection between sensations and
the external objects to which they are referred.
The mind was to Locke simply the paper on which
these images, together with the secondary states
which they called forth, were received. Thus the
power of mind stood at its minimum, and the power
of matter at its maximum.

As, however, the sensation is known to the
mind only as a sensation, an image, not at all as an
external, physical fact, Berkeley denied that there
was present any sufficient proof of the being of this
fact to which the sensation had been so confidently
ascribed. He affirmed that the sensation is to the
mind a first and final product, and that there is no
going back of it to some material source, to which
admittedly the senses can gain no access. Thus
the mind was instantly divorced again from its
thraldom to matter, and its own states were conceived as more wholly its own, and of a more truly
spiritual nature than ever before. This was an
adroit turning of the flank of the enemy ; but it
gave entrance to idealism, so uncongenial to Eng-

lish thought. It beat down the old difficulties only to raise up as many more new ones.

Such was the resistance offered to materialism in the period between Locke and Hume. It was straggling in its character, and tended rather to the more rapid unfolding of the obnoxious view than to its arrest. In the progress of materialism itself, we are brought up to the time of Hume, of Hartley and Priestley. Hartley was a little earlier than Hume, and Priestley a little later. Hartley's contribution was made in connection with the association of ideas. This subject had been treated by Locke, but Hartley gave it an enlargement, a rigid physical development, that made it henceforth a characteristic doctrine of materialism.

If all the material of thought is furnished to the mind, thought itself, it might be said, remains. It is the mind, after all, that analyzes, compares, unites this material, and builds it together in the rational structures of thought. This power of the mind to institute and order its own processes became the point on which the attack was now opened by Hartley. Not only is the material of thought given it, the very nature and flow of that thought, it was said, is determined by the external connections of the things which ideas represent. Objects come to the mind in sensation, already grouped in place and time. The repetition of a sensation, inducing in each instance a like physical activity of the brain as its condition, tends to make that activity in its completeness easy and natural to the organization which is subject to it. Such a sensation, returning to the mind without the presence of the external object, through this easy proclivity to it already induced in the nervous centres by its frequent repetition, is an act of imagination; if immediately associated in the mind with its previous presence, it becomes an act of memory. To the mind as blank paper there is now added a receptive, retentive repeating power.

But these first associations of objects are not stable. The same object reappears in many external connections. The varying history of the individual serves also to unite objects in many internal collocations of thought and of feeling. Moreover, one, two, three or four intervening objects may be dropped, and the remainder form a new secondary union, and thus with flexible conditions the juxtaposition, the association, of objects, is constantly varied, and weaker and stronger connections of every grade of intensity are formed between them. Ideas thus become, through external connections, through past dependencies, through accidental conjunctions, united in various ways in the mind, and there, in connection with their repeated appearance, gain a certain determinate power over it, by a tendency fastened on the brain to renew its previous states. If by the force of a new sensation, any one of these ideas is plucked at, it comes up from the depths of the mind, like a net secured by a single strand, drawing after it many others, through various lines of attachment. These connections have all been woven into the material of thought by the swift unobserved shuttle of past events, and hence the mind is no more indebted to itself for the flow of its thought, and the junction of particular ideas, than is a river to some presiding deity that congregates, disperses and arranges its particles. Here was a long stride toward materialism.

A German or Frenchman would have readily and quickly taken the shorter steps that remain, but the English mind is religious, practical, and will hold stolidly fast on the steepest declivities, if a flat denial of the ordinary truths of life and morality must accompany the descent. Priestley, in farther expanding this view of Hartley's, could talk of God and duty, when the words were scarcely more applicable to his psychological mechanism than to a power-loom.

Hume, by far the greatest, and by far the most unscrupulous, philosopher in this school of thought, was retarded by no such outside considerations. With a singularly clear and quiet mind, never to be abashed by its own conclusions, he ripened and made to burst forth as in a single summer day, the thousand winged seeds of mischief that lay hid in this one pregnant pod,—this composite thistle-head, —that all knowledge is the product of experience.

We shall give concisely the leading propositions of the system of Hume in their order of dependence. We do this because of its logical completeness, its central position and historical value in English philosophy. Opposed and concurrent systems have alike been shaped by it. Hume restates the doctrine of Locke as regards the origin of knowledge in this form. The phenomena of mind are divisible into impressions and ideas. "The difference betwixt these consists in the degrees of force and liveliness with which they strike upon the mind."[*] Impressions include sensations, emotions; ideas, "the faint images of these in thinking." His fundamental proposition is that all ideas are "derived from impressions which are correspondent to them, and which they exactly represent."[†] "All our ideas are copied from our impressions."[‡] Thus Hume makes those impressions, which we attribute to the external world, echo and re-echo themselves in the mind, and these first voices with their receding, fainting responses, are all the facts of mental science. Hence, as a first conclusion, space and time are not distinct ideas, but "merely of the manner or order in which objects exist."[§] Space and time as we accept them are flatly denied, and they are identified with that order which they in fact impart and explain. Other conceptions are pushed aside in like fashion. "The idea of existence is the very same with the idea of what we conceive to be existent."[||] "We have no other notion of cause and effect but that of certain objects, which have always been conjoined together."[¶] In this fashion is all the original furniture of the mind disposed of, and it is left, swept and garnished, for the unobstructed entertainment in reflection and re-reflection, of those images which date their origin from sensation only. The next weighty conclusion, there-

* Hume's Philosophical Works, vol i. p. 15.   † Ibid., p. 18.
‡ Ibid., p. 99.   § Ibid., p. 60. || Ibid., p. 92.   ¶ Ibid., p. 124.

fore, is that "all reasoning consists in nothing but comparisons,"* an observation of the agreement or disagreement of these fleeting impressions. At this point it is, that the theory of Hartley helps out that of Hume, for impressions by their very association, their reiterations, are made to compare themselves ; to sort, locate and put themselves into union, like boulders, gravel and sand in a river-bed.

The next deduction is still more striking. Belief turns upon the liveliness of the impression and hence of the idea. "Belief is nothing but a strong and lively idea derived from a present impression related to it."† Hume is thus led to admit that belief is a thing of sensation rather than of thought. In his own words, "Belief is more properly an act of the sensitive than of the cogitative part of our nature."‡ A good echo is audible, a weak one is not ; a lively idea is believable, a feeble one is not. The mind has no more agency in its own beliefs, than the ear in the sounds it receives ; a clear voice can be heard, an obscure one cannot. The notion of continued, distinct, external existence, as that of our own personal identity, is due entirely to the imagination. This acquires a certain tendency, a kind of momentum, by which it reproduces objects not present in sensation, and leads us to believe therefore in their continuous being. The upshot of this system is absolute skepticism. For nothing is a subject of belief, that is not at the moment vividly impressed on the mind, and every-

* Hume's Philosophical Works, vol. i. p. 100.
† Ibid., p. 140.   ‡ Ibid., p. 233.

thing that chances to be so impressed, is worthy, at
least for the moment, of acceptance. Belief necessarily shifts like the shadows of each passing day.
The noonday light of belief,—that is, of vivid impression,—travels round and round the earth, but it
tarries nowhere ; and each position is in turn over
taken by the darkness and shadows that follow hard
in the rear. Argument, knowledge, is a barren
transfer of the mind from point to point ; the mental, like the physical, eye takes in new views only
to lose old ones. He says, " The skeptic still con-
tinues to reason and believe, even though he
asserts that he cannot defend his reason by reason."* The weary traveller travels by a fatality
of unrest without hope or real joy. Nothing can
exceed the candor of Hume's conclusions. He says,
" I have already shown that the understanding,
when it acts alone and according to its most general principles, entirely subverts itself, and leaves not
the lowest degree of evidence in any proposition,
either in philosophy or common life. We save
ourselves from this total skepticism only by means
of that singular and seemingly trivial property of
the fancy by which we enter with difficulty into remote views of things."† That is to say, the vividness of ideas is constantly changing, therefore
nothing is worthy of permanent belief. We must
give ourselves in floating fancies to the impression
uppermost, and lucky is it that we drift on so very
slowly. Out of this fortunate sluggishness of our
faculties, by which they hold at least for a little the

* Hume's Philosophical Works, vol. i. p. 237.   † Ibid , p. 330.

impressions made on them, spring the congruity and order of daily life; near and passing impressions having this advantage, that they are at harmony with themselves. We are indebted to our dulness for what we seem to know. Hume touches on his own feelings under these irrefragable deductions, " The *intense* view of these manifold contradictions and imperfections in human reason, has so wrought upon me, and heated my brain, that I am ready to reject all belief and reasoning, and can look upon no opinion even as more probable or likely than another."* His farther pursuit of philosophy was a mere matter of pleasure, therefore, and diversion.

Hume did not stop with these purely speculative results; he touched on all sides practical questions, the immateriality of the soul, miracles, future life. He denies the possible proof of miracles, legitimately enough from one view of his doctrine, strangely enough from another. He starts with referring all knowledge to experience, this knowledge, in its most solid form, a miracle contradicts; very well, but has not our philosophy issued in the conclusion that all belief is a question of liveliness of ideas? Those, therefore, who accept miracles, show by this very fact a belief grounded on ideas sufficiently vivid to occasion it, and thus to justfy them in it. Thus Hume cannot be more rational in denying miracles under his ideas, than are his opponents in accepting them under the impression present to their minds. In short, a philosophy that makes it absurd to hold fast to any conclusion, cannot destructively criticise

* Hume's Philosophical Works, vol. i. p. 331.

any opinion ; for one opinion is at least as good as
another, and vindicates its right to be by the mere
fact that it exists. That I hear a voice, proves to me
the being of the voice.

The practical conclusions of Hume's philosophy,
self-destructive as they were, were, nevertheless,
very nettlesome to the religious and philosophical
world, and called forth, on the one side, farther expansion, and, on the other, more systematic attack.
We will turn first to affiliated views. It may be
asked, why should the system of Hume, and those
systems in continuation of his, be called materialistic, when they do not so much as decide on the
existence of the external world? We answer, because their whole constructive force is derived from
the sensational side of our being. Sensations, which
represent matter and material law, control mind,
completely subordinate it to the fixed, necessary
forces or tendencies contained in them. This is
the sense in which we say of Hume, of Spencer,
they are materialistic.

In ethics, the utilitarian view has been defended
by Paley, Bentham, Bain. Paley was an able
writer on the proofs of Christianity, yet bases his
ethical system on the skeptical, materialistic view
of obligation. He found in his spiritual philosophy, no higher inspiration, no weightier law for the
duties of ordinary life, than came to Hume in absolute unbelief, generalizing a transient law of action,
from the unsubstantial fleeting facts afloat about
him,—the gains and losses that fall to us under
them. The belief and unbelief of England often

strike hands on this question of morals, intimate as it is to daily life and character.

Bentham is most remarkable for bold, dogged assertion, English-wise. One might think the question of the foundation of obligation in morals had ceased to his mind to be one of abstruse inquiry, and was regarded as a point involving good sense and veracity, to be disposed of by positive averment, so contemptuous is he of his adversary. He settles the question as one Englishman says of another, with " a masculine, muscular, graphic, narrow, thick-headed ability."

Bain is the latest, most elaborate and thorough defender of utilitarian morals.

His works are to be read with great advantage, though the reading should be accompanied with the most complete dissent. English morals, though muddy and murky with the soiled sediment of self-interest, have their commercial value. The river Thames, vexed and turbid, though not much as a mirror of the heavens, floats a deal of shipping, and is every way a godsend to trade. English philosophy has worked hard at the utilities involved in ethics. Yet, it is a pity that one's home should be lighted with ground-glass, not because he cannot thus see the dinner on his table, but because he loses the long range of vision of the outside world. A law of morals that is deduced shrewdly from passing events may give a good deal of successful guidance in daily life, but we cease to discover in it the far-reaching light of eternity. Æsthetics has shared these sensual limitations of ethics in

England, and beauty has become, as to Jeffrey and Alison, the fruit of associations fleeting and accidental.

The opposite view of morals has also had its defenders, but their works have been less united, less the part of a system, and have possessed secondary power over the national mind, at least as represented in the agents of progress. Chief among these defenders, should be put Sir James Mackintosh and of later writers, Whewell. The former had the support which sprang from his connection with Scottish philosophy, the only continuous speculation, aside from materialism, that constitutes, on British soil, a school.

The philosophy of Hume has found its line of descent to our own time through James Mill, John Stuart Mill, and Spencer. The philosophy of Spencer is essentially an independent, vigorous reconstruction and re-argumentation of the doctrines of Hume; though, it must be said, with far more belief and consequently with far more momentum. The novelty of impression which begot such skepticism of his own conclusions in the mind of Hume, seems, in consistency with the theory that iteration breeds conviction, to have disappeared on farther familiarity, and the assertions of Spencer have apparently a very sufficient and undoubted hold on his own mind. Every reader of the two philosophies must be struck with their general identity, and with the fact that the germ of the one is wholly contained in the other; and yet with this great diversity of conviction between them. Their agreement is not the general agreement, that both refer knowledge to experience, but a close correspondence of secondary propositions. Thus, the evolution of the ideas of space and time is similar, though the discussion of Spencer is more patient and complete. Their resolution of all knowledge into resemblance is the same; also their reference of belief to what may be called the sensational, physical hold of ideas on the mind; their assertion of an inability to affirm anything of the existence of the external world, of mind and of God, or of the nature of any of them. Both alike deal only with impressions, and the ideas or states of mind directly consequent upon them, and thus wholly identify physical, social, mental events in their evolution, their law of progress. To this evolution Spencer has devoted much time in very fruitful labors, and has chiefly used his philosophy as an instrument in this field of inquiry. Evolution in man and in society is with him only a more complex, physical process than that which has from the beginning proceeded in inorganic and organic matter.

Between Hume and Spencer, lie the works of two powerful minds in close sympathy with them. The Mills, in vigor of thought, worthily stand between the two. The leading work of James Mill is an Analysis of the Phenomena of the Human Mind. He gets much the old start in sensations, and in ideas the lingering traces of sensations, and, under the fruitful law of association, proceeds to develop these into imagination, memory, belief. The road is one which many feet have travelled from the time of Locke, till it has become the beaten path of sensationalism, each succeeding investigator bringing new relations and a little new light to its details.

The leading philosophical work of John Stuart Mill is one on logic, the inductive logic, which he strives to establish to the exclusion of fundamental truths,—of deduction as primitive proof. Therein, and in many other ways, he shows his adherence to the school whose development we have briefly traced. (1) The initial feature of it is sensation as the exclusive source of knowledge. (2) From this follows the resolution of mental facts into floating phenomena, united only by laws of association; (3) phenomena, from which nothing in any direction can be predicated concerning real being. (4) One ultimate relation includes all others, that of resemblance; while (5) belief is the transient force of existing connections in the mind. (6) Every idea that will not accept this solution is denied, or modified or falsely referred. These conclusions may be reached in different forms or partially missed. They are none the less in the system. To these John Stuart Mill added (7) induction or observation as the complete, exclusive source of proof. This also is undeniable, if experience is our only means of knowledge, and all knowledge is expressed under resemblances; for induction is the union by experience of agreeing things and facts. For inductive logic, Mill has done much, and here lies his chief merit. The deductive logic, however, returns instantly to us as the moiety of a complete system, when we recognize intuitive truths.

14

It remains now only to speak of the opposing Scottish school, immediately called forth by Hume, and whose chief philosophers were first Reid, last Hamilton, with Stewart and others associated with them.

Reid took his appeal against the conclusions of Hume afresh to the common-sense, or common-consciousness of the race. He claimed anew the intuitive force of the mind, and strove to lead by means of it to a fresh view of the doctrine of perception. Locke and Hume had neither of them any means of establishing a belief in the external world. There are two ways by which this space between mind and matter, sensations and the objects to which they pertain, can be bridged over. The sensation can be regarded as exclusively a mental fact or state, and then, by the idea of causation, referred to external being as a source or cause ; or the sensation may be regarded as a conjoint product in which both mind and matter are present and directly recognizable. Neither explanation was open to the philosophy of Locke. He did not accept the intuitive act of mind by which it reaches the cause in the effect, he could not, therefore, pass from the sensation to a real exterior source of it. Neither did he find in the sensation itself two constituents which the mind immediately perceives. He accepted the traditional view of perception, that it is a detached state confined wholly to the mind itself. His philosophy had then no method of establishing the being of matter. Reid and

Hamilton have both labored at length this doctrine of perception. Reid's appeal to the common-
sense of men, was taken without sufficient analysis, and hence bears a dogmatic character. He
has left it uncertain, whether he regarded sensation itself as a direct contact with the external world, or whether it is instantly completed
by an intuitive action of the mind, and the
reference of effects to causes becomes the medium
by which this union is effected. We suppose him
to have obscurely held this last view. Hamilton
ascribes to him the first. Hamilton maintained
staunchly, and, as it seems to us, very mis-
takenly, the doctrine of immediate, direct knowledge of physical objects in perception.

The Scottish school, more especially Hamilton,
while far in advance of the Lockian philosophy,
was most unfavorably affected by it, and was unable to construct a consistent, complete system.
We feel more inclined to censure than to praise it.

The action it assigns the reason, the central, intuitive faculty of the soul, is very insufficient. The
division recognized by Coleridge, of the sense, the
understanding and the reason, is more fertile in
growth than the entire philosophy of Hamilton.
We make complaint of inadequacy against this
philosophy, and of limitations cast upon it by previous thought, at many points. Hamilton and
Mansel are both enslaved by the idea of the con-
ceivable and inconceivable, the imaginable and
unimaginable, as setting the limits of belief; and
on this ground, reject, as against the insight of

the reason, a knowledge of the infinite. Here, they are virtually back in the old slough of sensations, and ideas their shadows, as the sum of knowable things.

Again, the idea of causation does not arise with Hamilton from the power of the mind, but from its impotency rather, its inability to think or conceive a thing into nonentity. Here he is practically with Hume, and makes causation a notion fastened upon us by the imagination, instead of a cardinal fruit of the reason. Once more, having thus removed the idea of causation, he strives to make sensation do its work, and affirms us to be directly conscious of matter and mind. This, we believe, to be pure assertion, thrown in to help out the self-constituted weakness of his system. Having closed up the door to the real being of mind and of matter, he makes this rent in the wall to supply its place. The doctrine is plausible only because sensation is a complex process which results in a knowledge of the outside world, and, falsely looked on as a single, simple act, may be said directly to reach that result.

The drift of English thought down through Hobbes, Locke, Hartley, Hume, J. Mill, J. S. Mill and Spencer, we have seen to be steadily toward materialism. The chief resistance has been offered by the religious convictions of the nation. It is these that have made the word, *materialist*, opprobrious, and one which few of the school have been willing to accept.

The reluctance of this school to admit the

adjective, *materialistic*, while struggling to make absolute and universal those necessary connections which are the characteristic of the physical world, and the complete expression of physical force, is but one of its inconsistencies. It is true, the possibility of strict materialism or strict idealism has been lost to it, since the existence of matter and mind are both unproved; but the appearances with which this philosophy does occupy itself, are, in every one of their connections, those ascribed to physical being. Though the floating facts of our experience are only film deep, in the depth and coherence that do belong to them, they are fixed, necessary, and hence, in essence, physical.

This philosophy also started with a predilection for induction, and later, through Mill, declares this to be the sum of logic. Yet no system has been more exclusively deductive, more in the face of all experience, than that of Hume, who, after all, is the central mind of the school. Start with his simple, assumed premise, the nature of knowledge, and every subsequent step is evolved with almost the exactness and the freedom from observation which belong to mathematics.

Again, this philosophy, so purely deductive, so skeptical of the very being of the external world, strikes hands with natural science as its coadjutor, and stands in close affinity with it. Religion, on the other hand, as over-speculative, and dealing with unsubstantial ideas, it censures and shuns. This from a philosophy that has to do with images only, and cannot transcend the merest film of being in any direction ; that confessed in its corypheus, that its pursuit was a question of pleasure merely ! Contradictions and inconclusiveness can scarcely go farther. If all is dream, one should certainly be left to dream the dream most pleasant to him. A philosophy of dreams, what has it to do with science ? It should stand affiliated with any easy wayward thought ; if that thought be either brilliant or consoling.

There is in this development of the English mind, especially if we regard the ethical bearing of the points in discussion, a slow, sedimentary settling of commercial sentiment and principles, which turn on a sense of present well-being, from among the loftier, more lucid and spiritual elements of thought, and their patient, half-mechanical combination into those stratified products, those growing deposits of successive generations, known as sensationalism. Indeed, if the system be true, this is rather an exact physical, than a figurative statement of the process. This philosophy is strictly a resultant habit, a slowly acquired chronic tendency of brain, depositing and completing its beliefs in residuary fashion from age to age.

We trust that the implied half of the simile will also prove true, and that the clarified waters above, the elements relieved of this sordid contact, will be only the more thoroughly and brilliantly permeated with the light of Heaven, that direct light, which the reason of man mediates to the human soul.

THE END.

www.ingramcontent.com/pod-product-compliance
Lightning Source LLC
Chambersburg PA
CBHW020946030726
47496CB00005B/1370